THE CREATIVE LIFE PROJECT

Your Personal Guide to Creative Self Discovery, Development, and Expression

BY RICHARD ALTMAN

Copyright © [2025] Richard Altman. All rights reserved. No part of this publication may be reproduced, stored in a retrieval system, or transmitted in any form or by any means—electronic, mechanical, photocopying, recording, or otherwise—without the prior written permission of the author, except in the case of brief quotations used in critical reviews, educational commentary, or scholarly works.

Creative Life Project® is a registered trademark of Richard Altman (U.S. Reg. No. 5,921,758). The following terms are used throughout this guide as proprietary components of the Creative Life Project® system: Blueprint to Fingerprint™, Cloud of Confusion™, Creative Continuum™, Creative Life Project Philosophy™, Creative Life Project Framework™, Creative Life Project & Story™, Creative Life Project Vision™, Creative Self™, Creative Self Blueprint™, Creative Self Development™, Creative Self Development Framework™, Creative Self Development Process™, Creative Self Discovery™, Creative Self Expression™, Creative Self Expression Practice™, Creative Self Fingerprint™, Creative Self Fundamentals,™ Creative Self Management™, Creative Self Mindset™, Creative Self Mindset Principles™, Creative Self Navigation™, Creative Self Potential™, Fundamentals of Creativity™, Learning Spiral™, Life Force of Creation™, Life Skill of Being Creative™, and Storytelling Self-Talk™.

These terms are used without repeated trademark symbols in the body of the text for clarity and ease of reading. Their usage, structure, and integration are protected as original elements of the Creative Life Project® intellectual property system. Unlicensed reproduction or commercial use of these terms as part of a training system, curriculum, framework, or branded methodology is strictly prohibited. Reference to these terms in public discussion, citation, or commentary (including social media) is permitted, provided they are not used in a way that implies affiliation, authorship, or endorsement.

Public discussion, citation, or commentary—including on social media, podcasts, blogs, or forums—is welcomed and encouraged, provided it respects the original source and context of the terms and ideas. Individuals are encouraged to reference the Creative Life Project® by name when discussing these terms to help maintain their intended meaning and purpose. Use of the ™ or ® symbols is not required in casual or conversational public use, but the original authorship and framework context should be acknowledged whenever possible. Misrepresentation of the concepts as original works or use in a way that implies affiliation, endorsement, or co-authorship without permission is prohibited.

Diagrams and illustrations in this publication are copyrighted original works and integral to the Creative Life Project® Framework. They may be personally shared or referenced in non-commercial, informal conversations—including with friends, family, or peers—provided no modifications are made and proper attribution is given to the author. Use of diagrams in any formal educational, coaching, training, or commercial setting is not permitted without explicit permission or licensing. These visuals are designed to be interpreted within the full context of the Creative Life Project® system, and this usage restriction exists to preserve their integrity, intended meaning, and transformative value. Unauthorized or decontextualized use may result in misunderstanding or misrepresentation of their purpose, which runs counter to the core aims of Creative Self Development™. The goal is to ensure these tools are used to empower individuals, not to mislead, dilute, or distort their original function.

Disclaimer: This publication is intended for informational and educational purposes only. It is not intended as psychological, therapeutic, medical, legal, or financial advice. The author and publisher make no guarantees regarding specific outcomes and disclaim any liability for decisions made or actions taken based on the content of this work.

For serious inquiries regarding licensing, collaboration, or authorized use, please contact the author through the website.

For more information about the Creative Life Project® system and its applications, visit www.CreativeLifeProject.com.

CONTENTS

Preface 5

Part 01. Defining the Problem
01. Before We Begin 13
02. Orientation 23
03. Cloud of Confusion 29

Part 02. Category—Creative Life Project Philosophy
04. The Life Force of Creation 51
05. Fundamentals of Life 56
06. Fundamentals of Creativity 73
07. Functional Definition of Creativity 88

Part 03. Category—Creative Self Mindset
08. What is the Creative Self? 110
09. What is the Creative Self Mindset? 130
10. Creative Self Mindset Principles 151

Part 04. Category—Creative Life Project Vision
11. Preparing to Craft Your Vision 173
12. Crafting Your Vision 184

Part 05. Category—The Life Skill of Being Creative
13. The Strategic Life Skill of Being Creative 201
14. Learning to Learn 215
15. The Biology of Being Creative 230
16. The Life Skill of Being Creative Fundamentals 253

Part 06. Category—Creative Self Management
17. The Roles of Creative Self Management 275

Part 07. Category—Creative Life Project & Story
18. Viewing Life as a Creative Project 303
19. Your Creative Life Project & Story—The Hero Returns 317

Part 08. Category—Creative Self Expression Practice
20. Creative Self Expression Practice Components 330
21. Creativity in Cultures and Relationships. 359
22. Revisited—Before We Begin... and What's Next 365
23. Final Thoughts 373

PREFACE

Creativity is at the core of what makes us human, what separates us from other living things, and the technologies crafted to emulate it. The ability to be creative fuels our growth, transformation, and our capacity to build lives that matter. Yet for many, the idea of creativity remains elusive—either narrowly defined or quietly dismissed—as though it belongs to the artists, inventors, or a chosen few.

This guide is an invitation to see creativity differently, not as a rare talent or occasional spark but as a universal life force within you, waiting to be recognized, developed, and expressed. It's a call to remember that being creative is not something separate from who you are but central to how you live, learn, and lead your life.

My journey into this understanding began more than fifty years ago when a college psychology class introduced me to thinkers like Carl Rogers, Abraham Maslow, and Carl Jung. They opened the door to something I had sensed but hadn't yet named: the idea that we are not merely shaped by our circumstances—we are capable of shaping them. That realization became the seed of a lifelong pursuit: learning how to live creatively and helping others do the same.

This guide is the result of that pursuit. It presents a fresh perspective on creativity—one that is grounded in personal growth, lifelong learning, and intentional practice. It honors what has come before while offering a new framework for understanding and expressing creative potential across all areas of life. It moves beyond inspiration or technique to offer a full system of Creative Self Development that empowers you to do the best with what you have, wherever and however you are.

The Creative Life Project® (CLP) is both personal and collective. It's about discovering what makes you unique—and using that understanding to build a meaningful life while encouraging others to do the same. Whether you're just beginning to explore your creativity or already deeply engaged in creative work, this guide is here to support and challenge you.

There will be reflection and reframing. There will be structure—but not prescription. And always, there will be an invitation to return to your *Creative Self*™, not as something you need to become but as something you already are.

You don't need to be extraordinary to begin. You simply need to start.

A View of Life from Steve Jobs

In the domain of modern innovation and impact, few figures have emerged as significantly as Steve Jobs. His journey exemplifies the transformative power of embracing creativity not just as a skill but as a way of life. Jobs faced many challenges and setbacks, including being forced out of Apple, the company he co-founded. Yet, these obstacles became stepping stones in his creative journey—what he later referred to as "connecting the dots."

After being forced out of Apple, Jobs founded NeXT Computer. Although NeXT didn't achieve commercial success, his growth experience starting and running the company, along with its operating system, proved to be significant assets when Jobs returned to Apple. This illustrates how even our most challenging experiences can yield unexpected and valuable results when approached with a creative mindset.

Jobs' vision extended beyond computers. His acquisition of Pixar from George Lucas showcased his belief in the power of storytelling through 3D computer animation. This venture revolutionized the film industry and brought joy to millions worldwide. By following his curiosity and connecting seemingly unrelated domains—technology and storytelling—Jobs created something uniquely his own that transformed multiple industries.

Many of you reading this guide may be doing so on devices that Jobs helped create. His relentless pursuit of making complex technology simple and accessible has transformed how we communicate, work, and express ourselves creatively. Jobs' innovations broke down barriers, democratizing creative tools that were once the domain of specialists, supporting the creation of a new digital marketplace and opening access to digital creative expression around the world.

I was one of those individuals empowered by Jobs and his inventions. I purchased one of the first-generation Mac computers in 1984 and have since purchased and influenced consulting clients to purchase hundreds of Apple products. The first generation of Mac computers helped to launch my business, providing me with the tools to explore and integrate technology in education, art, and business.

It's with this context of Jobs' far-reaching influence that we turn to a profound statement he made in a 1995 interview. This statement encapsulates the essence of living a creative life, as defined in this guide, and challenges us to "Think different," the advertising slogan used by Apple from 1997 to 2002:

> *"When you grow up, you tend to get told that the world is the way it is and your life is just to live your life inside the world, try not to bash into the walls too much... But that's a very limited life. Life can be much broader once you discover one simple fact: Everything around you that you call life was made up by people who were no smarter than you. And you can change it, you can influence it... you can build your own things that other people can use. Once you learn that, you'll never be the same again."*[1]

These words reflect the essence of what it means to live a creative life. Not to passively accept the world but to shape it. Not to wait for permission but to discover what you can do with what you have. Not to wonder whether you are creative but to recognize that creativity is your birthright.

---

1   Steve Jobs, interview with the Santa Clara Valley Historical Association, 1995. Available in Steve Jobs: Visionary Entrepreneur, Santa Clara Valley Historical Association (DVD), 2001.

Challenging the Status Quo

Jobs begins by pointing out how we're often conditioned to accept the world as it is, living within prescribed boundaries. He immediately challenges this notion, calling it a "very limited life." This reflects the core challenge addressed in the CLP: the need to break free from mass-mindedness and rediscover our creative potential.

Empowerment Through Awareness

The pivotal moment comes with the realization that the world around us is not fixed but rather a construction created by people "no smarter than you." This awareness dismantles the myth of creative exceptionalism and replaces it with the truth of shared human potential. It is a call to wake up to our own creative capacity.

The Power to Change and Influence

Jobs emphasizes that we have the power not just to exist in the world but to shape it actively. This aligns with the Creative Life Project's perspective that we are not just passive recipients of life but creators of it. Through Creative Self Development, we learn to influence, adapt, and build—not only for ourselves but for others as well.

Creating Value for Others

He highlights that our creative efforts can extend beyond personal expression. They can become tools, systems, ideas, and artifacts that other people use and benefit from. This is the essence of living a creative life with purpose: turning our creative potential into meaningful contributions.

Transformative Realization

Jobs concludes by stating that this understanding fundamentally changes a person. Once you realize that the world is malleable, that you can shape it, and that your voice matters, "you'll never be the same again." This is the gateway to Creative Self Development—a mindset shift that changes how we live, learn, work, and lead.

The CLP begins here—with this realization. You are creative. You can change things. You can build things. You can shape your life and contribute to the world in ways that are both meaningful and necessary.

And once you truly believe that, you'll never be the same again.

The Journey of Creative Self Discovery, Development, Management, and Expression

As we begin this journey, consider where you currently stand in relation to the ideas Jobs has shared. Do you see yourself as a passive recipient of circumstances or as an active creator? Do you perceive clear boundaries around what's possible in your life, or do you approach those boundaries with curiosity and creativity?

Like the questions in "Before We Begin," these reflections aren't about judgment but awareness: wherever you are now is the perfect starting point for your journey. The path ahead isn't about becoming someone different—it's about reconnecting with the creative capacity you already possess and learning to express it more fully in your daily life.

Jobs' own journey illustrates these principles in action. From his beginnings creating Apple in a garage to his later reinvention of multiple industries, his statement proclaims that creativity isn't a special gift but a way of engaging with the world by doing the best with what you have, when, where, and however you are.

I invite you to join me on this transformative journey. Together, we can clear the "Cloud of Confusion™" surrounding creativity, unlock the boundless creative potential within ourselves, and celebrate the Life Force of Creation™ that lives in each of us.

You Can't Judge a Book by Its Cover (But Since You Already Have...)

While you can't judge a book by its cover, it does serve as your one chance to make a first impression. So here's the story behind this cover, so that while judging, you at least understand my intent.

Creating a visual representation of creativity's essence and its vital role in our lives proved to be no trivial creative task. After collaborating with other designers and artists, I realized that to achieve the expression I envisioned—one that truly captures the essence of this guide—I had to create it myself. As reinforced throughout these pages, while others may judge our creative work, we alone can determine whether it authentically represents what we're trying to share. This cover, along with the diagrams throughout the book, embodies the feeling of what I'm sharing and serves as a visual springboard for conversations about creativity and being creative—conversations that hopefully cultivate creative individuals who build creative communities and help make the world a better place for everyone.

The first criterion was to avoid the common depictions of creativity, like light bulbs, stacks of paint supplies on a workbench, or large blobs of multicolored paint. Instead, I was looking for imagery representing the Life Force of Creation—the universal energy that animates all living things and serves as the wellspring of creativity itself. The resulting image is composed of dynamic waves of overlapping light, alluding to the Life Force of Creation that is neither static nor predictable. It moves, shifts, and evolves, manifesting uniquely through each individual.

Notice how the translucent layers blend and intersect, creating new colors and patterns where they meet. This visual metaphor reflects how your own creative potential emerges—not as an isolated phenomenon, but through the dynamic interplay of your experiences, perspectives, and the creative energy that flows through you. Each wave of color represents a different aspect of this force: imagination, curiosity, innovation, and authentic expression, all flowing together in an endless dance of possibility.

The gradient transitions from vibrant purples and blues to warm pinks and greens mirror the spectrum of creative expression available to you. Just as no two moments in this flowing image are identical, your creative journey will be uniquely yours—shaped by your individual blueprint yet connected to the universal source that animates all creative beings.

The transparency and luminosity of these forms remind us that creativity is not something solid and fixed, but rather a living, breathing force that flows through you right now, ready to be discovered, developed, and expressed through your daily choices and actions.

This cover image invites you to see beyond traditional boundaries. Just as these flowing forms transcend any single shape or color, your creative potential transcends any single domain or definition. Whether you're solving everyday problems, building meaningful relationships, or pursuing ambitious dreams, the same Life Force of Creation that illuminates this cover is available to guide and empower your personal creative journey.

This visual journey from the universal Life Force of Creation on the cover to a deeply personal moment of creative recognition at the guide's end mirrors the transformation you'll experience—from understanding creativity as an abstract concept to recognizing your own Creative Self reflected back at you through your own experiences.

The journey from your genetic and cultural blueprint to your distinctive creative fingerprint begins with this recognition: you are born creative and made to create. You are already connected to the source of all creation. Your task is not to manufacture creativity, but to become a conscious conduit for the Life Force of Creation that seeks expression through your unique perspective and circumstances. In our AI-driven world, your Creative Self is your superpower—the one thing that cannot be replicated or automated. This guide will help you strengthen that connection and learn to express it authentically in service of navigating, building, and living your best life.

PART 01

DEFINING THE PROBLEM

"If I had an hour to solve a problem, I'd spend 55 minutes thinking about the problem and 5 minutes thinking about solutions."
— **Albert Einstein**

CHAPTER 1:
BEFORE WE BEGIN

Welcome to the starting point of your journey through the Creative Life Project® (CLP). Before we dive into this exploration of creativity and Creative Self Development™, there are a couple of important things we need to go over.

First, you should consume this guide from beginning to end on your first journey through it. This sequential approach ensures a progressive exploration of concepts and ideas, where each section builds upon the previous, allowing for a comprehensive and integrated understanding of creativity as it pertains to Creative Self Development. Once you've navigated through the content in order, the guide becomes a versatile, random-access resource for revisiting, refreshing, or reconsidering any aspect of the content as needed.

Second, before we begin with the content of the guide, take a moment for some self-reflection related to your current understanding and beliefs about creativity. This reflection will help you acknowledge your current perspective on creativity, your personal relationship with it, and the experiences that have shaped your viewpoint. This moment of reflection will help you recognize the evolution of your thoughts and beliefs as you progress through this guide.

By taking time to review these questions now, and again at the end of the guide, you'll be able to observe how your understanding has evolved and deepened through your engagement with the Creative Life Project Framework™.

Current Perspective on Creativity

The questions that follow are designed to trigger a comprehensive reflection on creativity in various aspects of your life. They are meant to stimulate your thinking and encourage a deeper exploration of your beliefs, experiences, and attitudes toward creativity.

As you read through these questions, allow yourself to pause and notice the thoughts influencing your response. You may choose to write down your thoughts on those that spark the strongest reactions or bring up significant memories. The goal is to create a personal snapshot of your current relationship with creativity—an honest starting point from which you can measure your growth and transformation.

Be open and honest, and don't shy away from recalling potentially uncomfortable memories or conflicting thoughts. Remember, there are no right or wrong answers—this is about your unique perspective and experiences.

Creativity in General

How well do you understand the concept of creativity?

- Not at all
- Slightly
- Moderately
- Very
- Extremely

How important do you believe creativity is in today's rapidly changing world?

- Not important at all
- Slightly important
- Moderately important
- Very important
- Extremely important

To what extent do you believe creativity can be applied in everyday life, beyond traditional artistic domains?

- Not at all
- To a small extent

- To a moderate extent
- To a great extent
- To a very great extent

How often do you consciously engage your creativity to solve problems or generate new ideas in your daily life?

- Never
- Rarely
- Sometimes
- Often
- Always

How strongly do you believe that developing and expressing creativity should be a priority for personal growth and well-being?

- Not at all
- Slightly
- Moderately
- Very
- Extremely

To what extent do you believe that creativity can be learned and developed by anyone?

- Not at all
- To a small extent
- To a moderate extent
- To a great extent
- To a very great extent

How often do you actively encourage and support others in their creative endeavors?

- Never
- Rarely

- Sometimes
- Often
- Always

How often have you received encouragement or praise for your creative ideas?

- Never
- Rarely
- Sometimes
- Often
- Always

How often have you experienced criticism or discouragement from others regarding your creative expressions or abilities?

- Never
- Rarely
- Sometimes
- Often
- Always

How much do you believe societal norms and expectations influence your willingness to think and act creatively?

- Not at all
- Slightly
- Moderately
- Very much
- Extremely

How strongly do you believe that learning about creativity and engaging in creative practices can enhance one's overall creativity?

- Not at all
- Slightly

- Moderately
- Very
- Extremely

Your Creative Potential

How strongly do you believe in your own creative potential?

- Not at all
- To a small extent
- To a moderate extent
- To a great extent
- To a very great extent

To what extent do you identify yourself as a creative individual?

- Not at all
- To a small extent
- To a moderate extent
- To a great extent
- To a very great extent

How would you assess your current level of creativity compared to what you believe is possible for you?

- Very low
- Low
- Moderate
- High
- Very high

How much time, energy, and resources do you currently invest in developing and expressing your creative potential?

- None
- A little
- A moderate amount

- A lot
- A great deal

How integral is creativity to your sense of self and your daily life?

- Not at all
- Slightly
- Moderately
- Very
- Extremely

Your Journey Begins: From Blueprint to Fingerprint

You've just completed a simple but essential first step—taking an honest look at yourself. Through the questions above, you've examined your relationship with creativity without the comfort of pretense or the safety of avoiding difficult truths. Whether your responses revealed confidence or uncertainty, excitement or hesitation, you've done something that's required for any meaningful journey: you've shown up authentically to explore your potential.

This act of honest self-reflection? It's exactly how every transformative adventure begins. And you're about to discover that your path follows the same powerful pattern found in humanity's most compelling stories.

The Hero's Journey: The Universal Pattern of Transformation

For thousands of years, storytellers across cultures have recognized a powerful pattern in the stories that move us most deeply. Scholar Joseph Campbell called it "The Hero's Journey"—a universal template that describes how ordinary people become extraordinary through facing challenges, gaining wisdom, and ultimately transforming not just themselves but their world.

You've seen this pattern in stories you know and love. In *Star Wars*, Luke Skywalker begins as a restless farm boy living a routine life until he discovers he has extraordinary abilities and is called to save the galaxy. In *The Lord of the Rings*, Frodo Baggins starts as a comfortable hobbit content with his quiet existence until he must undertake an epic quest to save his world. In *The Karate Kid*, Daniel begins as a bullied teenager feeling powerless until he discovers inner strength through an unexpected mentor.

In each story, the hero begins uncertain, even reluctant. They don't feel special or chosen. They question whether they're capable of what lies ahead. But what defines them isn't their confidence at the beginning—it's their willingness to answer the call and take the first step into the unknown.

That's exactly where you are right now.

Your Call to Adventure

The very fact that you're here, questioning and exploring how to develop your creative potential, represents your response to a call to adventure. Something deep within you recognizes that your life could be more intentional, more expressive, more authentically yours. You sense that you have the power to actively shape your experience rather than simply drift through situations others have arranged.

This sensing, this stirring, this recognition that brought you to this guide—this is your invitation to the adventure of creative transformation.

Your Blueprint to Fingerprint Adventure

The CLP is your personal version of this Hero's Journey—specifically, the adventure of transforming your blueprint into your fingerprint. Like Luke discovering the Force within him, like Frodo finding courage he never knew he possessed, like Daniel learning he could defend himself, you're about to discover creative capabilities that have always been part of you but may have been dormant or unrecognized.

Your blueprint represents everything you inherited—your genetic makeup, cultural background, family circumstances, and the conditions you were born into. This blueprint provides your starting point, just as those heroes had their own beginning circumstances. But your blueprint is not your limitation—it's your launching pad.

Your fingerprint is what you do with the individual potential you already possess when you intentionally discover, develop, and express it to navigate, build, and live your best life—leaving a mark through your creative choices, actions, and expressions. No one else can create your fingerprint because no one else will live your exact story, face your unique combination of challenges, or develop your specific gifts in quite the same way.

This transformation process is your personal adventure of becoming the creator in your life and of your life.

The Fresh Perspective That Opens New Worlds

Central to your adventure is establishing a fresh perspective on creativity itself. Most people think creativity belongs to artists, writers, or "creative types," but this limited view keeps them disconnected from their own creative potential. The truth that will transform your entire experience is this: creativity is the trait empowering humans to imagine and craft clever and strategic solutions to survive, thrive, and flourish in a constantly changing world.

This isn't about making art—it's about making life. Every time you solve a problem, adapt to change, or figure out a better way to approach a situation, you're being creative. Your ancestors didn't take creativity classes to create fire, build civilizations, or solve the challenges that brought us to where we are today. They used their inherent creative capacity to transform their circumstances, just as you can transform yours.

When you truly understand this, everything changes. Your life becomes your most important creative project, and every challenge becomes an opportunity for creative growth rather than something that simply happens to you.

Your Guide for the Path Ahead

Like the mentors in great stories who provide heroes with tools, wisdom, and encouragement at crucial moments, this guide serves as your companion for the transformation ahead. The CLP provides a Creative Self Development Framework™—a structured approach composed of philosophy, process, and practice that work together to support your growth from Blueprint to Fingerprint™.

This framework will guide you through seven integrated stages that take you from confusion to creative confidence. You'll discover how to cultivate your Creative Self—that essential part of you that transforms imagination into reality and dreams into action. Each stage prepares you for the next, building the strength and wisdom needed for what comes ahead.

The Adventure of Daily Transformation

What makes this practical rather than merely inspirational is understanding that every project you undertake, every challenge you face, and every opportunity you pursue becomes part of your transformation story. Whether you're navigating work situations, building relationships, or pursuing personal goals, each experience contributes to your ongoing development from Blueprint to Fingerprint.

As you progress through this guide, you'll discover what it truly means to become the creator in your life and of your life. You'll develop the capability to approach change with resilience, solve problems with innovation, and express yourself with authenticity. Most importantly, you'll learn to see your entire life as an ongoing creative project that reflects your values and aspirations.

The Adventure Begins

Like every hero standing at the threshold of their great adventure, you may feel a mixture of excitement and uncertainty about what lies ahead. That's not just normal—it's necessary. The combination of anticipation and apprehension signals that you're about to embark on something meaningful, something that will stretch you beyond your current boundaries and help you discover who you're truly capable of becoming.

This guide represents your crossing of the threshold—the moment where you step from your ordinary relationship with creativity into the realm of conscious creative development. From this point forward, you're not merely reading about creativity; you're beginning the active adventure of discovering, developing, and expressing your creative potential.

Your blueprint—genetic, cultural, and circumstantial—brought you to this moment. But the fingerprint you'll leave on the world through your creative choices and expressions? That story is about to unfold, and you are its author.

The adventure of transforming your blueprint into your fingerprint begins now.

Take a deep breath. Feel the excitement and possibility of what lies ahead. You're about to begin an adventure that has the potential to transform not just what you do, but who you are.

When you're ready, turn the page and take your first step into this journey of discovery and development of your Creative Self. Your adventure starts now.

CHAPTER 2:
ORIENTATION

The Creative Life Project: A Fresh Perspective on Creativity

Creative Self Transformation™

Life Force of Creation

Genetic Imprint
Cultural Imprint

Creative Self Expression
Creative Skill Development
Creative Self Exploration /Discovery

Creative Self Expression Practice™

Creative Self Development Framework™
Blueprint to Fingerprint™

Creative Self **Blueprint**

Creative Life Story **Fingerprint**

In our rapidly developing world, creativity stands as a fundamental human trait essential for our survival, growth, and fulfillment. Yet, a pervasive Cloud of Confusion surrounding the concept of creativity itself poses a significant obstacle for many seeking to harness their creative potential. This cloud, composed of misconceptions, misrepresentations, paradoxes, and societal influences, interferes with our ability to discover, develop, and express our creativity in ways that can help us navigate, build, and live what we consider our best lives. It is this critical challenge and the need to dispel it that has fueled the creation of the CLP and the Creative Self Development Framework.

The Essence of Creativity and Being Creative

At the core of all humanity is a dynamic, ever-present energy that fuels every act of creation in the universe—the Life Force of Creation. This force does not confine itself to any domain. It is the essence that empowers us to survive, thrive, and flourish. The CLP supports this perspective, acknowledging this universal force and exploring how we can intentionally channel it to build a meaningful life and contribute to a better world.

The CLP is a philosophy, process, and practice that empowers you to connect with the Life Force of Creation, develop your unique creative potential, and express it through your life and work. By understanding and engaging with this creative energy, you are better equipped to navigate, build, and live your best life while encouraging others to do the same, contributing to a world where creativity is celebrated and nurtured.

The Life Force of Creation is the source from which all creative acts evolve. This life force is more than artistic expression or intellectual innovation; it is the fundamental energy that drives all living things to grow, evolve, and express themselves. It is the source of both the mundane and the extraordinary, present in every aspect of life and available to everyone.

As a co-creation, you result from a creative collaboration between two individuals, each contributing a unique strand of DNA that merged, and you are the result. You join a population of other unique individuals who are fundamentally the same, yet different, as each stands alone with their own genetic and cultural blueprint. You are a unique creation endowed with the capacity to be a creator and collaborator, possessing the innate potential to shape both your own reality and contribute to shaping the reality of the world around you.

At birth, we are all connected to this Life Force of Creation, and at death, our bodies are disconnected from it. This life force enables us to create; it's the source of our creativity.

Creativity is the trait empowering humans to imagine and craft clever and strategic solutions to survive, thrive, and flourish in a constantly changing world.

This is the CLP's functional definition of creativity, and we will explore it in detail in the coming chapter. It serves as the foundation for everything that follows in this guide.

During our lives, we each have a choice to discover, develop, and intentionally use this empowering energy...or not.

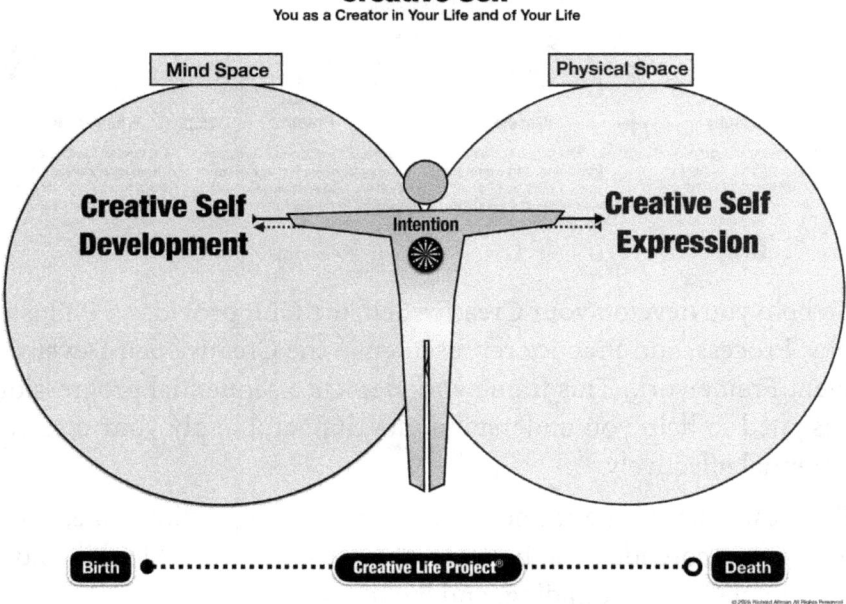

Central to CLP is the concept of the Creative Self: you as a creator in your life and of your life. You channel the Life Force of Creation through your individual genetic and cultural blueprint to transform the fruits of your imagination into meaningful actions that are your fingerprint and the story of how you survived, thrived, and flourished throughout your life.

The Creative Self is not static; it evolves as you do. It grows through your experiences, learning, and practice, continually refining the ability to channel the Life Force of Creation in meaningful ways. By developing your Creative Self and Creative Self Mindset™, you enhance your ability to harness this universal energy and use it to shape your reality and contribute positively to the world around you. This idea will be repeated many times throughout this guide as a reminder and to provide context from the various perspectives presented in the guide.

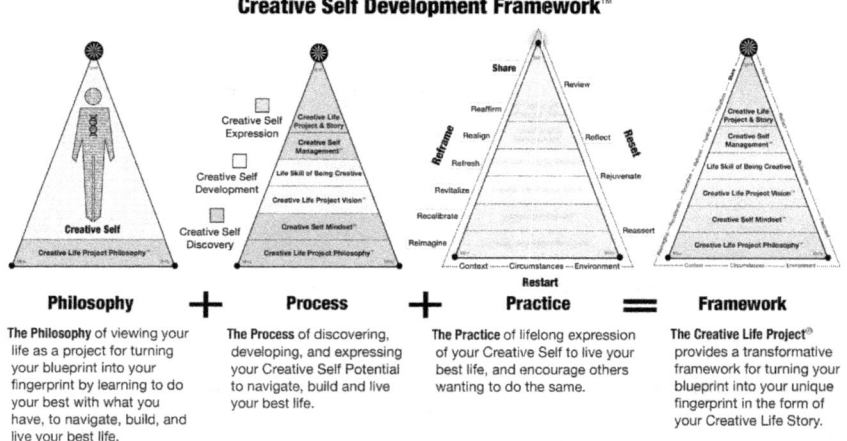

To help you develop your Creative Self, the CLP provides a Philosophy, Process, and Practice represented in the Creative Self Development Framework. This framework depicts a sequential progression designed to help you understand, develop, and apply your creative potential effectively.

Each category of the framework builds on the previous one, reinforcing the core idea that being creative is an essential life skill and a path to navigating, building, and living your best life.

This guide is a category-by-category exploration of the framework that follows a natural sequence of Creative Self Development. We begin by examining our fundamental beliefs about creativity and reimagining what it truly means to be creative. This fresh understanding then transforms how we think about creativity in our daily lives, shifting our mindset from limiting beliefs to empowering perspectives.

With this new foundation in place, we can envision new possibilities for our lives, considering how our creative potential might shape our future. This vision naturally leads us to develop the practical skills needed to bring our creative aspirations to life, followed by effective approaches to managing our creative resources and energies.

As our journey continues, we learn to view our entire life as a creative project unfolding through daily choices and actions. Finally, we discover how to establish sustainable practices that keep our creativity flowing throughout our lives.

Your CLP is your personal commitment to being creative by embracing the Life Force of Creation to navigate life's challenges, build meaningful experiences, and live what you consider to be your best life. This journey is about cultivating a philosophy, process, and practice that highlights creativity as a way of being. It involves recognizing the interconnectedness of all things and understanding that your creative actions have the power to shape both your own life and the lives of others.

By beginning your CLP journey, you are working toward personal fulfillment while also contributing to a collective effort to make the world a better place for everyone. This project encourages you to inspire and support others in their creative journeys, fostering a culture of creativity, collaboration, and innovation.

One of the key realities of the CLP is the paradox that creativity is both a personal and a collaborative endeavor. As you develop and express your Creative Self by practicing the Life Skill of Being Creative™, you naturally begin to inspire and empower others. Your creative actions, whether big or small, become a catalyst for change, encouraging those around you to explore their own creative potential.

In this way, your CLP extends beyond individual growth. It becomes a collective journey toward a more creative, compassionate, and connected world. By committing to this path, you build a future that values and nurtures creativity, empowers individuals to express themselves freely, and recognizes the Life Force of Creation as foundational to being human.

By adopting your own CLP, you go beyond just learning about creativity—you live it by being creative. You are becoming a part of a broader movement to empower individuals, build communities, and create a world where everyone can tap into their creative potential and use it to impact our world positively. This is the ultimate vision of the CLP: a world where creativity is a shared journey, a powerful force for good, and a fundamental celebration of what makes us human.

CHAPTER 3:
CLOUD OF CONFUSION

With a general understanding of your Creative Self and the Creative Self Development Framework in place, we are now ready to begin a deeper exploration of the obstacles that cloud our understanding of creativity. This journey starts by confronting the pervasive Cloud of Confusion surrounding creativity—a dense fog of misconceptions, paradoxes, and societal influences that distort how we perceive and engage with creativity and our creative potential.

This Cloud of Confusion forms the central problem that the CLP addresses. Throughout this guide, we will systematically deconstruct these misconceptions, demystify the creative process, and reimagine what creativity truly means and how it can be developed. The CLP Philosophy, process, and practice have been specifically designed to clear this cloud—helping you reclaim your innate creative potential, which has been obscured by these misunderstandings.

You've likely encountered this cloud in your own life. Perhaps you've struggled to articulate what creativity truly means to you or found it challenging to reconcile your understanding of creativity with how it shows up in different areas of your life. You may have questioned your own creative abilities, unsure of how they compare to others or how, or if, you can develop them further. Even those well-acquainted with creativity often find it difficult to provide a clear, comprehensive definition that encompasses all aspects of creative expression.

Chapter 1, "Before We Begin," encouraged you to reflect on your beliefs about creativity, drawing inspiration from Steve Jobs' transformative perspective and exploring the Creative Self and the Creative Self Development Framework. This foundation has prepared us to move forward with greater clarity and purpose. Now, we turn to understanding the critical barriers that stand between us and the realization of our creative potential.

The Cloud of Confusion is more than a collection of misunderstandings; it is the common story of creativity, which becomes a significant obstacle that can prevent you from recognizing and developing your creative potential. Rooted in societal myths, cultural norms, and internalized beliefs, this confusion can create doubt and hesitation, limiting your ability to imagine, create, and innovate. Recognizing and dispelling this cloud is essential for unlocking your Creative Self and embracing creativity as a fundamental life skill.

In this chapter, we will do the following:

- Identify several of the misconceptions and myths that contribute to the Cloud of Confusion.
- Examine how societal influences and mass-mindedness shape our perceptions of creativity.
- Lay the groundwork for deconstructing, demystifying, and reimagining these barriers and replacing them with a more empowering understanding of creativity.

By exploring the elements that contribute to this confusion, we will begin to see through the fog that obscures our creative potential. This clarity is the first step in reclaiming our creativity and using it to navigate, build, and live our best lives. Let's begin the process of clearing the confusion and stepping fully into the journey of Creative Self Development.

Two Root Causes Contributing to This Cloud of Confusion

A root cause is the most fundamental reason behind the occurrence of a problem or condition—the "source" from which other issues emerge. In exploring the Cloud of Confusion surrounding creativity, two distinct root causes can be identified as the foundation for the misconceptions and barriers we face:

The Paradoxical Nature of Creativity: The Judgment Disconnect

Creativity, and being creative, inherently contains contradictions—not only in how we perceive it but in its very essence.

One of the most profound paradoxes is this: all acts of creation flow from the Life Force of Creation through our creative selves, yet not all acts of creation are viewed by others as being creative.

This core contradiction shapes how we experience, express, and value creativity in every aspect of life.

Consider the journey of Vincent van Gogh, whose work epitomizes this paradox. During his lifetime, van Gogh sold just one painting and was largely dismissed by the art establishment as amateurish and lacking merit. The same paintings that critics once rejected now hang in the world's most prestigious museums, celebrated as revolutionary masterpieces of creative genius. Nothing changed about the paintings themselves—only the judgment applied to them.

This paradox continues to play out in modern times. George Lucas's original Star Wars concept was rejected by multiple major studios—United Artists, Universal, and Warner Bros. all passed on what they viewed as a bizarre, unmarketable space fantasy. Even 20th Century Fox executives had little faith in the project, agreeing to it largely to maintain their relationship with Lucas after his success with American Graffiti. Today, *Star Wars* stands as one of the most successful and influential creative franchises in history, having transformed filmmaking, merchandising, and popular culture.

Similarly, J.K. Rowling's manuscript for *Harry Potter and the Philosopher's Stone* was rejected by twelve publishing houses before being accepted by Bloomsbury, and even then, only after the eight-year-old daughter of the chairman begged her father to publish it. The series went on to become a global phenomenon that has sold over 500 million copies worldwide, been translated into over 80 languages, and spawned a multi-billion-dollar entertainment franchise. The same creative work that was repeatedly judged as unpublishable transformed the landscape of children's literature and entertainment.

This paradox extends beyond art and entertainment into everyday life. A child solving a math problem using an unconventional approach might be praised as ingenious by one teacher and criticized for not following proper procedures by another. A business proposal might be rejected as impractical by one company and embraced as visionary by another. A home cook's improvised recipe might be dismissed as "just throwing things together" by some family members while being celebrated as culinary creativity by others.

The confusion created by this paradox leads many people to doubt their creative abilities when their expressions aren't recognized or valued by those around them. It creates uncertainty about what "counts" as creative and whether one possesses that quality. **Yet, at the heart of this paradox lies a liberating truth: the value of the creative process exists independently of external judgment. The act of creating benefits the creator regardless of how others evaluate the outcome.**

Mass-Mindedness: The Collective Narrowing of Creative Potential

Mass-mindedness is the powerful social force that gradually narrows our understanding of creativity through collective agreement. It occurs when society collectively embraces oversimplified definitions and rigid categories that limit what "counts" as creative. These shared assumptions spread through education, media, and everyday conversations until they become invisible boundaries that shape how we see ourselves and others.

Dr. George Land's landmark creativity study provides compelling evidence of this phenomenon. In 1968, Land administered the same creativity test he had developed for NASA to 1,600 children aged five years old. He then retested the same children at ages 10 and

15. The results were stunning: 98% of five-year-olds scored at the "genius level" of creative thinking. By age 10, only 30% of the same children maintained this level. By age 15, the number had dropped to just 12%. When the same test was given to 280,000 adults, only 2% scored at the genius level.[2]

This dramatic decline in creative capacity isn't the result of a natural developmental process—it's mass-mindedness in action. As children progress through traditional education and socialization, they absorb collectively reinforced messages about what constitutes "proper" thinking. They learn that there are "right" and "wrong" answers, that certain subjects are "creative" while others are "analytical," and that creativity belongs to those with special talents in specific domains.

The natural human desire to belong further reinforces these divisions. Children and adults increasingly identify with socially recognized categories rather than embracing their multifaceted capabilities. "I'm a numbers person, not a creative type" becomes both a self-description and a self-fulfilling prophecy.

Mass-mindedness operates not through any individual's intention but through our collective participation in these simplified systems of understanding. It creates a powerful form of resistance to change precisely because it feels like "common sense" rather than a perspective that could be questioned. Land's study reveals not a natural loss of creative ability but the systematic impact of mass-minded thinking on our innate creative potential.

Understanding and addressing this Cloud of Confusion is essential for anyone seeking to embrace their creative potential fully.

Through the CLP and the Creative Self Development Framework, we will do the following:

- *Deconstruct* the complex factors that obscure our understanding of creativity.
- *Demystify* the true nature of creativity and our own creative potential.
- *Reimagine* what it means to be creative in today's world.

---

2   George Land and Beth Jarman, BREAKPOINT AND BEYOND: MASTERING THE FUTURE TODAY (San Francisco: HarperBusiness, 1993).

By examining these root causes, we begin to clear the fog that clouds our understanding of creativity. This clarity lays the foundation for a fresh and empowering perspective—one that acknowledges creativity's essential role in shaping our lives and cultures.

In the following explorations of specific elements contributing to this Cloud of Confusion, we will illuminate cultural myths and misunderstandings about creativity. This process will pave the way for transforming these barriers into stepping stones for Creative Self Development, empowering you to embrace and express your creative potential fully.

Factors Contributing to the Cloud of Confusion

There are numerous factors that contribute to the Cloud of Confusion. Together, they blur our understanding of creativity and leave many people disconnected from their creative potential. Among these, one of the most fundamental is the absence of a clear and functional definition of creativity—a gap that undermines everything built upon it. Let's begin there and then explore several other factors that reinforce the confusion.

Lack of a Functional Definition of Creativity

The absence of a clear, practical definition of creativity significantly contributes to our confusion. Without a well-defined understanding, creativity becomes an abstract and elusive concept that is difficult to recognize, measure, or develop intentionally. Rather than seeing creativity as a natural and accessible human capacity, many perceive it as a mysterious or innate quality possessed by a select few.

This definitional void affects how creativity is taught, understood, and applied across various domains—from education and workplace innovation to personal development. Without a functional definition, individuals struggle to see how creativity fits into their daily lives, leading to disengagement or undervaluation of their own creative abilities. The lack of clarity makes creativity remain an ambiguous concept, limiting its role in personal growth, problem-solving, and innovation.

Misconceptions and Stereotypes About Creativity

Widespread misconceptions and stereotypes profoundly deepen the Cloud of Confusion. Common beliefs—such as creativity being a rare, innate talent possessed only by artists, inventors, or "creative types"—create barriers for individuals who don't view themselves as naturally creative. These barriers discourage the exploration of creative potential and limit personal growth.

Stereotypes like the "tortured artist" or the belief that creative people are impractical further alienate individuals from engaging in creative pursuits. When creativity is portrayed as accessible only to certain personality types or domains, people naturally question their own creative capacities. These myths foster a culture that views creativity as inaccessible or frivolous, preventing many from recognizing it as a developable skill applicable to daily life. The belief that one must be born creative or that creativity is only valuable in certain fields significantly limits opportunities for meaningful creative expression and innovation.

Focus On Product over Process

Society's emphasis on end products over the creative process fuels confusion about creativity. Success is often measured by tangible results—awards, recognition, or marketable outcomes—rather than the journey of exploration, learning, and iteration that fuels creative growth. This product-centric mindset discourages experimentation and risk-taking, as individuals become overly concerned with producing "perfect" outcomes.

This focus fosters a fear of failure that causes many to abandon creative efforts prematurely. The emphasis on results undervalues the time and effort invested in developing ideas, building skills, and learning from mistakes. This perspective can make creativity feel unattainable, as the pressure to succeed stifles the curiosity and playfulness essential to creative thinking. When we prioritize outcomes exclusively, we neglect the importance of the creative process as a valuable space for personal development, innovation, and discovery.

Self-Assessment vs. External Assessment of Creativity

The tension between personal evaluation and the external judgment of creative work adds considerable confusion to our understanding of creativity. Individuals often struggle to balance their internal sense of creative accomplishment with feedback from others, leading to self-doubt and excessive reliance on external validation. This conflict discourages people from pursuing creative endeavors, especially when others don't immediately recognize or value their work.

The subjective nature of creativity makes consistent evaluation difficult—what one person finds innovative, another may see as ordinary. This variability in feedback can erode confidence and hinder creative risk-taking. The overemphasis on external assessment can shift focus away from intrinsic motivation, making individuals hesitant to explore creative ideas unless they meet societal or professional standards. This imbalance between self-assessment and external validation creates confusion about how to measure and trust one's own creative progress.

Paradox of Technology

Technology presents a complex duality that both enhances and complicates our engagement with creativity. Advanced digital tools, resources, and online platforms provide unprecedented opportunities to create, innovate, and collaborate, empowering individuals to explore new creative frontiers with ease. However, this technological surge brings significant challenges—particularly from artificial intelligence (AI), which, despite its immense potential, adds to our confusion about what truly constitutes human creativity.

As AI-generated art, writing, and creative outputs become increasingly indistinguishable from human-produced work, it raises complex questions about originality, authenticity, and authorship. Many individuals now find themselves uncertain about how to utilize technology creatively without losing the essence of genuine human expression. This tension creates hesitation and confusion, leaving many to wonder how to harmoniously integrate emerging technologies, including AI, into their creative endeavors.

A designer who once spent weeks perfecting hand-drawn illustrations now has access to AI tools that can generate similar images in seconds. While this technology expands what's possible, it also raises profound questions: Is the designer still being creative when using AI assistance? Does the value of human creativity diminish when machines can produce similar results? Where is the line between tool and collaborator? This uncertainty can either paralyze creative action or, when properly understood, open new frontiers for human–technology creative partnership.

Misunderstandings About Intelligence and Thinking in Creativity

A widespread misconception is that intelligence and creativity are interchangeable, leading to confusion about who is considered creative. Many assume that high intelligence automatically equates to high creativity, while those who struggle academically may see themselves as less creative. In reality, creativity involves diverse cognitive processes that extend beyond traditional measures of intelligence. It draws from emotional intelligence, intuitive thinking, and the ability to connect seemingly unrelated ideas.

This misunderstanding limits how people recognize and cultivate their creative potential, especially in educational and professional settings where intelligence is often prioritized over imaginative thinking. By conflating intelligence with creativity, individuals may either underestimate or overestimate their creative capabilities, preventing them from fully engaging with creative processes. This misconception also affects how educators and employers foster creativity, often valuing logical reasoning over imaginative exploration, further narrowing opportunities for diverse forms of creative expression.

Shortage of Accessible Creative Role Models

Accessible and relatable role models who demonstrate creativity's everyday applications are lacking for many people. The popular media often highlights extraordinary creative figures—renowned artists, inventors, and entrepreneurs—making creativity seem unattainable to the average person. This overemphasis on exceptional talent creates a gap between everyday creativity and what society deems "true" creativity.

Without visible examples of how creativity operates in ordinary contexts, individuals may struggle to recognize or value their own creative efforts. This absence of relatable creative role models fosters the misconception that creativity must be exceptional to be meaningful, discouraging many from exploring or expressing their creative abilities. Everyday examples of creativity in problem-solving, innovation, and personal expression are often overlooked, perpetuating the belief that creativity is exclusive to a select few rather than an essential and accessible human trait.

Consider how cooking illustrates this problem. The media celebrates celebrity chefs creating elaborate dishes with exotic ingredients while overlooking the creative ingenuity of a parent who transforms leftovers into a new meal that pleases picky eaters. Both involve creative problem-solving, adaptation, and originality, yet only one is typically recognized as "creative." This lack of validation for everyday creativity prevents many from recognizing their own creative acts and developing confidence in their creative abilities.

Creativity Across Life and Disciplines

Creativity is often narrowly viewed as being relevant only in traditionally "creative" fields like art, music, and writing. This limited perception overlooks how creativity functions across a wide range of disciplines, including science, technology, engineering, business, and even daily life. Such a narrow focus contributes to the belief that creativity is only valuable in certain contexts, causing individuals in non-creative industries to dismiss the importance of creative thinking.

This misunderstanding prevents many from applying creative problem-solving skills in diverse situations. Recognizing the broad applicability of creativity across various domains is essential for fostering innovation and adaptability in both professional and personal contexts. A limited view of creativity can hinder growth, collaboration, and the development of new ideas, ultimately reinforcing the Cloud of Confusion.

Professional vs. Non-Professional Creativity Perspectives

The divide between how creativity is perceived in professional versus personal settings adds to the Cloud of Confusion. In professional environments, creativity is often associated with productivity, innovation, and measurable outcomes. Conversely, in personal contexts, creativity is frequently viewed as a leisurely or non-essential activity. This contrast leads many to undervalue creative pursuits that don't have direct financial or professional rewards, discouraging exploration and experimentation.

The pressure to monetize creativity can diminish its intrinsic value, causing individuals to neglect creative hobbies or passions that contribute to personal fulfillment. This separation creates a false hierarchy between "serious" and "casual" creativity, limiting opportunities for meaningful engagement with creative activities in both spheres.

Stereotypes Associated with Creativity

Stereotypes about creativity contribute significantly to confusion by promoting narrow or distorted views of who can be creative and what creativity looks like. Common stereotypes—such as the "tortured artist," the belief that creativity is impractical, or the idea that it's purely innate—limit the understanding of creativity as a diverse and accessible human trait.

These stereotypes prevent individuals who don't fit these molds from exploring creative pursuits, reinforcing the notion that creativity is reserved for a select few. This narrow framing also excludes non-artistic domains where creativity thrives, such as engineering, business innovation, and scientific discovery. These limiting beliefs distort how creativity is valued and expressed, creating barriers to engaging with creative potential in personal and professional contexts.

Creativity in Relationships and Well-being

The role of creativity in fostering healthy relationships and enhancing personal well-being is often overlooked. Creativity improves communication, deepens emotional connections, and supports conflict resolution, but people rarely recognize its value in personal interactions. Creative activities contribute to mental health by providing outlets for self-expression, stress relief, and emotional processing.

Failing to acknowledge creativity's role in relationships and overall well-being limits opportunities for personal growth and fulfillment. Ignoring this aspect of creativity contributes to the misconception that it is solely for artistic or professional purposes rather than an essential life skill that can enrich all aspects of the human experience.

A couple facing communication challenges might benefit enormously from creative approaches to expressing needs and resolving conflicts. Simple creative acts—like writing letters instead of arguments, creating a shared vision board, or establishing playful rituals for difficult conversations—can transform relationship dynamics. Yet these applications of creativity are rarely recognized or encouraged, leaving many to struggle with conventional approaches that don't serve their unique relationship needs.

Commercialization of Creativity

The increasing commercialization of creativity adds to the Cloud of Confusion by prioritizing marketability over authentic creative expression. This trend encourages creators to focus on producing work that sells or gains social approval, often at the expense of originality and personal fulfillment. The pressure to monetize creative efforts can discourage experimentation and risk-taking, leading individuals to create content that aligns with trends rather than pursuing meaningful or innovative ideas.

This commercialization narrows the perception of creativity to economically valuable outputs, overlooking the intrinsic value of creative expression for personal growth and societal enrichment. As a result, many people may feel their creativity is only worthwhile if it leads to financial success, which can suppress authentic and exploratory creative work.

Process and Practice of Creativity

People often portray creativity as a spontaneous or innate trait, leading to the misconception that it cannot be intentionally developed.

This misunderstanding minimizes the importance of consistent practice, persistence, and structured development in cultivating creativity. Many individuals give up on being creative when they don't experience immediate success, failing to recognize that expression of creativity, like any skill, requires deliberate effort, iteration, and feedback.

The romanticized notion of sudden inspiration overshadows the reality that creativity involves hard work, experimentation, and ongoing refinement. This belief discourages people from engaging in creative practices that demand patience and resilience. By neglecting the process-oriented nature of creativity, individuals may feel disconnected from the steps necessary to nurture and expand their creative potential.

Nurturing Creativity by Influencers

A significant barrier to creative growth is the lack of effective support and encouragement from those in influential positions—teachers, parents, mentors, and leaders. Many influencers struggle to foster creativity in others because of their own misconceptions or limited understanding of creative development. Without proper resources or training, well-intentioned efforts to encourage creativity can inadvertently reinforce harmful stereotypes or restrictive thinking.

The absence of clear frameworks for nurturing creativity in educational, professional, and personal settings leaves individuals without the guidance they need to explore and develop their creative potential. This gap in understanding contributes to the Cloud of Confusion by limiting how creativity is modeled, supported, and encouraged across various environments.

Being Creative as a Fundamental and Strategic Life Skill

People often view creativity as a luxury or an optional talent rather than a critical life skill. This perception limits its integration into education, professional development, and daily living. Viewing creativity as non-essential prevents people from recognizing its relevance in problem-solving, adaptability, and innovation.

The undervaluation of creativity in life skills education leaves individuals ill-equipped to navigate complex, evolving challenges. This misunderstanding also fosters the belief that creativity is only applicable to certain professions or hobbies rather than being a universally valuable skill that enhances all aspects of life. Failing to recognize creativity as a fundamental life skill diminishes opportunities for personal and professional growth.

Broader Importance of Creativity for Society and Evolution

The broader societal role of creativity is often overlooked, reducing its perceived value to personal expression or artistic endeavors. Creativity is a driving force behind human progress, cultural evolution, and global problem-solving. Failing to recognize creativity's impact on societal advancement limits investment in creative education, innovation, and cultural development.

This narrow perspective undervalues how creativity contributes to technological breakthroughs, social movements, and economic growth. Without acknowledging creativity's role in shaping history and driving future advancements, society risks neglecting a critical component of sustainable development and collective well-being.

Lack of a Cohesive Teaching Framework

The absence of a unified, cohesive approach to teaching creativity significantly contributes to confusion about how creativity can be developed. Educational systems often present fragmented and inconsistent methods for fostering creativity, with some emphasizing technical skills and others focusing on mindset. The lack of alignment between different teaching philosophies confuses learners, making it hard for them to understand how to develop and use creativity in various fields.

Additionally, creativity is often treated as secondary to more traditional academic subjects, leaving it underdeveloped in formal education. Without a comprehensive framework that integrates both creative thinking and practical application, individuals struggle to engage with and develop their creative abilities fully.

A student might experience vastly different approaches to creativity across their education—an art teacher who emphasizes technical skill and reproduction, a science teacher who values creative problem-solving but doesn't name it as creativity, and a literature teacher who encourages creative interpretation but only within strict analytical frameworks. Without a cohesive understanding of how these various approaches connect to creativity development, the student struggles to transfer creative skills across domains or develop a confident, creative identity.

Summary

As we conclude our exploration of the Cloud of Confusion, we've uncovered the complex web of factors that obscure our understanding and expression of creativity. From the lack of a functional definition to the pervasive influence of mass-mindedness and from misconceptions about creativity to the challenges posed by traditional education systems, we've seen how these interconnected elements form a formidable barrier to fully embracing our creative potential.

This confusion extends beyond artistic domains—it influences how we approach problem-solving, innovation, and personal growth across all aspects of life. It shapes our self-perception, affects decision-making, and can limit our ability to adapt and thrive in a constantly changing world. The paradoxes inherent in creativity, such as the tension between discipline and spontaneity or between personal expression and external validation, add layers of complexity that can lead to self-doubt and hesitation.

The CLP and the Creative Self Development Framework are intentionally designed to clear this confusion. They offer an organized framework for individual Creative Self Discovery, Development, Management, and Expression in ways that are meaningful and personally fulfilling. This structured approach empowers you to navigate challenges, build meaningful experiences, and live what you consider to be your best life.

By deconstructing and demystifying the barriers to creativity, the CLP and the Creative Self Development Framework encourage you to reimagine a more empowering and comprehensive understanding of creativity—one that acknowledges its complexity while recognizing its universal accessibility and importance. Through engaging with this framework, you will learn to intentionally develop and express your creative potential, transforming creativity from a misunderstood concept into an essential life skill.

As you confront this Cloud of Confusion, you may feel a mixture of emotions—frustration with past barriers, excitement for growth, or curiosity about the path forward. These emotions are natural and signal the beginning of a meaningful journey toward unlocking your creative potential.

In Part II, we begin our journey through the CLP Framework by exploring its foundation: the *Creative Life Project Philosophy*™. This foundational element will introduce the guiding principles that support Creative Self Discovery and set the stage for living a more intentional and creative life.

PART 02

CATEGORY–CREATIVE LIFE PROJECT PHILOSOPHY

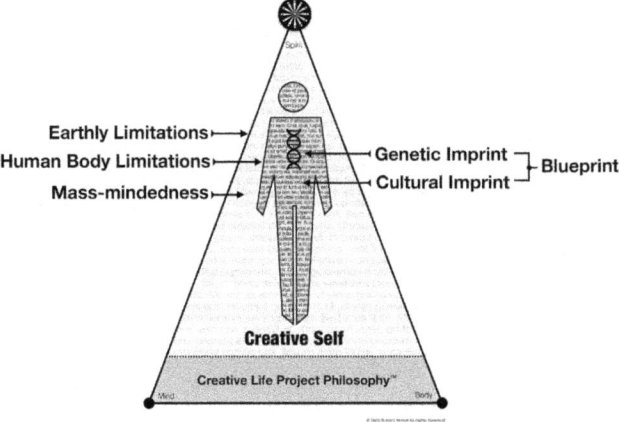

Introduction to the Creative Self Development Framework

The CLP begins with a simple but powerful truth: while we are all born into a specific set of conditions—biological, cultural, and environmental—we are also born with the capacity to shape our lives through Creative Self Expression™ and intentional development. This capacity is at the heart of the Creative Self Development Framework.

The framework is introduced through a foundational diagram representing the essential elements each of us must work with throughout life. The triangle symbolizes physical space—the environment we inhabit, shaped by natural forces such as gravity, air, water, and time. This space provides both the raw materials for life and the boundaries within which we must create. At the three corners of the triangle are mind, body, and spirit—the core dimensions of our human experience and the cornerstones of our ability to perceive, act, and pursue meaning.

At the center of this space is the *Creative Self*—you, as the creator in your life and of your life. Visually represented by the human figure, the Creative Self embodies our evolving potential. Within this figure lies a symbolic strand of DNA layered over a backdrop of text, representing our blueprint: the combination of genetic and cultural imprints that influence how we think, feel, and engage with the world. These inherited elements do not define us completely, but they do shape the starting point for our journey.

Behind the figure is a textured field composed of mass-minded cultural text—the background influence of social norms, dominant beliefs, and communal expectations we encounter throughout our lives. This field represents mass-mindedness, a force that subtly encourages conformity and often limits creative growth through various forms of resistance. In contrast, the text within the Creative Self represents the inner imprint formed through conscious reflection, lived experience, and personal evolution. It symbolizes the difference between what the broader culture dictates and what we come to value as true and meaningful for ourselves.

The Creative Self—the part of you that actively shapes your life—is grounded in both the philosophy and mindset introduced in the first two categories of this framework. Together, they form the internal foundation that empowers you to engage with your blueprint, respond to mass-mindedness with awareness, and bring your mind, body, and spirit into alignment with a life of purpose and direction. The CLP logo at the apex of the triangle represents this aspiration: the ongoing process of navigating, building, and living your best life through intentional creative expression.

This philosophy and the visual framework that supports it set the stage for everything that follows. It acknowledges the realities of physical life—our limitations, our circumstances, and the conditions we inherit—while asserting our potential to grow beyond them. It reminds us that although we are influenced by what we've been given, we are not confined by it.

This is the foundation of the Creative Self Development Framework, and it is where the guide begins. The remaining categories will explore how to build upon this foundation—providing tools, perspectives, and practices that support a lifelong process of Creative Self Discovery, Development, Management, and Expression. With philosophy as your base, the journey ahead is about learning to create a life that is not only authentic and fulfilling but uniquely your own.

Building a Foundation for Understanding Creativity

We begin this journey with the Creative Life Project Philosophy category of the framework. This section is where we explore the fundamentals that form the bedrock for a fresh perspective on creativity and Creative Self Development. As we begin, you are invited once again to adopt a beginner's mind—setting aside preconceived notions and assumptions about creativity—and join me in deconstructing, demystifying, and reimagining what creativity is and the essential role it plays in our lives.

The premise of this work is to clear the pervasive Cloud of Confusion surrounding creativity that we just explored, which often leads to misunderstandings, misrepresentations, and even mystification of this crucial human trait. To achieve this, the CLP Philosophy introduces the concept of creative literacy—a foundational tool for navigating the complexities of learning about and talking about creativity and being creative.

Just as traditional literacy enables individuals to read, write, and engage with written information, creative literacy empowers individuals to understand, express, and harness their creative potential in meaningful and impactful ways. It involves understanding creativity's nature, function, cultivation, and application in diverse contexts.

As Albert Einstein famously stated, "If I had an hour to solve a problem, I'd spend 55 minutes thinking about the problem and five minutes thinking about solutions." In the spirit of this quote, the CLP Philosophy dedicates significant attention to clearly defining and understanding the nature of creativity before exploring strategies for enhancing it. By establishing a strong foundation of creative literacy, we can more effectively harness the power of creativity to navigate, build, and live what we consider to be our best lives—while encouraging others to want to do the same.

Part II unfolds in four interconnected chapters that support this foundational process.

Chapter 4: The Life Force of Creation

The next chapter introduces the foundational concept of the Life Force of Creation—a universal energy that animates all living things and serves as the origin of all creativity. It sets the stage for understanding the deep connection between life and creativity, emphasizing that this life force is not limited to artistic expression or innovation but is the animating energy behind every act of survival, growth, and self-expression. This chapter invites us to reflect on the miracle of being alive and the innate potential we all have to create in alignment with this life force.

Chapter 5: Fundamentals of Life

This chapter explores the realities of being alive and human. It further explores the concept of the Life Force of Creation—a universal energy that animates all living things—and how this energy gives rise to our potential to create. It also introduces the idea that we are each born as unique expressions of this life force, shaped by our individual genetic and cultural blueprints. This context lays the foundation for understanding what it means to be a creator of one's life and of life. It reinforces a simple yet profound truth: we are all the same, but different. We are fundamentally connected by life itself, yet individually distinct in how we are expressed.

Chapter 6: Fundamentals of Creativity

Here, we examine the essential qualities and behaviors that define creativity as a universal human capacity. This chapter identifies the foundational traits we are all endowed with—the inherent aspects of creativity present in everyone—and places them within the context of life. It dispels limiting beliefs and cultural myths that confine creativity to a select few or certain domains. Instead, it presents creativity as a strategic life trait—a learnable, expandable capacity we all possess that is essential for problem-solving, meaning-making, and purposeful living.

Chapter 7: Functional Definition of Creativity

Bringing together the foundational ideas from the previous two chapters, this chapter offers a functional definition of creativity that grounds the entire CLP Framework. It combines the logic of life's fundamental sameness and diversity with the shared endowment of creative potential. The definition becomes the "stake in the ground" around which all subsequent content is organized. It provides the philosophical and practical clarity needed to understand creativity as a life skill, a mindset, and a practice that plays an essential role in every life. This definition also anchors our understanding of creative literacy and serves as the central reference point for everything that follows.

Each chapter builds on the one before, reinforcing the belief that creativity is not an occasional act but an ongoing process of becoming—a lifelong, intentional engagement with life itself. The CLP Philosophy and the concept of creative literacy serve as catalysts for profound personal and societal change. By embracing creativity as a fundamental human trait and a powerful tool for positive transformation, we can work together to dispel the Cloud of Confusion, unlock our creative potential, and build a future in which we can all move beyond survival—to thrive and flourish in our constantly changing world.

CHAPTER 4:
THE LIFE FORCE OF CREATION

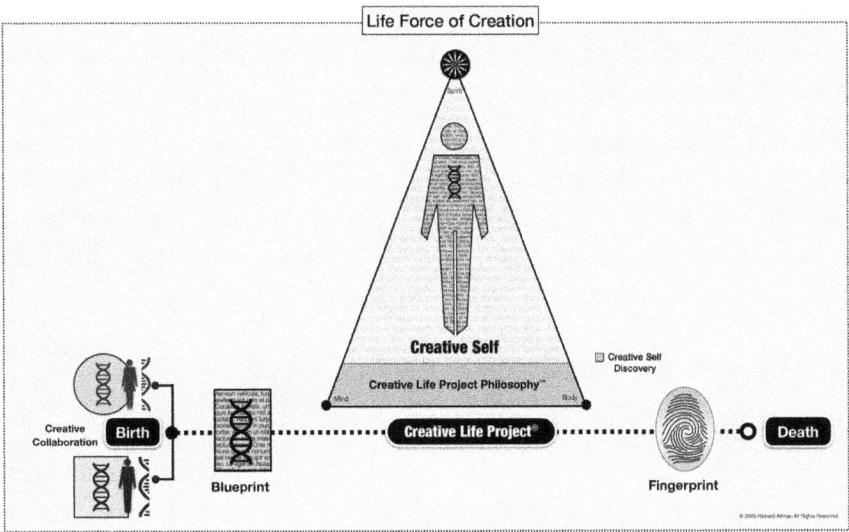

The Life Force of Creation

The Life Force of Creation is the universal energy that drives all acts of creation—from the smallest biological processes to the grandest artistic and scientific achievements. At its core, the Life Force of Creation is the energy that fuels life itself, propelling everything in the natural world to grow, evolve, and express itself in unique and creative ways.

The Life Force of Creation serves as both the starting point and the underlying power that guides every individual's creative journey. This energy is accessible to all living beings, and it is by tapping into this force that we can unlock our creative potential, navigate the challenges of life, and build the world we want to live in.

Defining the Life Force of Creation

The Life Force of Creation is an ever-present, dynamic energy that flows through all living things. It is the vital force that gives life to every organism, from plants and animals to humans. It is also the source of all creative potential, the driving force behind every thought, action, and expression of creativity.

This context does not limit creation to artistic or intellectual endeavors. It encompasses everything that brings something new into existence, whether it is a scientific breakthrough, a social movement, a piece of art, or the simple act of nurturing a relationship. The Life Force of Creation is the energy that drives us to survive, thrive, and flourish in a constantly changing world.

This life force is dynamic; it is in constant motion, influencing and shaping our world. Every time we engage with this energy—whether consciously or unconsciously—we are participating in the process of creation. It is the energy that fuels our thoughts, sparks our imagination, and motivates us to turn ideas into reality.

The Universal Accessibility of the Life Force

One of the most empowering aspects of the Life Force of Creation is its universal accessibility. Every individual, regardless of their background, talents, or circumstances, can tap into this life force. It is not reserved for a select few; it is a resource that is available to all of us.

Accessing the Life Force of Creation does not require special skills or knowledge. It is an inherent part of being alive. Just as every living organism draws upon the life force to grow and thrive, every human being can draw upon this creative energy to fuel their thoughts, actions, and expressions. The key to unlocking this potential lies in becoming aware of the life force and learning how to channel it intentionally.

The Role of the Life Force in Human Development

The Life Force of Creation makes human development possible, both individually and collectively. The most fundamental and consequential act of creation starts with a creative collaboration between two humans, each contributing a single strand of DNA, which merges and triggers the beginning of the life of a new and unique human being. This new life is both a co-creation and a creator with the capacity to discover, develop, manage, and express their Creative Self.

This creative journey extends beyond personal fulfillment. Through their actions, expressions, and contributions, they have the power to inspire and encourage others to embark on their own creative paths. Together, as creators and collaborators, humans can collectively channel the Life Force of Creation to build a world where everyone can survive, thrive, and flourish—a world enriched by the diverse expressions of creativity that make it a better place for all.

As individuals, we are constantly evolving. Our experiences, environment, and choices shape who we are and how we express our creative potential. The Life Force of Creation is the driving force behind this evolution, urging us to grow, explore new ideas, solve problems, and adapt to the ever-changing world around us.

At a collective level, this life force also shaped human cultures and societies. Every innovation, social movement, and cultural development is a product of this creative energy that flows through individuals and communities. By tapping into the Life Force of Creation, humans have been able to build civilizations, create art, and solve some of the most pressing challenges of our time, most of which result from our own acts of creative expression.

Tapping Into the Life Force: Intentional Engagement

While the Life Force of Creation is universally accessible, it requires intentional engagement to be harnessed fully. Many people go through life without fully realizing their creative potential, often because they are unaware of the life force or do not know how to channel it effectively. It involves recognizing that this energy exists within you and that it can fuel your thoughts, actions, and creative endeavors. From there, it requires a commitment to engage with the life force intentionally. This means cultivating habits and practices that support your connection to this energy, such as mindfulness, self-reflection, and creative exploration.

When you intentionally engage with the life force, you unlock your creative potential. You start to see opportunities for growth and innovation in every aspect of your life. You become more adaptable, resilient, and open to new experiences. This is the power the Life Force of Creation allows you to continually develop, learn about, and create in response to the world around you.

The Life Force of Creation and the Blueprint to Fingerprint Analogy

Each individual begins life with a unique genetic and cultural imprint, often referred to as their blueprint. A combination of genetics, family background, and early life experiences shapes this blueprint. However, this blueprint is not static. Through intentional engagement with the Life Force of Creation, individuals have the power to transform their blueprint into a fingerprint—a unique expression of their creative potential that leaves a lasting impact on the world.

The process of transforming your blueprint into your fingerprint is the essence of the CLP, and we will refer to it throughout this guide. By channeling the Life Force of Creation, you can shape your life in ways that align with your deepest values and aspirations, leaving a unique and meaningful legacy. We will return to this "Blueprint to Fingerprint" analogy on multiple occasions throughout this guide.

The Life Force of Creation and the Creative Self Development Framework

As you move forward in your journey with the CLP, you will explore how your Creative Self channels the Life Force of Creation. Your Creative Self serves as the conduit for this life force, allowing you to transform your creative potential into tangible outcomes intentionally.

Through the Creative Self Development Framework, you will learn how to discover, develop, manage, and express your Creative Self, using the Life Force of Creation to build your best life and contribute to the world around you.

In the next section, we will explore the Creative Self Fundamentals™ to understand how to channel the life force effectively and begin your Creative Self Development journey.

CHAPTER 5:
FUNDAMENTALS OF LIFE

Having explored the Life Force of Creation as the universal energy that animates all living things and fuels our creative potential, we now turn our attention to the landscape in which that potential is developed and expressed: everyday life. If the Life Force of Creation is the shared power we are all born with, then the *fundamentals of life* are the shared conditions through which we come to understand and apply it.

These fundamentals of life represent a collection of the core experiences, challenges, and opportunities that every human being must navigate. They serve as the common ground upon which our individuality plays out. While each of us is shaped by a unique genetic and cultural blueprint, we are all operating within a basic set of human realities that shape our thoughts, actions, emotions, and relationships.

This chapter frames the life side of the CLP—not simply as a philosophical concept but as a daily reality. It reminds us that life presents every person with problems to solve, decisions to make, relationships to manage, and responsibilities to carry. It is within this space that our creative potential is both tested and developed.

In short, the fundamentals of life establish the basic context for Creative Self Development. They are the recurring themes and structural conditions we encounter throughout life—the canvas on which the Life Force of Creation must operate.

As the saying goes, "same, same, but different." We are all confronted with the same categories of life experience, though we face them in unique ways. Recognizing this dual truth helps us cultivate empathy, perspective, and personal agency.

By identifying and reflecting on these life fundamentals, we develop an awareness of the landscape in which creativity becomes meaningful. They allow us to understand how our creative potential can be actively engaged to navigate life with more clarity, adaptability, and purpose.

As you explore these fundamentals, consider how they are showing up in your life. How do they support your creative expression? How do they challenge your growth? And in what ways might deepening your understanding of these elements allow you to navigate life more effectively, with greater creative insight and intention?

These fundamentals are not rigid truths but living guideposts. Embrace them as tools for Creative Self Development, catalysts for creative growth, and foundational aspects of a life that seeks not only to survive but to thrive and flourish through creative engagement.

The Fundamentals of Life

Here are seventeen fundamental principles that can help you build your CLP Philosophy.

1. We are all the same but different because of our genetic and cultural blueprint and the human consciousness we share.

As human beings, we share a common foundation of humanity, characterized by our human mind, body, and spirit. This shared essence binds us together and highlights our fundamental similarities. However, while we are all the same at our core, we are also unique individuals shaped by the complex interplay of our genetic makeup, cultural background, and personal experiences.

Our genetic inheritance provides the blueprint for our physical attributes, predispositions, and potential, setting the stage for our individual development. Cultural imprints, including family dynamics, societal norms, and educational experiences, further mold our perspectives, values, and behaviors. The combination of these factors contributes to the diverse tapestry of human existence, allowing for a rich array of talents, interests, and ways of perceiving the world.

Recognizing our shared human consciousness while acknowledging and celebrating our individual differences is essential to the CLP Philosophy. By embracing the idea that we are all the same yet different, we can cultivate empathy, understanding, and collaboration, harnessing the power of our collective creativity to navigate challenges and create meaningful change. This understanding serves as a foundation for appreciating and leveraging our unique strengths while being open to learning from and connecting with others, fostering a more vibrant and innovative society.

2. Life is neither fair nor unfair; it just is. The challenge for all of us is to make the best of what we have whenever, wherever, and however we are.

Life, in its essence, is a canvas upon which we paint the story of our lives. It does not inherently favor or discriminate against any individual; rather, it presents a variety of experiences, challenges, and opportunities that we must navigate. Accepting that life is neither fair nor unfair liberates us from the mental and emotional burdens of victimhood or entitlement, empowering us to focus on what we can control: our actions, responses, and the meaning we ascribe to our experiences.

The CLP Philosophy emphasizes the importance of embracing our current circumstances and making the most of the resources available to us. By adopting a proactive and empowering mindset, we can transform perceived limitations into opportunities for growth and innovation. This approach enables us to harness our creative potential and develop the resilience necessary to overcome obstacles and thrive in the face of adversity.

Recognizing that life is a shared journey, we can find strength and inspiration knowing that everyone faces their own unique set of challenges. By cultivating compassion and understanding for ourselves and others, we create a supportive environment that encourages collaboration, empathy, and mutual growth. Ultimately, the challenge lies not in lamenting the perceived unfairness of life but in leveraging our creativity and resourcefulness to make the best of our circumstances and create a life of purpose and fulfillment.

3. We all must deal with our own innate potential, limitations, and personal circumstances, along with the natural realities of sharing and living on planet Earth.

As human beings, we are subject to a complex interplay of factors that shape our existence and the ways in which we navigate through life. These factors encompass the inherent potential and limitations of our physical, mental, and spiritual selves, as well as the universal realities that govern our shared experience on Earth.

Our bodies, with their unique genetic makeup and physical attributes, provide the vessel through which we experience the world. While we each possess an inherent potential for growth, development, and expression, we must also contend with the limitations imposed by our physical forms, such as the effects of aging, illness, and injury.

Similarly, our minds and spirits are subject to their own unique sets of potentials and limitations. Our cognitive abilities, emotional capacities, and spiritual beliefs shape our perceptions, decisions, and interactions with the world around us.

Furthermore, we must acknowledge and adapt to the natural realities that govern life on Earth, such as gravity, the need for sustenance, and the importance of relationships. These universal constants shape our daily experiences and provide a shared foundation upon which we build our lives.

The CLP Philosophy encourages individuals to embrace their potential, work within their limitations, and navigate their personal circumstances with grace, resourcefulness, resilience, and creativity.

By recognizing the interconnectedness of our physical, mental, and spiritual selves, as well as our shared experiences as inhabitants of Earth, we can cultivate a more holistic and empowering approach to life.

4. We all spend our days doing something, sometimes intentional and productive, other times not so much.

All of us have the challenge and responsibility of choosing each day how we invest the currency of life, our time and energy, which, over the course of our lives, defines our life story.

The fabric of our lives is woven from the threads of our daily actions and choices. Each moment, we are presented with the opportunity to invest our time and energy in pursuits that can either contribute to our personal growth and fulfillment or detract from it. While some of our activities may be intentional and purposeful, others may be less so, often driven by habit, impulse, or external pressures.

The CLP Philosophy emphasizes the importance of recognizing the value of our time and energy as the most precious currencies we possess. By cultivating awareness of how we spend these resources, we can make more conscious and deliberate choices that align with our values, goals, and aspirations. This requires a willingness to assess our priorities regularly, eliminate or delegate tasks not serving our higher purpose, and invest in activities promoting our personal and professional development.

Over the course of our lives, the cumulative effect of these daily choices and actions shapes the narrative of our existence. By consistently making decisions that honor our values and contribute to our growth, we can craft a life story that is rich in meaning, purpose, and fulfillment. Conversely, if we allow ourselves to be swept along by the currents of mass-mindedness without intentional direction, we risk looking back on a story that feels disconnected from our true selves and our innate potential.

5. We all have the power to shape our own story and create meaning in our lives.

By actively engaging in self-reflection, setting intentions, and making conscious choices, we can craft a life story that aligns with our values, purpose, and desires.

One of the most empowering aspects of the human experience is our ability to shape the narrative of our lives. While we may not have control over every circumstance that arises, we always have the power to choose how we interpret, respond to, and create meaning from these experiences. This fundamental truth lies at the heart of the CLP Philosophy, which encourages individuals to take an active role in authoring their own life stories.

The process of crafting a meaningful and fulfilling life narrative begins with self-reflection. By taking the time to examine our thoughts, feelings, and beliefs, we can gain a deeper understanding of our authentic selves and the values that drive us. This introspection enables us to identify the core elements that we wish to embody and express in our lives, serving as a compass for our intentions and actions.

Setting clear intentions is another crucial aspect of shaping our life narrative. By defining our goals, aspirations, and desired outcomes, we create a direction for our personal and professional development. These intentions act as a filter through which we can evaluate our choices and decisions, ensuring that they align with our overarching purpose and values.

Making conscious choices is the final key to crafting a life story that resonates with our deepest desires. Every decision we make, from the smallest daily habits to the most significant life changes, contributes to the overall narrative of our lives. By approaching these choices with mindfulness, creativity, and a commitment to our authentic selves, we can actively shape our experiences and create a life that is rich in meaning and fulfillment.

6. We all face problems, challenges, and opportunities as part of life, and we are called upon to make choices related to these circumstances.

We can choose to react emotionally or respond mindfully to our situations, which often present themselves as binary choices yet frequently require critical and creative thinking to reframe them into more appropriate alternatives. Life is a complex set of problems, challenges, and opportunities.

These situations arise as an inevitable part of our human journey, testing our resilience, adaptability, and problem-solving skills. How we choose to perceive and respond to these circumstances plays a crucial role in shaping the outcome of our experiences and the overall quality of our lives.

The CLP Philosophy encourages us to cultivate a flexible and open-minded approach to changing circumstances. Rather than resisting or avoiding the inevitable difficulties of life, we learn to embrace them as integral parts of the creative journey and to find ways to use them to our advantage.

When faced with difficulties or opportunities, our initial instinct may be to react emotionally, driven by fear, anxiety, or excitement; while these emotional responses are natural and valid, they can often lead to impulsive decisions or binary thinking that limits our options and hinders our ability to find optimal solutions. Instead, the CLP Philosophy encourages individuals to cultivate the skill of mindful response, which involves pausing, assessing the situation objectively, and exploring creative alternatives.

This practice of adaptability within the CLP Philosophy is about developing the mental and emotional flexibility needed to thrive in the face of ever-changing circumstances. By cultivating a responsive and resilient approach to the situations we encounter, we become more capable of navigating the twists and turns of life's journey with grace, courage, and authenticity.

7. We all possess the human resource of a creative potential that we can discover, develop, and express to help us navigate, build, and live our best lives... or not.

Although it's not the easiest path, choosing to engage in the development and expression of our creative potential not only leads to greater well-being, personal fulfillment, adaptability, and resilience in the face of life's challenges but also contributes to the collective well-being of our communities, cultures, and society.

At the core of every individual lies their creative potential, waiting to be tapped and harnessed for personal and collective growth. This inherent creativity doesn't limit itself to artistic pursuits; rather, it encompasses our ability to generate novel ideas, solve problems, and adapt to life's ever-changing circumstances. The CLP Philosophy frames this creative potential as a valuable asset, cultivating and applying it to enhance our overall well-being and resilience.

Discovering and developing our creative potential is a journey of self-exploration and personal growth. It requires a willingness to step outside of our comfort zones, embrace curiosity, and engage in the process of experimentation and learning. By dedicating ourselves to the cultivation of our creative abilities, we unlock new possibilities for self-expression, problem-solving, and innovation, enabling us to make the most of the resources and opportunities available to us.

8. We all have the capacity for self-awareness, reflection, and assessment, which are essential for creative growth and making conscious choices that align with our values and goals.

Self-awareness and self-reflection are two of the most powerful tools we possess for personal growth and the successful navigation of life's challenges and opportunities. These introspective practices enable us to gain a deeper understanding of our thoughts, emotions, values, and behaviors, providing a foundation for making conscious choices that align with our authentic selves and desired outcomes.

Self-reflection involves taking the time to contemplate our experiences, examine our responses, and evaluate the outcomes of our actions. By engaging in regular self-reflection, we can identify patterns in our thinking and behavior, recognize areas for improvement, and gain insights into our strengths and weaknesses. This process of introspection allows us to learn from our mistakes, celebrate our successes, and make informed decisions about our future actions.

Self-awareness, on the other hand, is the ongoing practice of being attuned to our internal states, thoughts, and emotions as they arise in the present moment. By cultivating self-awareness, we develop the ability to observe our experiences as objectively as possible, without judgment or reactivity. This heightened sense of awareness enables us to respond to situations more mindfully, regulating our emotions and making choices that are grounded in our values and long-term goals.

The CLP Philosophy emphasizes the importance of self-reflection and self-awareness as essential skills for personal growth and effective decision-making. By regularly engaging in these practices, we can develop a clearer sense of purpose, align our actions with our values, and navigate life's challenges and opportunities with greater wisdom and resilience.

9. We all can cultivate a beginner's mind, openness, and eagerness to learn and experience new things.

Faced with life's complexities and ever-changing circumstances, cultivating a beginner's mind is a powerful tool for personal growth, creativity, and successful navigation of challenges and opportunities. The beginner's mind, a concept rooted in Zen Buddhism, refers to the practice of approaching situations with openness, curiosity, and a willingness to learn, unencumbered by preconceptions or experiences. When we embrace a beginner's mind, we release our attachment to being an expert and instead adopt a stance of humility and receptivity.

This approach allows us to see the world with fresh eyes, noticing details and possibilities that may have gone unnoticed when clouded by our assumptions and biases. By letting go of our need for certainty and control, we open ourselves up to the joy of discovery and the potential for unexpected insights and solutions.

Cultivating a beginner's mind is essential for personal growth, as it enables us to approach new experiences and challenges with a sense of wonder and enthusiasm. Rather than being limited by our past successes or failures, we can engage with each moment as an opportunity to learn, grow, and expand our understanding of ourselves and our world.

The CLP Philosophy recognizes the cultivation of a beginner's mind as a fundamental practice for navigating life's complexities and unlocking our full potential. By consciously choosing to approach situations with openness, curiosity, and a willingness to learn, we equip ourselves with the mental flexibility and resilience necessary to adapt to change, overcome obstacles, and seize opportunities for personal and collective growth.

10. We all operate within a framework of values, ethics, and moral principles that guide our actions and interactions with others.

Being mindful of these principles and striving to live in alignment with them can contribute to a greater sense of integrity, purpose, and social responsibility. As human beings, we are inherently social creatures who navigate the complexities of life within our own self-constructed framework of values, ethics, and moral principles. These principles guide our actions and interactions, shaping the way we perceive and respond to the world around us. The CLP Philosophy recognizes the importance of being mindful of these principles and striving to live in alignment with them or adjust them to cultivate a greater sense of integrity, purpose, and social responsibility.

Our values, ethics, and moral principles are shaped by a combination of personal experiences, cultural influences, and inherent human qualities such as empathy and compassion. They form the foundation of our character and serve as a guide for making decisions that honor our authentic selves and contribute positively to the lives of others. By being mindful of these principles and consciously choosing to align our actions with them, we develop a strong sense of integrity and purpose, knowing that we are living in accordance with our most deeply held beliefs.

Living in alignment with our values, ethics, and moral principles enables us to become more socially responsible citizens. When we act with integrity and compassion, we create a ripple effect of positive change in our relationships, communities, and the world at large. By modeling ethical behavior and considering the impact of our choices on others, we inspire trust, collaboration, and a shared sense of purpose, fostering a more harmonious and fair society.

The CLP Philosophy encourages individuals to reflect regularly on their values, ethics, and moral principles and to make conscious choices that honor these guiding principles. By cultivating mindfulness and intentionality in our actions and interactions, we can navigate life's challenges and opportunities with greater clarity, purpose, and social responsibility.

11. We are all influenced by the social, economic, and political systems in which we live.

These systems can either support or hinder our ability to navigate, build, and live our best lives. It is important to be aware of how these systems affect our choices and opportunities. As individuals, we exist within a complex web of social, economic, and political systems that shape the context of our lives. These systems, including institutions, policies, and cultural norms, exert a powerful influence on our experiences, opportunities, and overall well-being. The CLP Philosophy recognizes the importance of being aware of these systemic influences and how they impact our lives.

Social systems, such as family structures and societal norms, shape our identities and relationships. Economic systems influence our financial stability and career opportunities. Political systems define our rights, freedoms, and responsibilities as citizens. By understanding how these systems affect us, we can make more informed choices and work toward creating positive change.

Being aware of these systems allows us to recognize opportunities and constraints within our environment, make informed decisions about our personal and professional lives, and advocate for policies and practices that promote fairness and equality. By actively engaging with these systems, we can work toward shaping a world that supports the creative potential and well-being of all individuals.

12. We all have the capacity for empathy, compassion, and connection with others, and fostering these qualities can lead to more meaningful relationships, a greater sense of belonging, and a more fulfilling life.

Our inherent wiring as human beings includes connection, empathy, and compassion. These qualities form the foundation of meaningful relationships and a sense of belonging that is essential to our well-being and fulfillment. The CLP Philosophy reinforces the importance of fostering these qualities to create a more meaningful and satisfying life, both personally and collectively.

Empathy allows us to understand and share the feelings of others, enabling us to build stronger, more authentic relationships. By cultivating empathy, we develop a deeper understanding of those around us, leading to more effective communication, conflict resolution, and collaboration. Compassion, flowing from empathy, drives us to ease the suffering of others and promote their well-being. When we approach others with compassion, we create a supportive environment that enhances both individual and collective flourishing.

Connection, fostered by empathy and compassion, fulfills our need for belonging and relatedness. Strong connections provide emotional support, opportunities for growth, and a sense of community. By actively cultivating these qualities, we can develop deeper, more fulfilling relationships, enhance our emotional intelligence and social skills, and contribute to a more compassionate and understanding society.

13. We all live in an increasingly digital world where technology and media play a significant role in our daily lives and relationships.

It is important to acknowledge the impact technology has on our well-being, communication, and personal connections, and to use it in a way that supports our growth and values.

In today's rapidly evolving digital landscape, technology and media have become ubiquitous forces, shaping our daily experiences, communication patterns, and relationships. The CLP Philosophy recognizes the profound influence of these digital tools and platforms on our lives and emphasizes the importance of mindful engagement with technology.

While digital technologies offer unprecedented opportunities for connection, learning, and creative expression, they also present unique challenges to our well-being and interpersonal relationships. It's crucial to maintain a balanced and intentional approach to our digital interactions. This includes being aware of how technology affects our mental health and productivity, balancing online and offline interactions to maintain authentic connections, and using digital tools to enhance creativity and personal growth.

By acknowledging the double-edged nature of technology, we can harness its benefits while mitigating potential negative impacts. This mindful approach allows us to use digital tools to enhance our creative expression, fostering meaningful connections and supporting our personal growth. The CLP encourages individuals to assess and regularly adjust their relationship with technology, ensuring that it aligns with their values and contributes positively to their creative journey and overall well-being.

14. We all have the potential to contribute to the well-being of others and our world. By recognizing our interconnectedness and taking responsibility for our actions, we can create positive change in our communities and beyond.

The CLP Philosophy emphasizes our inherent capacity to make a positive impact on our world. This fundamental recognizes that each individual has the power to contribute to the collective well-being, highlighting the interconnected nature of our existence and the ripple effect of our actions.

By recognizing our interconnectedness, we understand that our actions and choices affect not only ourselves but also others and the environment. Taking responsibility for our role in shaping our communities and the broader world through our daily decisions and behaviors is crucial. This involves cultivating awareness of how our actions impact others and the environment, both locally and globally.

Embracing this principle allows us to tap into the transformative power of collective action. Whether through minor acts of kindness, community involvement, or larger-scale initiatives, each contribution adds to the creation of a more compassionate, sustainable, and thriving world. The CLP Philosophy encourages individuals to view their creative journey not just as a path to personal fulfillment but as an opportunity to make a meaningful difference in the lives of others and the world at large.

15. We all face moments of uncertainty, fear, and doubt. Cultivating creative courage, resilience, independence, and a sense of purpose can help us navigate the problems, challenges, and opportunities of being human.

The CLP Philosophy recognizes that uncertainty, fear, and doubt are inevitable aspects of the human experience.

These challenging emotions can arise in various contexts, from personal relationships to professional endeavors and even in our creative pursuits. However, by developing certain qualities, we can navigate these difficult moments more effectively and use them as opportunities for growth and self-discovery.

Embracing courage means facing our fears and taking action despite feeling uncertain. Building resilience allows us to bounce back from setbacks and adapt to change. Cultivating a sense of purpose connects our actions to our deeper values and long-term goals. These qualities, along with self-awareness and effective coping strategies, help us transform moments of uncertainty and doubt into catalysts for personal development.

By practicing self-awareness, we can recognize our emotional states and understand their origins. Developing coping strategies helps us manage stress and anxiety effectively. It's also important to recognize when to seek support from others for help and guidance. Reframing challenges as opportunities for learning and personal growth allows us to face life's difficulties with greater confidence and clarity.

16. We all have the responsibility to respect and take care of our mind, body, and spirit.

The CLP Philosophy emphasizes the fundamental importance of self-care and self-respect. This principle recognizes that we are holistic beings, composed of interconnected mental, physical, emotional, and spiritual aspects, each requiring attention and nurturing. By taking responsibility for our own well-being, we not only improve our quality of life but also enhance our capacity to contribute positively to the world around us.

Caring for our mental well-being involves engaging in activities that stimulate our minds, like acquiring knowledge and engaging in situations that challenge our thinking and the application of our knowledge. Physical health requires prioritizing proper nutrition, regular exercise, adequate sleep, and preventive healthcare. Emotional health involves recognizing, understanding, and managing our emotions in ways that promote resilience and well-being, which may include developing healthy coping strategies for stress, fostering positive relationships, and expressing emotions constructively. Spiritual nourishment comes from cultivating practices that provide meaning, purpose, and connection to something greater than ourselves. Self-awareness plays a crucial role in this process, allowing regular check-ins to understand our needs and feelings. Learning to set boundaries and say no to demands that compromise our well-being is an essential aspect of self-care. Continuously seeking opportunities for learning and self-improvement contributes to our personal growth.

It's important to view self-care not as selfish but as an essential practice that enables us to show up fully in our lives and creative endeavors. By respecting and nurturing ourselves, we set a foundation for sustainable creativity and personal fulfillment. When we are well-cared for, we have more energy, creativity, and resilience to face life's challenges and pursue our goals.

17. We all share this world and the resources it provides, and just as we care for ourselves, we are responsible for caring for the world we share and the people we share it with.

The CLP Philosophy recognizes our interconnectedness with our world and our collective responsibility to care for our shared environment and communities. This principle extends our sphere of care beyond ourselves to encompass the planet and all its inhabitants. It acknowledges that our actions have far-reaching consequences and that we play a crucial role in shaping the world in which we live.

Environmental stewardship is a key aspect of this responsibility, involving actions to protect and preserve natural resources and ecosystems. Adopting sustainable living practices helps minimize our ecological footprint and promotes long-term environmental health. This mindset encourages us to consider the impact of our choices on the planet and future generations.

Our responsibility extends to our communities as well. Actively taking part in and contributing to the well-being of our local and global communities fosters a sense of social responsibility. This involves considering the impact of our actions on others and striving to make positive contributions to society. It also includes appreciating and honoring diverse cultures and ways of life, promoting a more inclusive and harmonious world.

By embracing this responsibility, we contribute to creating a more sustainable, fair, and harmonious world. This approach aligns our personal creative journey with the greater good, enabling us to find fulfillment not just in personal achievements but in our contributions to the world we share. We have a responsibility to view our creative endeavors as opportunities to positively impact both their immediate surroundings and the broader world, fostering a sense of global interconnectedness and shared responsibility.

The Power in the Fundamentals of Life

As we complete our exploration of these fundamentals, it becomes clear they are not just abstract concepts but powerful idea tools for personal transformation and creative growth. These fundamentals form the guidelines of the CLP Philosophy, providing a comprehensive framework for understanding and navigating the complexities of human existence.

By embracing these fundamentals, we gain a deeper appreciation of the interconnected nature of our lives and the world around us. Our daily experiences, relationships, and broader societal and environmental contexts are inextricably linked to our creative journey. This holistic understanding empowers us to approach our creative pursuits with greater authenticity, purpose, and resilience.

The implications of integrating these fundamentals into our creative practice are profound. They challenge us to move beyond narrow definitions of creativity, encouraging us to see our entire life as a canvas for creative expression. Whether we're navigating personal relationships, confronting societal challenges, or exploring our inner landscapes, these fundamentals provide us with the tools to do so with greater awareness, empathy, and innovation.

In our CLP journey, these fundamentals equip us with a powerful lens to view and shape our experiences as we carry them forward. They serve to guide us toward more intentional, fulfilling, and impactful lives. They remind us that creativity is not separate from life but is life itself—a dynamic, ever-evolving process of growth, expression, and connection.

CHAPTER 6:
FUNDAMENTALS OF CREATIVITY

Building on the fundamentals of life—the shared realities and challenges of human experience—we shift our focus to the human capacity that allows us to interact and respond to those realities with intention, adaptability, and imagination: creativity.

The CLP Philosophy approaches creativity from a unique and transformative perspective. Unlike much of the psychological research with a focus on the degree to which a product or process can be labeled as "creative," the CLP shifts the focus to creativity as a fundamental human trait—one that exists in all of us and can be intentionally developed. This chapter explores creativity not as a personality trait or artistic quality but as a human resource for surviving, thriving, and flourishing in a constantly changing world.

We examine the foundational aspects of creativity that are inherent in all people, regardless of background, profession, or skill. These universal fundamentals form the basis of creative literacy—the ability to understand, learn about, talk about, access, and apply our unique creative potential with clarity and purpose.

By exploring these fundamentals, we deconstruct and demystify creativity and become open to reimagining this core human capacity. As you engage with these ideas, you are invited to reconnect with your own Creative Self and reimagine what's possible as the creator in your life and of your life.

To illustrate this distinction, consider the analogy of the sun as a developable resource. Just as the sun's energy can be harnessed and processed to function as solar energy, the human trait of creativity can be cultivated and expressed to generate outcomes that hold value for the individual creator and, in certain cases, for specific domains or society as a whole.

The Fundamentals of Creativity™, as presented in the CLP Philosophy, are not concerned with assigning labels of "creative" or "not creative" to the products of creative endeavors. Instead, these fundamentals explore the very nature of creativity as a universal human trait and developable resource, one that has played a crucial role in our species' ability to survive, thrive, and flourish throughout human history.

By focusing on creativity as a fundamental aspect of human existence, the CLP Philosophy provides a framework for understanding how this trait functions within the context of our daily lives, our personal and professional growth, and our overall well-being. It encourages us to view creativity not as a rare or exceptional quality possessed by a select few but as a resource that every individual can access, develop, and apply in meaningful ways.

This fresh perspective on creativity has far-reaching implications for how we approach Creative Self Development and creative literacy. Rather than striving to reach an externally defined standard of "creativeness," we are empowered to cultivate and express our creativity in ways that align with our personal values, goals, and aspirations. We are invited to evaluate our creative outcomes based on their significance to us as individuals while also recognizing the potential for our creative expressions to contribute to the collective knowledge and progress of specific domains or society as a whole.

By engaging with these fundamentals, you will gain a deeper understanding of creativity as a fundamental human trait and a powerful resource for self-discovery, problem-solving, and positive transformation. You will be challenged to rethink your assumptions about creativity and to embrace a perspective that celebrates the inherent creative potential within yourself and others.

As we move through this exploration, I encourage you to approach these fundamentals with an open and curious mind, reflecting on how they resonate with your own experiences and aspirations. By doing so, you will begin to develop a strong foundation for creative literacy, one that empowers you to harness your creative potential and apply it in meaningful and impactful ways throughout your life.

So, let's start this journey by opening to a fresh perspective that recognizes the inherent value and potential of this essential human trait. Together, we will unlock new possibilities for personal growth, self-expression, and positive change as we strive to cultivate a more creative and fulfilling life for ourselves and those around us.

Fundamentals of Creativity

Here are the fundamental principles of creativity.

1. Creativity is the human trait driving the evolution of humankind.

Creativity is an inherent human characteristic, not just a rare gift or special talent. This fundamental challenges popular misconceptions that often describe creativity as a muscle, habit, compass, or gift from the muse. While these analogies can be useful, they can contribute to confusion about creativity's true nature.

Creativity is a trait and the underlying resource that enables us to create, think creatively, and produce creations. It's distinct from the outcomes of creative processes. The term "creativity" refers to the human capacity for creative thought and action, while "creation" describes the tangible or intangible result of the creative process. Acknowledging creativity as the driving force behind human evolution underscores its transformative power in shaping our world.

Throughout history, human creativity has led to groundbreaking discoveries, inventions, and cultural developments that have propelled our species forward. From tool creation and language development to space exploration and the digital revolution, creativity is responsible for human progress.

2. Creativity is at the core of what makes us human, what separates us from other living things, and the technologies crafted to emulate it.

Creativity lies at the essence of human nature, distinguishing us from other living organisms and the technologies designed to mimic human capabilities. It's the unique combination of curiosity, imagination, and creation that enables us to shape our world in unprecedented ways.

At the heart of human creativity is our remarkable capacity for curiosity and imagination: the ability to wonder about and envision things that don't yet exist. The power of curiosity and imagination allows us to transcend current reality and explore unbounded possibilities. We can conceive novel ideas, dream up innovative solutions, and create entirely new concepts.

Coupled with curiosity and imagination is our ability to translate these visions into tangible realities through creation. We possess or can develop the skills and determination to craft our ideas into practical solutions, addressing diverse problems, challenges, and opportunities we encounter in life. This blend of curiosity, imagination, and creation enables us to transform the world around us and shape our own destiny.

Unlike other creatures that exhibit curiosity yet rely primarily on instinct and adaptation, humans can intentionally design and create tools, systems, and environments that enhance our abilities and improve our quality of life. From the wheel's invention to complex technologies, our creativity has driven remarkable advancements throughout human history.

While we've made significant strides in developing AI and technologies that aim to emulate human capabilities, the essence of human creativity remains unmatched. Our ability to combine curiosity, imagination, emotion, intuition, and contextual understanding with the intention to fuel the creative process is something that machines, at least for now, cannot replicate.

3. Creativity is the ultimate tool for human survival, thriving, and flourishing.

Creativity serves as a vital tool for ensuring human survival, enabling us to thrive, and ultimately facilitating our flourishing. As human beings, we possess a remarkable capacity to assess our environment and circumstances, using our imagination to envision potential outcomes and project ourselves into a future that transcends our current reality. This ability to create a vision and establish a strategy sets us apart, empowering us to actively shape our lives rather than being passive recipients of circumstance.

By harnessing our creativity, we can develop innovative solutions to the challenges we face, both as individuals and as a species. Whether it's finding ways to adapt to changing environments, overcoming resource scarcity, or addressing social and economic inequalities, creativity enables us to devise strategies that ensure our survival and well-being.

Creativity is not just a tool for mere survival; it is the key to thriving and flourishing. When we engage our creative capacities, we unlock the potential for personal growth, self-expression, and fulfillment. By envisioning and pursuing our dreams, we can create lives that are rich in meaning, purpose, and joy.

On a collective level, creativity is the driving force behind human progress and the advancement of civilizations. Throughout history, creative individuals have pushed the boundaries of what was thought possible, leading to groundbreaking discoveries, artistic masterpieces, and social movements that have transformed the world. By nurturing and applying our creativity, we can continue to push the frontiers of human potential and create a future that surpasses our current limitations.

4. Creativity is among, if not the most powerful, human traits and is available as a catalyst for the enrichment of all other human traits and resources.

Creativity stands as one of the most powerful human traits, if not the most powerful, serving as a catalyst for enhancing and amplifying all other human traits and resources. Alongside cognitive intelligence, creativity emerges as a vital human characteristic that can be developed into a strategic resource and life skill. By cultivating our creativity, we can approach life's challenges, opportunities, and complexities with a unique and valuable individual perspective.

Creativity acts as a catalyst by inspiring new ways of thinking, facilitating innovative problem-solving, and enabling us to see the world through a lens of possibility. When we apply our creative mindset to other human traits and resources, we unlock their full potential and enhance their usefulness in navigating life's challenges.

For example, combining creativity with cognitive intelligence allows us to generate original ideas, develop innovative solutions, and approach problems from unconventional angles. This synergy enables us to push the boundaries of knowledge and understanding, discovering new frontiers.

Similarly, infusing creativity into emotional intelligence helps us find novel ways to express ourselves, build stronger connections with others, and navigate complex social situations with greater ease. We can develop empathy, communicate effectively, and foster more meaningful relationships.

Creativity can also serve as a catalyst for extending our natural and human resources. By being creative with natural and human resources, we can find new ways to use them, combine them uniquely, and adapt them to suit changing circumstances and needs. This creative approach allows us to maximize the value of our resources and increase our overall effectiveness in various aspects of life.

5. Creative potential is our individual superpower, and its development and expression can range in value from personally meaningful to globally significant.

Learning to do the best with what we've got is embedded in the strategic Life Skill of Being Creative. Creative potential is a unique superpower that each individual possesses. The development and expression of this potential can have a wide-ranging impact, from personal fulfillment to global significance. Embracing creativity as a life skill transforms the way we perceive and interact with the world, empowering us to approach challenges with resilience and innovation.

Being creative is a choice, as is Creative Self Discovery and Development and the intentional expression of our innate gifts and talents. When we choose to engage in the process of Creative Self Development, we uncover our unique talents, passions, and perspectives. Through dedication and practice, we can develop and refine our creative skills, transforming our potential into tangible abilities.

The value of developing and expressing our creative potential is multifaceted. On a personal level, engaging in creative pursuits can bring immense joy, fulfillment, and a sense of purpose. When we tap into our creativity, we discover new aspects of ourselves, explore our passions, and find ways to express our unique perspectives and experiences.

However, the impact of our creative potential extends far beyond personal gain. As we develop and refine our creative skills, we can apply them to make significant contributions in various domains of life. Whether it's through artistic expression, scientific innovation, entrepreneurial ventures, or cultural development, our creativity has the power to shape the world around us and create positive change on a local, national, or even global scale.

Learning to do the best with what we've got is part of the strategic Life Skill of Being Creative. It involves recognizing and appreciating our unique strengths, talents, and resources and finding ways to leverage them effectively. This approach fosters resilience, resourcefulness, and the ability to thrive in the face of adversity.

6. Creative potential is something we all share, but the timing, manner, and degree to which we develop and use it are unique to each of us.

While creative potential is a universal human trait, the way it manifests and develops within each individual is distinct and personal. This fundamental highlights the importance of honoring our own unique creative journey and avoiding the pitfalls of unhealthy comparisons.

Every human being possesses creative potential. However, the timing and manner in which this potential emerges and evolves can vary greatly from person to person. Some individuals may discover their creative passions early in life, while others may uncover them later or experience a more gradual awakening of their creative abilities.

The motivation to engage in Creative Self Development is a deeply personal matter. Each individual is faced with the choice of whether to cultivate and express their creative potential actively or to leave it untapped. The factors that drive us to pursue creative growth can be diverse, ranging from a burning desire for self-expression to a yearning for personal fulfillment or a drive to make a positive impact on the world.

It's crucial to recognize that comparing our creative journey with that of others can be counterproductive. While it can be inspiring to observe and learn from the creative successes of others, it's important to distinguish between emulation and inspiration. Attempting to emulate someone else's creative path or achievements can lead to frustration, anxiety, and a sense of inadequacy, as we each have our own unique set of talents, experiences, and circumstances.

Instead, we should embrace our own creative uniqueness and focus on our personal growth and development. By acknowledging and celebrating the diversity of creative expression, we can find inspiration in the work of others without falling into the trap of unhealthy comparisons. This approach allows us to cultivate a more authentic and fulfilling creative journey.

7. Creative potential can be discovered, developed, and intentionally expressed to help navigate, build, and live what we consider to be our best lives while helping make the world a better place to live for everyone.

This fundamental emphasizes the transformative power of creative potential when it is intentionally discovered, developed, and expressed. It highlights that our creativity can serve as a guiding force in navigating life's challenges, building the lives we desire, and contributing to the betterment of the world around us.

The heart of this principle is the idea that creative potential is not a stagnant trait but a dynamic resource that can be actively cultivated and harnessed. By engaging in the process of Creative Self Development, we can uncover our unique talents, passions, and perspectives. Through dedication and practice, we can develop and refine our creative skills, transforming our potential into tangible abilities that can be applied in meaningful ways.

When we intentionally express our creativity, we unlock its power to enrich and transform our lives. We can navigate the complexities of life with greater ease, finding innovative solutions to problems, overcoming obstacles, and seizing opportunities that align with our values and aspirations.

This fundamental emphasizes that the intentional expression of our creative potential can extend beyond personal gain to create a positive impact on the world. By channeling our creativity toward causes that matter to us, we can contribute to shaping a better future for all.

8. Curiosity, imagination, and creation form a synergy fueling lifelong Creative Self Discovery, Development, and Expression.

This fundamental highlights the dynamic interplay between curiosity, imagination, and creation. These three elements are not separate entities but interconnected opportunities to nurture and sustain Creative Self Discovery, Development, and Expression.

- *Curiosity* serves as the spark that ignites our desire to explore, learn, and discover. It drives us to ask questions, seek out new experiences, and venture into uncharted territories. Without curiosity, our creative potential can remain dormant, and we may lack the motivation to pursue new ideas and possibilities.
- *Imagination* is the space where our creative visions go to play. It allows us to freely explore the "what ifs" and "what could be," unencumbered by the constraints of reality. Our imagination gives us the latitude to take any thought, idea, inspiration, or feeling

and manipulate it in any way, shape, or form that may lead to something previously unimaginable.
- *Creation* is the transformation of our curiosity and imagination into things in physical space that can be shared and used to enrich ourselves, others, and the world in which we live.

Curiosity, imagination, and creation work in harmony, each one feeding and amplifying the others. Curiosity fuels our imagination, providing it with new inputs and perspectives to explore. Imagination gives form to the possibility of our creative ideas, and creation is the force that brings these ideas to life, translating them from thoughts into things.

By cultivating and practicing these interdependent skills, we create a self-reinforcing cycle of creative growth. This ongoing process of exploration, ideation, and creation becomes the foundation for lifelong learning and development, continually expanding our creative potential and deepening our relationship with our creative selves.

9. Creativity can be developed or depressed, so engaging in Creative Self Development and Expression is a personal choice.

This fundamental emphasizes the role of personal choice in the cultivation or suppression of our creative potential. It acknowledges that creativity is not a fixed trait but a malleable capacity that can be actively developed or inadvertently depressed, depending on our own choices and the influences we allow to shape our lives.

Engaging in Creative Self Discovery, Development, and Expression requires intentional effort and commitment. It's a choice that each individual must make, weighing the value and significance of their creative potential against the challenges and sacrifices that may be involved in pursuing it.

Choosing to cultivate our creativity actively can lead to immense personal growth, fulfillment, and achievement. By investing time and energy into exploring our creative passions, developing our skills, and expressing our unique perspectives, we can tap into a deep well of potential and create lives that are rich in meaning and purpose.

Conversely, our creative potential can be depressed or suppressed, either by external influences or our own internal dialogue. External factors such as mass-mindedness that reinforce accepted cultural norms or the opinions of others can sometimes discourage or undermine our creative pursuits. Similarly, our own internal dialogue, our *Storytelling Self-Talk*™, shaped by self-limiting beliefs, fears, or past experiences, can act as a barrier to our creative development and expression.

This fundamental emphasizes that it is ultimately up to each individual to determine the value they place on their creative potential and to make the choice to nurture or neglect it. It requires a conscious decision to prioritize creativity in our lives, to carve out the time and space for creative exploration, and to resist the external and internal forces that may seek to depress it.

10. Creativity can be expressed to support good or evil; use it mindfully.

This fundamental addresses the ethical dimension of creativity, emphasizing the importance of using our creative abilities mindfully and responsibly. It acknowledges that creativity is a powerful tool that can be wielded for both positive and negative purposes, and it is up to each individual to make conscious choices about how they direct their creative energies.

The core of this principle is the recognition that creative expression has the potential to enrich or degrade our lives and the world around us. When channeled toward growth-oriented pursuits, creativity can lead to remarkable innovations, artistic masterpieces, scientific breakthroughs, and cultural progress. It can uplift the human spirit, inspire positive change, and contribute to the betterment of society.

However, the opposite is also possible when our creativity is misused or misdirected, leading to destructive or harmful outcomes. When driven by malicious intent, greed, or a lack of ethical consideration, creative expression can cause significant damage on both a personal and societal level.

This fundamental challenges us to approach our creative pursuits with a deep sense of responsibility and mindfulness. It urges us to consider the potential ripple effects and unintended consequences of our creative expressions and to make choices that align with our values and the intent to bring about positive change.

It also emphasizes the importance of ethical considerations in the creative process, calling upon us to engage in critical reflection, ask difficult questions, and grapple with the moral dimensions of our creative endeavors. By considering the broader effects of our creations on individuals, communities, and the planet as a whole, we can strive to use our creativity as a force for good in the world.

11. Creativity is natural, neutral, non-ethnic, non-cultural, and non-political.

This fundamental asserts that creativity is an inherent human characteristic that transcends ethnic, cultural, and political boundaries. It emphasizes the universality of creativity, recognizing it as a natural and neutral trait shared by all human beings, regardless of their genetic or cultural blueprint.

Creativity is not the exclusive domain of any particular group or culture. It is not determined by race, ethnicity, nationality, or political affiliation. Instead, creativity is a fundamental aspect of our shared humanity, a capacity that is woven into the very fabric of our existence. Just as intelligence is a human trait that manifests in various ways across different individuals and cultures, creativity, too, is a universal attribute that finds expression in diverse forms and contexts. Whether it's through art, music, science, technology, or any other field of human endeavor, creativity knows no bounds and rejects artificial divisions.

By embracing creativity as a natural, neutral, and universal human trait, we open ourselves up to a world of possibilities. We recognize that every person is a manifestation of the Life Force of Creation with the capacity for creative development and expression, regardless of their background or circumstances. This understanding fosters a more open-ended creative landscape where all voices and perspectives are valued and celebrated.

12. Mass-mindedness is the opposition to creativity characterized by conformity, rigidity, and a lack of independent thought.

The tension between being creative and mass-mindedness can act as a significant obstacle to creative expression and innovation. *Mass-mindedness* is a resisting force of conformity, rigidity, and a lack of independent thought, which stands in direct opposition to the open, flexible, and original nature of being creative.

Creativity thrives on the ability to think independently, to question established norms, and to explore unconventional ideas and solutions. Being creative requires a willingness to break free from the constraints of mass-mindedness, challenge the status quo, and venture into uncharted territories of thought and expression.

The reality is that mass-mindedness exerts a force that can stifle creativity and discourage individuals from embracing their unique creative potential. When conformity and rigidity become the dominant modes of thinking and behavior, it creates an environment that is hostile to creative expression. Individuals who dare to think differently and who propose novel ideas or solutions often face resistance and pushback from both internal and external sources.

This fundamental challenges us to recognize and resist the forces of mass-mindedness that can hinder our creative potential. It encourages us to cultivate a mindset of independent thought, to question assumptions, and to embrace the discomfort that often comes with stepping outside of established norms.

By resisting mass-mindedness and embracing our unique creative voice, we contribute to a more diverse, innovative, and dynamic society. We create space for a wide range of perspectives to be heard, enriching our collective creative landscape and fostering a culture that values and supports creative expression.

13. Creativity has inherent value regardless of external judgments or evaluations, yet external domain-specific evaluations can provide targeted feedback and recognition.

The purpose of this fundamental is to emphasize the intrinsic value of creative expression while also acknowledging the role of external evaluations in providing domain-specific feedback and recognition. It distinguishes between the inherent worth of creative expression and the varying ways in which creative acts are perceived and assessed by others.

This view asserts that creativity has value in and of itself, regardless of external validation or classification. Every act of creation, whether it is a personal expression, a solution to a problem, or a contribution to a particular field, is a manifestation of an individual's unique perspective and has inherent worth and meaning to the creator.

However, this fundamental also recognizes that domain-specific evaluations can play a significant role in providing targeted feedback and recognition within specific fields.

These external assessments can offer valuable insights and guidance for creators seeking to refine their skills, push the boundaries of their craft, or contribute to the advancement of their chosen field. They can help creators understand the strengths and weaknesses of their work, identify areas for improvement, and gauge the impact of their creative contributions within a particular context.

This fundamental reinforces the inherent value of creative expression regardless of the nature of external judgments or evaluations.

14. Teaching about and strategically developing our creative potential is fundamental to the survival, thriving, and flourishing of our species, and it can no longer be ignored, misrepresented, taken for granted, or left to chance.

This final fundamental asserts the critical importance of prioritizing the education about and strategic development of our creative potential. It recognizes that in an era of rapid change and complex challenges, the survival, thriving, and flourishing of our species depend on our ability to harness the full power of human creativity.

This principle emphasizes that creativity is not a luxury or a frivolous pursuit but a vital necessity for navigating the challenges and opportunities now and in the future. As the rate of change accelerates and the complexity of our world increases, the ability to think creatively, generate innovative solutions, and adapt to new realities becomes increasingly essential.

Our fundamental challenge here is to reimagine the way we approach the education and development of creativity. It calls for a paradigm shift that places creativity at the center of our learning and growth rather than relegating it to the margins. This requires a comprehensive and strategic approach that encompasses not only formal education but also lifelong learning and practice, professional development, and cultural transformation.

This perspective emphasizes the urgency of this task, given the profound implications of being creative for the future of our species and the planet we inhabit. The stakes are high, and the consequences of inaction or misdirection are potentially catastrophic.

By embracing this responsibility and reimagining the value and impact of creativity, we can unlock the full potential of human ingenuity and work toward a future that is not only sustainable but also thriving and flourishing for all.

CHAPTER 7:
FUNCTIONAL DEFINITION OF CREATIVITY

With an understanding of the essential components of the CLP Philosophy—from the Life Force of Creation to the shared realities presented in the fundamentals of life to the Fundamentals of Creativity—we can now bring these elements together into a cohesive and actionable understanding of creativity.

Introducing the CLP's functional definition of creativity is the purpose of this chapter. This definition is a unifying synthesis that clarifies the nature, purpose, and value of creativity as it applies to all of life. This definition serves as a conceptual stake in the ground: a reference point for creative literacy and a foundation for all future exploration within the CLP.

By integrating life and creative fundamentals, this definition moves beyond abstract ideals or isolated moments of insight. It reframes creativity as a practical, strategic human trait—one that empowers us to meet challenges, make meaning, and bring purpose to how we live, learn, and contribute.

With this definition in hand, we can begin to develop a more intentional practice of creativity—not only as a means of self-expression but as a path to navigating, building, and living our best lives.

What is a Functional Definition?

A functional definition, in the context of the CLP, is a practical and accessible way of understanding a concept that emphasizes its real-world application and impact. For creativity, this approach moves beyond traditional, often limiting descriptions to provide a clear and actionable understanding of what creativity is and how it operates in our daily lives.

The need for a functional definition of creativity arises from the challenges faced by the psychological research community in establishing a comprehensive and widely accepted definition. Historically, much of the focus has been on evaluating the outcomes of creative processes, assessing whether a product or solution is novel, innovative, or effective. While this perspective has its merits, it fails to capture the full scope of creativity, particularly its role in everyday problem-solving and personal growth.

The CLP represents a fresh perspective on creativity, aligning more closely with the principles of positive psychology. Positive psychology focuses on the study of positive emotions, character strengths, and institutions that enable individuals and communities to survive, thrive, and flourish, reinforcing the importance of cultivating well-being, resilience, and personal growth.

In line with this perspective, the CLP supports a functional definition of creativity grounded in its practical application and integration into daily life. This approach goes beyond the evaluation of creative products and instead highlights the transformative power of creativity in shaping our experiences, relationships, and personal development.

The functional definition offered by the CLP serves several crucial purposes:

- It helps dispel the pervasive Cloud of Confusion surrounding creativity by providing a clear and accessible understanding of what creativity is and how it manifests in our lives.
- It establishes a meaningful context for the relationship between creativity and life, demonstrating how creativity is not merely an isolated skill or talent but an integral part of our existence.
- It reinforces the establishment of creative literacy by equipping individuals with the knowledge and tools necessary to recognize, develop, and harness their creative potential.

By understanding how the core elements of creativity manifest in real-world situations, we can develop a definition that not only captures the essence of creativity but also serves as a useful tool for positioning creativity as an essential element in navigating, building, and living our best lives. This approach focuses on the role of creativity in promoting personal growth, well-being, and flourishing rather than determining if and to what degree a creative expression is novel and effective.

Basically, this functional definition of creativity within the CLP Framework is designed to empower individuals, foster creative confidence, and promote the application of creative thinking to everyday challenges and opportunities. It provides a practical tool for understanding and harnessing the transformative power of creativity in our lives.

The CLP Functional Definition of Creativity

Creativity is the trait empowering humans to imagine and craft clever and strategic solutions to survive, thrive, and flourish in a constantly changing world.

Now that we have a functional definition, let's systematically deconstruct and demystify it to gain a deeper understanding and begin the process of reimagining creativity in general and, more specifically, our own creative potential. Let's dive into each component of the definition to unravel its depth and relevance.

Creativity is the Trait...

In the context of the CLP, creativity is defined as a fundamental human trait. This perspective is crucial as it positions creativity not as a rare gift or special talent but as an inherent characteristic shared by all humans. By framing creativity as a trait, the CLP challenges conventional notions and opens up new possibilities for personal growth and development.

As a trait, creativity is the underlying capacity that enables us to engage in a wide range of creative activities and processes. It's the innate human resource that allows us to create, to be creative, to be creators, to think creatively, and to produce creations. When we tap into our creative potential, we're drawing upon this powerful trait that distinguishes us as human beings and empowers us to generate novel ideas, solutions, and expressions.

It's essential to understand that creativity as a trait is distinct from the various manifestations and outcomes of creative processes. The term "creativity" refers to the underlying human capacity for creative thought and action, while "creation" describes the tangible or intangible result of the creative process. Similarly, "creator" denotes the individual or group responsible for bringing a creation into existence through the application of their creative abilities.

One of the key aspects of creativity as a trait is its universality. Every human being possesses creative potential, although the degree to which this potential is developed and expressed may vary from person to person. This means that creativity is not limited to a select few individuals or specific domains but is a fundamental characteristic of the human experience.

Another important consideration is that creativity, as a trait, is not inherently tied to the labels of novelty, innovation, cleverness, or uniqueness. While these qualities are often associated with creative outcomes, they are not necessarily inherent to the trait of creativity itself. Instead, the determination of whether a creation is novel, innovative, clever, or unique is a matter of evaluation, either by the creators themselves or by external sources.

This distinction is crucial because it highlights the fact that creativity, as a trait, is not defined by the judgments or assessments of others. An individual can engage in creative thinking and processes regardless of whether the resulting creation is deemed "creative" by external standards. The value and significance of Creative Self Expression lie fundamentally in the act of creation itself, including the personal meaning and fulfillment it brings to the creator. This does not diminish outcomes judged to be creative; it just reinforces that there is value in the process of creation for the creator for outcomes that are not creative.

By acknowledging that creativity is a fundamental human capacity, we can begin to cultivate a more relatable and empowering approach to Creative Self Development. We can focus on nurturing and expressing our creative potential in ways that align with our personal values, goals, and aspirations rather than striving to meet external benchmarks of "creativeness."

In the context of the CLP Philosophy, understanding creativity as a trait is essential for fostering a Creative Self Mindset and a sense of creative agency. It encourages individuals to embrace their inherent creative potential and to engage in creative activities as a means of personal growth, self-expression, and problem-solving. By recognizing that creativity is a fundamental aspect of the human experience, we can begin to cultivate a more creative and fulfilling life for ourselves and those around us.

This perspective on creativity aligns with the CLP's goal of empowering individuals to discover, develop, and express their creative potential. It invites us to see creativity not as something external or unattainable but as an integral part of who we are as human beings. This shift in understanding can be transformative, opening up new possibilities for personal growth, problem-solving, and self-expression across all areas of life.

...empowering humans...

The concept of empowerment is central to the CLP's understanding of creativity. Describing creativity as a trait that empowers humans emphasizes the transformative and enabling nature of creative thinking and expression in our lives.

Empowerment, in this context, refers to the process of gaining confidence, strength, and agency to take control of one's circumstances and exercise power over one's life. When we say that creativity empowers humans, we're acknowledging its role as a catalyst for personal growth, problem-solving, and the ability to shape our reality in meaningful ways.

This empowering aspect of creativity manifests in several key ways:

- **Problem-solving and adaptation:** Creativity empowers us to confront challenges with resourcefulness and ingenuity. It enables us to see beyond conventional solutions and develop innovative approaches to problems, both big and small. In a world of constant change, this adaptability is crucial for navigating uncertainties and overcoming obstacles.

- **Self-expression and identity:** Creative expression allows us to communicate our thoughts, feelings, and experiences in unique ways. This self-expression is empowering as it helps us understand ourselves better, assert our individuality, and connect with others on a deeper level.
- **Personal growth and self-actualization:** Engaging in creative activities often leads to a sense of accomplishment and self-discovery.

As we develop our creative skills, we also cultivate self-confidence, resilience, and a Creative Self Mindset. This journey of Creative Self Development can be profoundly empowering, helping us realize our potential and work toward self-actualization in several ways:

- **Shaping our environment:** Creativity empowers us to actively shape our surroundings rather than passively accepting them. Whether it's redesigning a living space, innovating in the workplace, or contributing to community projects, our creative actions allow us to influence and improve our environment.
- **Creating opportunities:** Creative thinking often leads to the identification of new opportunities or the creation of entirely new possibilities. This ability to generate options and chart new paths is incredibly empowering, especially in situations where conventional routes seem limited or unsuitable.
- **Emotional resilience:** Creative activities can serve as powerful tools for managing stress, processing emotions, and maintaining mental well-being. This emotional resilience is empowering as it helps us navigate life's ups and downs with greater ease and grace.
- **Social impact:** Creativity empowers us to make meaningful contributions to society. Through creative problem-solving, innovation, and artistic expression, we can influence others, spark important conversations, and contribute to positive change in our communities and beyond.
- **Breaking limitations:** By encouraging us to think beyond conventional boundaries, creativity empowers us to challenge limiting beliefs about ourselves and what's possible. This can lead

to breakthroughs in personal and professional realms that we might not have thought possible.

The empowering nature of creativity can help individuals navigate, build, and live their best lives. By recognizing creativity as an empowering force, we shift our perspective from seeing it as limited or rare to understanding it as a human resource that can be developed into a strategic life skill. This shift can be transformative, encouraging individuals to actively cultivate and apply their creative capacities across all areas of life.

...to imagine...

Imagination is a cornerstone of creativity, and its inclusion in the CLP's functional definition underscores its critical role in the creative process. To imagine is to form mental images or concepts of what is not present or has not been experienced. It's the cognitive ability that allows us to transcend the immediate, the visible, and the known, venturing into the realm of possibilities.

Imagination is not merely daydreaming or fantasy; it's a powerful cognitive tool that enables us to play with ideas and envision new possibilities, solutions, and ways of being. It's the spark that ignites the creative process, providing the raw material from which innovative ideas and strategic solutions emerge.

The act of imagining serves several crucial functions in the creative process:

- **Generating ideas:** Imagination allows us to generate a multitude of ideas, some conventional and others wildly innovative. It's the wellspring of possibilities that fuels brainstorming and ideation processes.
- **Problem-solving:** By imagining different scenarios and outcomes, we can mentally test various solutions to problems before implementing them. This mental simulation is a key aspect of creative problem-solving.
- **Envisioning the future:** Imagination enables us to project ourselves into the future, visualizing goals and aspirations. This abil-

ity is crucial for personal growth, strategic planning, and motivation.
- **Empathy and perspective-taking:** Through imagination, we can put ourselves in others' shoes, considering different viewpoints and experiences. This empathetic imagination is vital for social understanding and collaborative creativity.
- **Connecting disparate ideas:** Imagination allows us to make unique connections between seemingly unrelated concepts, often leading to innovative insights and solutions.
- **Challenging assumptions:** By imagining alternatives to the status quo, we can question existing norms and practices, paving the way for transformative thinking.
- **Emotional exploration:** Imagination provides a safe space to explore and process emotions, contributing to emotional intelligence and well-being.
- **Creating mental models:** We use imagination to create mental models of complex systems or abstract concepts, aiding in understanding and analysis.

Imagination within the CLP is not a passive or frivolous activity but an active and essential component of creative thinking. It's a skill that can be developed and honed through practice and intentional cultivation. By emphasizing imagination in its functional definition, the CLP encourages individuals to actively engage their imaginative faculties as part of their Creative Self Development. Importantly, the CLP's approach to imagination is grounded in practicality. While it values the expansive and sometimes fantastical nature of imagination, it also emphasizes the importance of channeling imaginative thinking toward tangible outcomes and strategic solutions. This balance between unfettered ideation and practical application is key to the CLP's philosophy of creativity as a life skill.

Imagination is closely linked with curiosity and creativity, forming a synergistic triad that fuels ongoing creative development. Curiosity prompts us to explore and question, imagination allows us to envision new possibilities, and creativity enables us to bring those possibilities into reality.

By cultivating a rich and active imagination, individuals can enhance their capacity for creative thinking across all areas of life. Whether facing personal challenges, professional obstacles, or societal issues, a well-developed imagination provides the mental flexibility and innovative thinking needed to craft strategic solutions.

Imagination also plays a crucial role in personal growth and self-actualization. By imagining different versions of ourselves and our lives, we can set ambitious goals, visualize success, and work toward becoming the best versions of ourselves. This aspirational aspect of imagination aligns closely with the CLP's goal of empowering individuals to navigate, build, and live their best lives.

...and craft...

Crafting is a vital component of the creative process, bridging the gap between imagination and tangible outcomes. In the context of the CLP, crafting refers to the intentional act of bringing ideas to life through skillful refinement and execution.

This aspect of the definition highlights several key points:

- **Intentionality:** Crafting implies purposeful action. It's not about haphazard creation but a deliberate process of shaping ideas into reality. This intentionality places an emphasis on creativity as a strategic tool for life management.
- **Skill development:** The concept of crafting acknowledges that creativity involves more than just having good ideas. It requires developing and applying specific skills to manifest those ideas effectively. This perspective encourages ongoing learning and skill refinement as part of the creative journey.
- **Iterative process:** Crafting often involves multiple attempts, revisions, and refinements. This iterative nature of creation is central to the CLP's view of creativity as a dynamic, ongoing process rather than a one-time event.
- **Tangible outcomes:** While creativity starts in the mind, crafting emphasizes the importance of producing concrete results. These outcomes might be physical objects, implemented strategies, or realized visions.

- **Personal investment:** The act of crafting involves investing time, effort, and personal meaning into one's creations. This investment can lead to a deeper sense of accomplishment and connection to one's creative work.
- **Adaptability:** Crafting requires adapting to the materials, constraints, and unexpected challenges that arise during the creative process. This adaptability is a crucial life skill that the CLP seeks to nurture.
- **Quality focus:** The idea of crafting implies a concern for quality and effectiveness. It's not just about creating but about creating well and with purpose. Crafting is seen as an essential link between creative potential and real-world impact. It transforms abstract ideas into strategic solutions that can address life's challenges and opportunities.

The emphasis on crafting also serves to demystify the creative process. It presents creativity not as a mysterious gift but as a combination of curiosity, imagination, and practical skills that can be developed over time. This perspective makes creativity more accessible and actionable for individuals at all stages of their creative journey.

Crafting also extends beyond traditional artistic domains. It applies to all areas of life where ideas are transformed into action. This could include crafting a business strategy, developing a personal growth plan, or designing innovative solutions to community problems.

By including crafting in its functional definition, the CLP emphasizes the importance of bringing creative ideas to fruition. It encourages individuals to move beyond ideation and engage in the rewarding process of making their visions a reality.

Crafting also aligns with the goal of fostering creative independence. As individuals become more skilled at crafting their ideas into reality, they become less reliant on others to implement their visions and more capable of directly influencing their world.

So, the concept of crafting underscores the practical, action-oriented nature of creativity. It celebrates the process of creation as much as the end result, recognizing that the act of crafting itself is a valuable part of the creative journey and personal growth.

...clever...

The use of "clever" in the functional definition of creativity is deliberate and meaningful. It reflects the CLP's commitment to making creativity accessible and relatable while acknowledging the ingenuity inherent in the creative process. Cleverness in this context refers to the ability to devise effective and often original solutions to problems or challenges. It implies a certain resourcefulness and wit that allows individuals to make the most of their circumstances, regardless of limitations or constraints.

Key aspects of cleverness in the CLP Framework include the following:

- **Resourcefulness:** Clever solutions often emerge from working within constraints. This resourcefulness encourages individuals to do their best with what they have, turning limitations into opportunities for unique solutions.
- **Personal assessment:** The concept of cleverness allows creators to evaluate their own work without relying solely on external validation. By comparing their approach to others, individuals can recognize the unique aspects of their solutions, fostering creative confidence.
- **Adaptability:** Clever solutions are often flexible and capable of evolving as circumstances change. This aligns with the CLP's emphasis on creativity as a tool for navigating a constantly changing world.
- **Unconventional thinking:** Clever solutions frequently involve looking at problems from new angles or making unexpected connections. This ability to work outside conventional boundaries is a key aspect of creative thinking.
- **Practical innovation:** While cleverness can lead to groundbreaking innovations, it doesn't require all solutions to be entirely novel. A clever solution might involve a new application of existing ideas or a unique combination of known elements.

By incorporating "clever" into the definition, we acknowledge that creativity isn't always about grand, world-changing ideas. It's often about finding smart, effective ways to address everyday challenges and improve our lives in both small and significant ways.

This approach to cleverness also recognizes the paradoxical nature of creativity. Limitations and constraints, while potentially problematic, can actually stimulate creative thinking by necessitating resourcefulness.

Importantly, cleverness and resourcefulness are fundamental components of innovation, even at the highest levels. Consider the development of the iPhone by Apple and Steve Jobs. They didn't invent the smartphone concept, but their approach was undeniably clever and resourceful. They ingeniously and strategically integrated the device with their existing ecosystem and cleverly packaged it with the revolutionary App Store marketplace.

This perspective empowers individuals to see their clever ideas and resourceful solutions not as lesser forms of creativity but as a valuable practice and expression of creative thinking, and doing that has the potential to lead to meaningful innovations. It reinforces the idea that creativity is about clever problem-solving and resourceful action operating on a Creative Continuum™, discussed in a later chapter.

...and strategic solutions...

The CLP functional definition of creativity emphasizes the importance of developing "strategic solutions" as a key aspect of the creative process. This element highlights the intentional and purposeful nature of creativity, moving beyond mere ideation to the thoughtful application of creative thinking in addressing life's challenges and opportunities.

A strategic solution is one that you, as the creator, determine to be appropriate and effective given your specific circumstances, resources, and constraints. This creator-centric approach empowers you to define and assess the strategic nature of your solutions based on your unique context rather than relying solely on external validation or predetermined criteria.

The concept of strategic solutions in the Creative Self Development Framework is inherently flexible and adaptable. A strategic solution might be a quick fix that addresses an immediate need, a temporary measure that buys time for a more comprehensive approach, or a long-term plan that considers future implications and unintended consequences. The key is that you consciously choose the approach based on your assessment of what's most appropriate for the situation at hand.

Developing strategic solutions involves several key steps:

- **Clarifying your objectives:** Before diving into problem-solving, take time to clearly define what you want to achieve. This clarity helps guide your creative efforts and ensures that your solutions align with your overall goals.
- **Gathering and analyzing information:** Collect relevant data, consider different perspectives, and look for patterns or insights that might inform your approach.
- **Generating multiple options:** Use your creative thinking skills to brainstorm a variety of potential solutions. Don't limit yourself to obvious answers—explore unconventional ideas that might lead to innovative strategies.
- **Evaluating and selecting the best approach:** Assess each potential solution against your objectives, available resources, and potential risks. Choose the option that offers the best balance of feasibility and impact for your specific situation.
- **Developing a detailed plan:** Once you've selected a strategy, create a step-by-step plan for implementation. Consider timelines, resources needed, and potential obstacles you might encounter along the way.
- **Remaining flexible and adaptive:** Remember that even the best-laid plans may need adjustment as circumstances change. Stay open to new information, and be prepared to modify your approach if needed.

This flexible, context-dependent approach to strategic solutions reinforces the idea that creativity is a practical, everyday skill applicable across all life domains. It encourages you to think critically about your circumstances, available resources, time constraints, and the complexity of the problem you're facing. By doing so, you can develop solutions that are not only innovative but also pragmatic and suited to your specific needs.

Importantly, this perspective on strategic solutions supports self-assessment in the creative process. While external feedback can be valuable, honest self-assessment is always available to evaluate the success of your solutions based on how well they meet the strategic needs you've identified. This self-assessment capability is crucial for building your creative confidence and independence.

Embracing this concept of strategic solutions in your creative process empowers you to approach life's challenges and opportunities with greater confidence and effectiveness. It transforms creativity from a purely abstract or artistic endeavor into a powerful tool for shaping your life and the world around you. By developing this aspect of your creative potential, you enhance your ability to both imagine a better future and actively create it through thoughtful, strategic action.

...to survive...

In the definition, "survive" represents the most fundamental application of our creative capacities. It acknowledges that creativity is a crucial tool for meeting our basic needs and overcoming life's challenges.

Survival, in this context, encompasses the following:

- **Basic needs:** Using creativity to secure food, shelter, and safety. This might involve finding innovative ways to stretch limited resources or adapting to harsh environments.
- **Problem-solving:** Applying creative thinking to overcome immediate threats or obstacles. It's about finding quick, effective solutions when traditional methods fail.
- **Adaptability:** Using creativity to adjust to changing circumstances or unexpected challenges. This adaptability is key to survival in an ever-changing world.
- **Resilience:** Creativity plays a crucial role in developing mental and emotional resilience, helping individuals bounce back from setbacks and persevere through difficult times.

- **Health and well-being:** Creative approaches to maintaining physical and mental health, especially in situations where traditional healthcare might be limited or unavailable.
- **Economic survival:** In modern contexts, this could involve using creativity to secure and maintain employment, manage finances, or create new income streams.
- **Social survival:** Creatively navigating social situations, building relationships, and maintaining support networks are crucial for emotional and sometimes physical survival.
- **Crisis management:** Using creative thinking to handle emergencies or unforeseen circumstances that threaten one's survival or well-being.

"Survival" underscores the practical, essential nature of creativity. It's not a luxury or a special talent but a fundamental human trait that has been crucial to our species' survival and evolution.

By linking creativity to survival, we highlight the universality of creative potential. Every human who has survived challenges has, by definition, exercised some form of creativity. This realization can be empowering, especially for individuals who might not traditionally see themselves as "being creative."

In the broader context, this understanding of creativity as a survival tool sets the foundation for its role in helping individuals thrive and flourish. It suggests that by honing our creative skills in meeting basic needs, we develop the capacity to apply these skills to higher-level goals and aspirations.

This perspective on creativity and survival makes creativity accessible and relevant to all individuals, regardless of their circumstances. It invites everyone to recognize and value their creative potential beyond artistic pursuits to include the fundamental task of navigating life's challenges.

...thrive...

The inclusion of "thrive" in the functional definition elevates the concept of creativity beyond mere survival, emphasizing its role in achieving a state of growth, success, and well-being. Thriving represents a proactive approach to life where individuals not only meet their basic needs but actively seek opportunities for personal and professional development.

In the context of the CLP, thriving through creativity involves the following:

- **Personal growth:** Using creative abilities to continuously learn, develop new skills, and expand perspectives.
- **Goal achievement:** Applying creative strategies to set and reach ambitious personal and professional goals.
- **Resilience building:** Developing creative coping mechanisms to bounce back from setbacks and adapt to new challenges.
- **Relationship enhancement:** Utilizing creative approaches to deepen connections, resolve conflicts, and build a supportive network.
- **Career advancement:** Leveraging creative thinking to innovate in one's field, solve complex problems, and create value in work.
- **Life satisfaction:** Finding creative ways to align daily activities with values and passions, leading to a sense of fulfillment.

The concept of thriving encourages individuals to view creativity as a catalyst for positive change and personal empowerment for crafting a life that is rich, meaningful, and aligned with one's aspirations.

..and flourish...

In this functional definition of creativity, "flourish" represents the highest level of creative application. While surviving is about meeting basic needs and thriving involves actively improving one's life, flourishing encompasses reaching one's full potential, achieving a state of optimal well-being, and making meaningful contributions to the world.

Flourishing through creativity involves the following:

- **Creative self-actualization:** Using creativity to fully realize one's potential, aligning actions with core values, and pursuing one's highest aspirations.

- **Innovation and impact:** Creating novel solutions or ideas that not only benefit oneself but also positively impact others or society at large.
- **Mastery and excellence:** Applying creativity to achieve exceptional skill or knowledge in chosen areas, pushing the boundaries of what's possible.
- **Wisdom and insight:** Creatively synthesizing experiences and knowledge to gain a deeper understanding of oneself, others, and the world.
- **Legacy building:** Using creative approaches to leave a lasting, positive mark on the world, whether through work, relationships, or community contributions.
- **Holistic well-being:** Creatively balancing and integrating all aspects of life—physical, emotional, intellectual, and spiritual—to achieve comprehensive wellness.
- **Transcendent experiences:** Engaging in creative pursuits that lead to moments of profound joy, flow, or connection to something greater than oneself.
- **Cultural contribution:** Using creativity to enrich one's culture, whether through art, innovation, or new ways of thinking.
- **Ethical living:** Creatively navigating complex moral landscapes to live in alignment with one's highest principles and contribute to the greater good.
- **Continuous growth:** Embracing creativity as a lifelong journey of learning, adaptation, and evolution, always seeking new horizons for personal and collective advancement.

The inclusion of "flourish" in the definition underscores that creativity is not just about solving problems or improving one's situation but about reaching the pinnacle of human experience and potential. It encourages individuals to see creativity as a pathway to their highest selves and their greatest possible impact on the world. This perspective aligns with the CLP's vision of creativity as a transformative force in human life. It suggests that by fully embracing and developing our creative capacities, we not only enhance our own lives but also contribute to the betterment of society and the world at large.

Within Creative Self Development, flourishing means using one's creative gifts in service of something greater than oneself, presenting creativity as a fundamental human capacity that can elevate all aspects of life—from basic existence to extraordinary achievement and fulfillment.

By linking creativity to flourishing, we invite individuals to dream big and pursue their highest aspirations. It encourages a view of life as a canvas for creative expression and impact, where each person has the potential to craft a life of deep meaning, joy, and significance.

This flourishing supports the goal of unleashing the full creative potential within each individual. It presents creativity not just as a skill or a tool but as a lifelong journey of growth, discovery, and positive impact.

...in a constantly changing world.

This final phrase of the functional definition of creativity emphasizes the dynamic context in which our creative capacities operate. It acknowledges that we live in an era of rapid technological, social, and environmental changes, which present both challenges and opportunities for creative expression and problem-solving.

Key aspects of this concept include the following:

- **Adaptability:** In a constantly changing world, creativity becomes a crucial tool for adapting to new situations, technologies, and paradigms. It enables individuals to remain flexible and resilient in the face of uncertainty.
- **Lifelong learning:** The ever-changing nature of our world necessitates continuous learning and skill development. Creativity plays a vital role in approaching new knowledge and experiences with an open, curious mind.
- **Innovation:** Constant change creates gaps and needs that can be addressed through creative innovation. This environment provides endless opportunities for those who can imagine and craft novel solutions.
- **Problem-solving:** As new challenges emerge with changing circumstances, creative problem-solving skills become increasingly

valuable. The ability to approach issues from fresh perspectives is essential in a dynamic world.

- **Future-oriented thinking:** Creativity helps in anticipating future trends and preparing for potential scenarios, allowing individuals to be proactive rather than merely reactive to change.
- **Resilience:** In a world of constant flux, creative thinking fosters mental and emotional resilience, helping individuals bounce back from setbacks and find new paths forward.
- **Cross-disciplinary approach:** As boundaries between fields blur in our changing world, creativity enables the cross-pollination of ideas and innovative interdisciplinary solutions.
- **Cultural navigation:** With rapidly evolving social norms and global interconnectedness, creativity aids in navigating diverse cultural landscapes and fostering understanding.
- **Sustainable thinking:** In a world facing environmental challenges, creative approaches are crucial for developing sustainable solutions and lifestyles.
- **Personal growth:** Constant change provides ongoing opportunities for personal reinvention and growth, with creativity serving as a key tool in this process.

By situating creativity within the context of a constantly changing world, we emphasize its practical, everyday relevance. This establishes creativity not as a luxury or a specialized skill but as an essential capacity for navigating modern life.

This framing also highlights the dynamic nature of creativity itself and suggests that our creative abilities aren't fixed but can and should evolve in response to the changing circumstances of our lives and the world in which we live.

Ultimately, by placing creativity in the context of a constantly changing world, the CLP functional definition emphasizes its role as a strategic life skill. It presents creativity as our most valuable tool for not just surviving but thriving and flourishing in an unpredictable and ever-evolving environment.

A Fresh Point of Departure

This functional definition of creativity serves as a cornerstone of the CLP, providing a practical and empowering framework for understanding and harnessing our innate creative potential. By presenting creativity as a fundamental human trait that empowers us to imagine and craft clever and strategic solutions at every stage of life, it invites each individual to recognize their creative capacity as an indispensable tool for navigating life's problems, challenges, and opportunities. The definition transcends traditional notions of creativity, extending its relevance across the entire spectrum of human needs—from basic survival to personal thriving and ultimately to flourishing. In doing so, it supports the CLP's mission of guiding individuals to discover, develop, and express their unique creative potential, regardless of their current circumstances or level of personal development.

In a world of constant change, this definition reminds us that creativity is our most valuable asset for shaping our lives, contributing to our communities, and collectively crafting a better future. Our creative potential empowers each of us to become active creators of our own stories, capable of not just adapting to change but of driving positive transformation in our lives and the world around us. By aligning creativity with the full range of human needs and aspirations, this definition invites us to cultivate and apply our creative potential continuously, fostering a lifelong journey of growth, innovation, and fulfillment.

PART 03

CATEGORY—CREATIVE SELF MINDSET

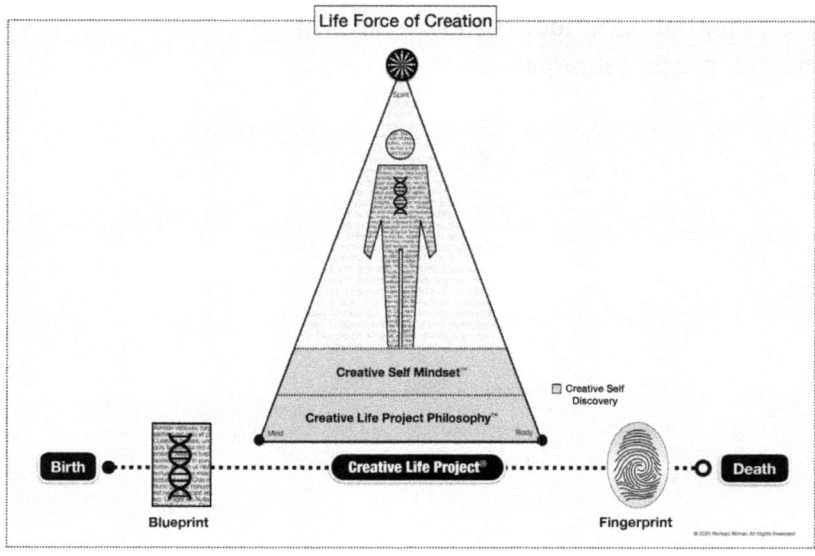

Following the foundation established in the CLP Philosophy, we now move into the dynamic space where creativity becomes intentional: the Creative Self Mindset.

The very nature of the CLP is the powerful interplay between your Creative Self and your Creative Self Mindset. While interconnected, these two concepts serve distinct roles in your Creative Self Development and Expression journey.

Your Creative Self is the essence of who you are as a creator in your life and of your life. It reflects your unique identity, values, aspirations, and the stories you tell yourself about your creative potential. It is your connection to the Life Force of Creation and the foundation of your creative identity.

Your Creative Self Mindset, by contrast, is the lens through which you perceive yourself as a creator. It encompasses the attitudes, beliefs, and perspectives that shape how you choose to use—or not use—creativity in your daily life. This mindset influences how you interpret experiences, recognize opportunities, respond to challenges, and engage with your creative potential across all domains of life.

Together, your Creative Self and Creative Self Mindset form a dynamic partnership. The mindset shapes the conditions for how the Creative Self emerges and evolves. One cannot fully develop without the other. By cultivating both, you become more resilient, imaginative, and authentically engaged in shaping your life and influencing the world around you.

The chapters that follow will explore these ideas in greater depth, offering you insight into the beliefs, narratives, and internal conditions that either strengthen or suppress creative expression. This journey will help you nurture your Creative Self and develop an empowering Creative Self Mindset—setting the stage for a life of intentional, purposeful, and meaningful creative engagement.

CHAPTER 8:
WHAT IS THE CREATIVE SELF?

Creative Self
You as a Creator in Your Life and of Your Life

- Mind Space
- Life Force of Creation / Spiritual Space
- Physical Space

Creative Self Potential
- Curiosity
- Imagination
- Creation

Creative Self Mindset

Mass-mindedness
- Cyber Space
- Natural Space
- Outer Space

Creative Self Development ← Intention → **Creative Self Expression**

Creative Self Management

Birth •·········· Creative Life Project® ··········○ Death

The Creative Self is you as a creator in your life and of your life. Channeling the Life Force of Creation through your Creative Self empowers you to transform the fruits of your imagination into meaningful actions, helping you survive, thrive, and flourish in a constantly changing world.

Understanding Your Blueprint

The Creative Self refers to the part of you that harnesses your unique creative potential and uses it to engage with the world in a creative and meaningful way. This concept acknowledges that each person is born with a genetic imprint and, through maturation, acquires a cultural imprint which fuses into their "blueprint". This blueprint does not wholly define your potential or limit your capacity for growth, yet it establishes the parameters in which your growth and development occur.

Your blueprint represents the inherited traits, both genetic and cultural, that shape the foundation of who you are. Some aspects of this blueprint are fixed, such as your physical features or certain genetic predispositions. These are the conditions with which you must work. However, the creative paradox is that, even within these fixed limitations, there is significant room for flexibility, adaptation, and growth outlined in the next chapter.

The key to the CLP Philosophy is to recognize and take advantage of this balance between the fixed and flexible aspects of your genetic and cultural blueprint. Although you may not be able to change certain innate qualities, you can creatively discover, develop, and express your gifts to the fullest extent. This involves accepting your blueprint, embracing it, and doing the best with what you have, where, when, and however you are.

The Role of the Creative Self

The Creative Self acts as the conduit through which the Life Force of Creation flows. This life force is the driving energy behind all creative acts, and the more open and receptive you are to it, the better your capacity to channel that energy toward meaningful outcomes. Openness, in this context, refers to an internal state of being where you allow the creative energy to flow through you without resistance. The ability to stay open to this flow is crucial to the development and expression of your creative potential.

One of the primary roles of the Creative Self is to relearn this openness that most people possess in early childhood but may lose because of societal pressures and mass-mindedness. Children, in their natural state, are curious, imaginative, and unafraid to explore. They allow the Life Force of Creation to flow freely. As we grow older, we often become more guarded, adopting rigid belief systems that limit our creative potential. Developing the Creative Self involves reviving that childlike state of openness while maintaining the wisdom and experience gained through adulthood.

Transforming Imagination into Action

The Creative Self is actively engaged in transforming imagination into action. While you may have ideas, dreams, and aspirations, it is through the Creative Self that these intangible thoughts are shaped into tangible realities. This process of transformation requires intention, effort, and the strategic use of your personal resources, energy, skills, and relationships.

Both solitary reflection and active collaboration play crucial roles in the development of the Creative Self. By balancing these two modes of creative engagement, you can draw strength from moments of introspection while also embracing the power of collective input to refine and expand your creative vision.

Creative Self and Personal Growth

The Creative Self is integral to the process of growth, both personal and collective. Growth occurs when you engage your creative potential to solve problems, overcome challenges, and seize opportunities. This growth is not linear; it is an evolving process where each experience contributes to your creative development.

Part of this process involves accepting that limitations exist but that they do not define the boundaries of your creative potential. In fact, creativity often flourishes within constraints. Your Creative Self allows you to see beyond limitations and turn them into opportunities for growth. Whether you are working with physical, intellectual, or environmental constraints, the ability to creatively navigate these boundaries is a hallmark of the Creative Self.

The Creative Self is the essence of who you are as a creator in your life and of your life and collaborator. It is the channel through which the Life Force of Creation flows, empowering you to transform your blueprint into meaningful actions that help you survive, thrive, and flourish in a constantly changing world. By embracing your unique blueprint, remaining open to the flow of creative energy, and developing the capacity to transform imagination into reality, you can navigate life's challenges and opportunities with confidence.

Fundamentals of the Creative Self

Here is an explanation for each of the Creative Self Fundamentals.

1. Channeling the Life Force of Creation

Chapter 4 introduced and explained the Life Force of Creation as part of the CLP Philosophy. In the fundamentals of the Creative Self, we are looking at the relationship between the Creative Self and the Life Force of Creation.

As previously discussed, the Life Force of Creation represents the universal energy that fuels all acts of creation, from personal transformation to societal advancements. It's the driving force behind innovation, artistic expression, problem-solving, and the ability to adapt to a constantly changing world. Your Creative Self is the conduit through which this force flows, giving you the power to transform thoughts, ideas, and dreams into reality. This fundamental aspect of creativity allows you to shape your life in meaningful ways, helping you navigate, build, and live what you consider to be your best life.

The Creative Self must be open and receptive to the force of creation to connect with possibilities that surround you, whether they come from your environment, experiences, or the people with whom you interact. This life force is always present, but it's up to you to cultivate the mindset and practices that enable you to open to its potential. By recognizing and actively engaging with this creative energy, your Creative Self becomes the tool for transformation, turning abstract thoughts into tangible outcomes.

- **Harnessing creative flow:** One of the most powerful ways to engage with the Life Force of Creation is through the state of creative flow. This is when you're fully immersed in the creative process, losing track of time as ideas effortlessly come together. In this state, you are aligned with the life force, and your creative energy flows freely, unimpeded by distractions or self-doubt.

Achieving flow requires a balance of focus, passion, and openness, and it's where your Creative Self thrives.

- **Expanding your vision:** Channeling the Life Force of Creation doesn't just apply to producing creative outputs; it's also about expanding your vision of what's possible. When you connect with this force, it opens up new perspectives and pathways that you may not have previously considered. This expanded vision allows you to see opportunities in challenges, solutions in problems, and growth in setbacks. The life force acts as a catalyst for innovation, pushing you beyond your comfort zone to explore new realms of possibility.

- **Personal and collective empowerment:** The Life Force of Creation is not just a personal resource; it's a shared force that connects all of humanity. By aligning with it, you're able to contribute to the collective creative energy of the world. Whether it's through collaborative projects, shared ideas, or collective problem-solving, the life force empowers you to make a positive impact on others. This collective empowerment is at the heart of creativity—it's not only about individual growth but also about making the world a better place for everyone.

- **Nurturing the conduit:** Just as a river must remain unobstructed to flow freely, the channel through which the Life Force of Creation flows your Creative Self must also remain open and nurtured. This involves developing practices that keep your mind, body, and spirit in alignment. Whether it's through meditation, physical exercise, creative rituals, or simply making time for reflection, nurturing the conduit ensures that your creative energy remains strong and unhindered.

- **Overcoming resistance:** Channeling the Life Force of Creation is not always an easy process. There are times when resistance, both internal and external, can block the flow of creative energy. Whether it's fear, self-doubt, societal pressures, or external obstacles, these resistances can make it difficult to engage with the life force fully. The role of the Creative Self is to overcome these barriers by cultivating resilience, persistence, and a mindset of openness. This allows you to push through resistance and stay connected to your creative energy, even when challenges arise.

Ultimately, the ability to channel the Life Force of Creation is what sets the Creative Self apart. It's the foundation of all creative acts, large or small, and the key to transforming ideas into reality. By remaining open, aligned, and focused, your Creative Self can harness this force to help you navigate life's complexities, build your best life, and contribute to the greater good.

2. Interface Between Mind Space and Physical Space

The Creative Self plays a crucial role as the interface between your mind space and physical space, transforming intangible thoughts into tangible actions, expressions, and creations. This process is essential to the act of creation, allowing you to take ideas from the abstract realm of your thoughts and turn them into realities that can be seen, touched, or experienced. As a creative being, you navigate between these two spaces constantly, and your Creative Self acts as the bridge that connects them.

- **Mind space—the realm of ideas:** The mind space is where your ideas, dreams, beliefs, and reflections reside. It is the birthplace of creativity and the origin of all acts of creation. Within this space, you can imagine new possibilities, explore hypothetical scenarios, and develop solutions to the problems you encounter. It's in the mind space that you gain clarity on your creative vision, set your intentions, and generate innovative ideas that will later be expressed in the physical world. However, without the active role of the Creative Self, these ideas remain conceptual, lacking the structure needed to bring them into being.

- **Physical space—the world of action:** Physical space is where your ideas take form. It's where your thoughts, plans, and intentions are turned into concrete actions, whether through physical creations, problem-solving, or expressions of emotion. The process of transforming thoughts into actions is what ultimately gives creativity its power. In the physical realm, the outcomes of your creative efforts become visible and measurable, whether it's a work of art, a completed project, or an innovative solution to a real-world problem.

- **The role of the Creative Self:** Acting as the interface between mind space and physical space, your Creative Self enables you to move fluidly between imagining and actualizing. It's the Creative Self that organizes, refines, and directs the energy generated in the mind and channels it toward productive, purposeful outcomes. The ability to seamlessly transition from idea generation to action is a hallmark of creative mastery. As the conduit for the Life Force of Creation, the Creative Self ensures that this energy doesn't remain stuck in the abstract but is instead used to manifest real, meaningful change in your life and the world around you.

- **Navigating both realms:** The act of moving between mind space and physical space is a constant process of adaptation. Your Creative Self learns to balance the abstract with the concrete, the internal with the external. This adaptability is essential because, while the mind space is infinite and boundless, the physical space is often limited by time, resources, and physical constraints. The Creative Self helps you navigate these limitations by finding innovative ways to bring your ideas to life despite the constraints of the physical world.

- **Visualization and manifestation:** One of the key functions of the Creative Self is the ability to use your imagination to visualize outcomes and then take steps to manifest those outcomes in the physical world. Visualization involves imagining a specific goal or solution, seeing it clearly in your mind space before it exists in physical space. This practice is a powerful tool for setting intentions and aligning your actions with your creative vision. The Creative Self facilitates this process by helping you refine and focus your mental energy, guiding your thoughts toward specific, achievable goals.

- **Bridging the gap between thought and action:** One of the greatest challenges in creativity is the gap that often exists between thought and action. It's easy to come up with ideas in your mind space, but far more difficult to bring those ideas to life in the physical space. This is where the Creative Self becomes invaluable. It helps you overcome obstacles such as fear, doubt, procrastination, or lack of resources, and pushes you to take action. The Creative Self bridges this gap by acting as a motivator and a problem-solver, ensuring that your creative ideas do not remain unrealized.

- **Intentional creation:** The process of transforming thoughts into things is not random—it is deeply intentional. The Creative Self channels the Life Force of Creation with purpose, ensuring that your actions in the physical space align with your goals and values. Every creative act becomes a reflection of your inner world, shaped by your intentions, beliefs, and desires. This alignment between thought and action is what allows you to build a life that is true to your creative vision.

The Creative Self, as the interface between mind space and physical space, is the key to turning imagination into reality. It is the conduit through which your ideas are transformed into tangible results, allowing you to shape your world in meaningful ways. By cultivating and managing this interface, you gain the ability to create with intention, solve problems effectively, and express your unique vision in the physical realm.

3. Cultivating and Managing Internal and External Resources

The Creative Self's ability to thrive and realize its potential is deeply linked to the effective cultivation and management of both internal and external resources. These resources form the foundation for creative expression, problem-solving, and decision-making. A key aspect of nurturing the Creative Self is learning to balance and utilize these resources efficiently, making the most of what you have, both within yourself and in the external world.

Internal Resources, Your Personal Assets

Internal resources include your cognitive, emotional, and physical capacities. They are the personal strengths and skills that empower you to navigate challenges, adapt to changing circumstances, and express your creativity. These assets need constant nurturing and development to remain effective.

- **Cognitive resources:** These include your ability to think critically, reason, and engage in fluid, adaptive thinking. Creativity thrives on cognitive flexibility—the capacity to shift perspectives, consider multiple options, and make connections between seemingly unrelated ideas. Developing your cognitive resources requires intentional practices such as learning new skills, challenging your assumptions, and regularly engaging in activities that stimulate your brain.
- **Emotional resources:** Your emotional resilience and intelligence play a significant role in how well you can manage the ups and downs of the creative process. The Creative Self relies on emotional stability to remain motivated, adaptable, and focused, even when facing setbacks. Emotional resources also include empathy and the ability to understand and collaborate with others. Developing emotional resources involves self-reflection, emotional regulation, and mindfulness practices that help you stay centered and responsive to your creative needs.
- **Physical resources:** Your physical health and energy are crucial for sustaining long-term creative efforts. Physical resources encompass your stamina, well-being, and the ability to maintain a healthy balance between activity and rest. Creativity often demands sustained effort, and ensuring that your body can support your creative work is key. Practices like exercise, healthy eating, and proper sleep all contribute to maintaining your physical resources.

External Resources

External resources include the tools, materials, environments, and networks that support your creative process. These are the resources outside of yourself that you can draw upon to bring your ideas to life.

- **Environmental resources:** The physical spaces you work in, the tools you use, and the materials at your disposal all contribute to your creative output. A well-organized, inspiring environment can significantly boost your ability to concentrate and produce meaningful work. Part of cultivating external resources is designing spaces that encourage creativity and reduce distractions. This could involve setting up a workspace that reflects your personal aesthetic or using tools that enhance your creative process.

- **Social resources:** Collaboration is often a vital part of creativity. Your relationships, professional networks, and communities are essential resources that can inspire, challenge, and support your work. Creative projects often benefit from feedback, collaboration, and partnerships, where others' perspectives and skills complement your own. Cultivating social resources means building and maintaining relationships with others who share your creative goals, as well as seeking out new opportunities for collaboration.
- **Financial resources:** Depending on the nature of your creative endeavors, financial resources can also play a significant role in your ability to pursue and sustain creative projects; managing external resources may involve budgeting, seeking funding, or making strategic investments in tools and materials that support your work.

Balancing Internal and External Resources

One of the central tasks of the Creative Self is learning to balance and integrate internal and external resources in a way that maximizes creative output. This balance requires awareness, intention, and adaptability. Internal resources, such as your mindset, focus, and motivation, need to align with external resources like tools, environments, and social support to create optimal conditions for creativity.

For instance, even if you possess strong internal resources, such as emotional resilience and creative thinking skills, if your external environment is chaotic or your tools are insufficient, your creative output may be limited. Conversely, even with the best external resources, if you are emotionally or cognitively drained, your ability to create will be diminished. The Creative Self thrives when both internal and external resources are cultivated and managed in harmony.

4. Creative Collaboration

Creativity, while often viewed as a solitary pursuit, is inherently collaborative. The Creative Self is not isolated; it thrives internally through interaction and externally with ideas, environments, and other people. This collaboration extends beyond traditional teamwork, encompassing the internal collaboration between your mind, body, and spirit, as well as external collaboration with the people, environments, and cultures around you. Understanding and cultivating creative collaboration is essential to unlocking your full creative potential.

Internal Collaboration: The Interaction of Mind, Body, and Spirit

At the heart of internal creative collaboration is the harmony between your mind, body, and spirit. These three aspects of your being are deeply interconnected and must work together to channel the Life Force of Creation effectively.

- **Mind:** Your mind is the space where ideas form, evolve, and mature. It is the realm of imagination, critical thinking, and problem-solving. Internal collaboration begins with the ability to harness your mind's power to generate new possibilities and refine these ideas through thoughtful reflection and analysis.
- **Body:** Your body is the instrument through which you express your creativity in the physical world. It enables you to bring ideas from your mind into tangible reality, whether through writing, painting, building, or other forms of creative expression. Collaboration between the mind and body is crucial for translating thoughts into action. Taking care of your physical health and energy levels is a key part of maintaining this internal collaboration, as a healthy body supports sustained creative effort.
- **Spirit:** The spirit represents your inner drive, purpose, and connection to something greater than yourself. It is the wellspring of passion and meaning that fuels your creative endeavors. When your mind and body are aligned with your spirit, your creativity is not just about producing work; it becomes an expression of your deeper values and aspirations. This spiritual alignment

gives your creativity direction and purpose, ensuring that it is not only functional but also fulfilling.

The Creative Self relies on the seamless collaboration of these three elements. When mind, body, and spirit are in sync, you are better equipped to engage in the creative process with clarity, energy, and motivation. Fostering this internal collaboration is an ongoing practice requiring mindfulness, self-care, and introspection.

External Collaboration, Engaging with the World Around You

External collaboration involves interacting with people, environments, and cultural contexts in ways that enhance your creative output. Creativity does not happen in a vacuum; it is influenced by the external world, and collaborating with others can significantly expand your creative horizons.

- **Collaboration with people:** Working with others, whether through direct teamwork, feedback, or simply exchanging ideas, enriches your creative process. Other people bring new perspectives, skills, and experiences that can challenge your assumptions and inspire you to think differently. Collaboration fosters innovation by combining diverse viewpoints and expertise, leading to more robust and creative solutions. Effective creative collaboration involves openness to feedback, active listening, and a willingness to adapt your ideas in response to others' contributions.
- **Collaboration with environmental places and spaces:** The surroundings you inhabit also play a role in your creative process. Whether it's the design of your workspace or the natural world around you, your environment can influence your thinking and productivity. An aesthetically pleasing space (according to your preferences) can stimulate creativity, while an inspiring natural environment can provide fresh ideas and new perspectives. Collaboration with your environment involves intentionally designing spaces that support your creative work and seeking out new environments that inspire and challenge you.
- **Cultural and social collaboration:** Engaging with different cultures and social contexts can broaden your creative horizons. Exposure to new cultural practices, values, and artistic traditions

can spark innovation and provide a rich source of inspiration. This form of collaboration requires cultural awareness and sensitivity, as well as an openness to learning from others whose experiences and viewpoints may differ from your own. In a globalized world, the ability to collaborate across cultural and social boundaries is increasingly important for fostering creative growth.

The Synergy Between Internal and External Collaboration

One of the most powerful aspects of creative collaboration is the synergy that arises when internal and external collaboration work together. External influences enrich and expand the ideas that your internal collaboration with your body and spirit generates. Similarly, your interactions with the external world, through people, environments, and cultures, feed back into your internal world, shaping your thoughts, beliefs, and creative process.

For example, a writer may generate initial ideas in solitude (internal collaboration), but those ideas might evolve dramatically through discussions with peers, exposure to different writing styles, or experiences in new environments (external collaboration). The final creative product is a result of this dynamic interplay between the internal and external realms of collaboration.

This synergy is a hallmark of the Creative Self. By actively engaging in both internal and external collaboration, you are able to draw on a wider range of resources, perspectives, and experiences, all of which contribute to richer, more innovative, creative outcomes.

Collaboration as a Mindset

Collaboration is not just a process but can also be a mindset. It requires openness, flexibility, and a willingness to embrace both the internal and external forces that shape your creativity. The Creative Self Mindset embodies this collaborative orientation, recognizing that creativity is enhanced through connection—whether that connection with your own inner resources, with other people, or with the environments and cultures around you.

Cultivating a collaborative mindset involves being receptive to new ideas, feedback, and experiences. It means approaching creative challenges with humility and a recognition that no one creates in isolation, even when they are alone. By fostering harmony internally and externally, you can unlock new levels of creativity and expand your capacity to navigate, build, and live your best life.

5. Cultivating the Power of Intention and Motivation

The Creative Self thrives on the energy that comes from having clear intentions and sustaining strong motivation. Both intention and motivation are essential forces that drive the creative process, turning thoughts into actions and aspirations into tangible outcomes. Intention shapes the direction of your creative journey, while motivation fuels your capacity to stay engaged and overcome obstacles along the way. Cultivating these forces is central to unlocking the potential of your Creative Self.

The Role of Intention in the Creative Process

Intention is more than just setting goals or having a plan; it is the conscious decision to direct your energy and focus toward a particular outcome or purpose. In the context of creativity, intention acts as the guiding force that shapes your actions and ensures that your efforts are aligned with your broader vision for your life and creative work.

- **Clarifying purpose:** At the heart of intention is the desire to create with purpose. Whether you are working on a specific project or developing your creative potential more broadly, having a clear sense of purpose gives your creative endeavors meaning and direction. Purpose allows you to make intentional choices about how to invest your time, energy, and resources. Without a clear purpose, creative work can feel aimless or unfulfilling. By cultivating intention, you can ensure that your creative efforts are focused and aligned with your highest values and aspirations.
- **Setting intentional goals:** Intention involves not only having a purpose but also setting clear, actionable goals that move you toward that purpose. These goals provide structure to your cre-

ative work, helping you break down larger aspirations into manageable steps. Intentional goals are flexible and adaptive, allowing you to adjust your approach as needed while maintaining focus on the overall outcome. Setting intentions for each stage of the creative process ensures that your efforts are consistent and purposeful, even when challenges arise.

- **Aligning intention with action:** Having intention is not enough; it must be translated into action. The Creative Self is empowered when intention and action are aligned, creating a seamless flow between what you want to achieve and the steps you take to make it happen. This alignment requires mindfulness and discipline, as it involves consistently checking in with yourself to ensure that your actions are moving you closer to your creative goals; when intention and action are in harmony, you are better equipped to make meaningful progress in your creative journey.

Motivation: The Driving Force Behind Creative Engagement

While intention provides direction, motivation is the fuel that sustains creative effort over time. Motivation is what keeps you engaged in the creative process, even when faced with setbacks, challenges, or periods of low inspiration. Cultivating strong motivation is essential for maintaining the momentum needed to bring your creative visions to life.

- **Intrinsic vs. extrinsic motivation:** Motivation can be divided into two main types: intrinsic and extrinsic. Intrinsic motivation comes from within, driven by a genuine interest or passion for the creative work itself. This type of motivation is deeply connected to the Creative Self, as it stems from a desire to express your unique creative potential and pursue activities that bring you fulfillment. Extrinsic motivation, on the other hand, comes from external rewards or pressures, such as recognition, approval, or financial gain. While both types of motivation can play a role in the creative process, intrinsic motivation tends to lead to more sustained and meaningful engagement with creative work.
- **Nurturing intrinsic motivation:** To cultivate long-term motivation, it is important to tap into intrinsic sources of motivation.

This involves identifying what excites and inspires you about the creative process itself, rather than focusing solely on external outcomes. By connecting with the deeper reasons behind your creative work, such as self-expression, personal growth, or the desire to contribute to others, you can sustain motivation even during challenging or monotonous periods. Nurturing intrinsic motivation requires regular reflection on what drives you creatively and making intentional choices that align with your passions and values.

- **Building resilience through motivation:** Motivation is not static; it fluctuates based on a variety of factors, including your emotional state, energy levels, and external circumstances. To maintain motivation over the long term, it is important to build resilience in the face of these fluctuations. This involves developing strategies to stay motivated during difficult times, such as setting smaller, achievable goals, celebrating progress, and reminding yourself of your larger purpose. Resilience allows you to stay engaged with your creative work even when external motivation wanes, ensuring that you can continue to make progress toward your goals.

The Interplay Between Intention and Motivation

Intention and motivation work together in a dynamic relationship. Intention provides the vision and purpose, while motivation supplies the energy and persistence needed to achieve that vision. Without intention, motivation can become scattered, leading to unfocused efforts. Without motivation, intention remains unrealized, as there is no sustained drive to bring it into action.

- **Motivation as a catalyst for intention:** Motivation can act as a catalyst for clarifying and deepening your intentions. When you feel motivated to create, you are more likely to reflect on why you are creating and what you hope to achieve. This process of reflection helps sharpen your sense of purpose and strengthens your commitment to your creative goals. In this way, motivation can help refine your intentions and ensure that they are aligned with your true desires.

- **Intention as a guide for motivation:** On the other hand, intention provides a framework for sustaining motivation. When you have a clear intention in mind, you are more likely to stay motivated because you understand the significance of your creative efforts. Intention acts as a reminder of why you started the creative journey in the first place, helping you push through challenges and maintain focus when motivation dips. By keeping your intention at the forefront of your mind, you can use it as a source of inspiration to stay motivated, even when the creative process feels difficult.

Cultivating Intention and Motivation in Daily Life

The practice of cultivating intention and motivation is not limited to major creative projects; it can be integrated into your daily life in small but meaningful ways. Setting daily intentions for how you want to approach your creative work, engaging in activities that spark your intrinsic motivation, and regularly reflecting on your creative goals can help you stay aligned with your purpose and energized in your efforts.

- **Daily intention setting:** Start each day by setting an intention for how you want to engage with your creative work. This could be as simple as committing to a specific task or as broad as cultivating a particular mindset, such as openness or curiosity.
- **Motivation check-ins:** Throughout the day, check in with yourself to assess your motivation levels. If you notice a dip in motivation, take a moment to reconnect with your larger purpose or reflect on what aspects of the creative process bring you joy.
- **Reflection and adjustment:** At the end of each day or creative session, take time to reflect on your progress. Were your actions aligned with your intentions? What motivated you, and how can you build on that motivation moving forward? Regular reflection helps you stay connected to both your intentions and your motivation, ensuring that you remain engaged and purposeful in your creative journey.

6. The Creative Self as a Conduit for Creative Expression

Creative expression extends beyond art and innovation; whether you're solving a problem, writing a story, designing a new product, or simply connecting with others, your Creative Self is always at work.

Creative Expression as a Daily Practice

Creative expression is not a one-time act or a skill reserved for specific moments; rather, it is a daily practice that is woven into the fabric of your life. The more you engage with this practice, the more attuned you become to the creative energy flowing through you. Over time, the daily cultivation of your Creative Self strengthens your ability to bring meaningful and impactful contributions to the world.

- **Intentional expression:** Every moment presents an opportunity for intentional creative expression. From how you solve everyday challenges to how you communicate with others, your Creative Self enables you to approach situations with innovation and imagination. By engaging intentionally with your Creative Self, you can transform routine tasks into opportunities for creativity and personal growth.

- **Spontaneity and playfulness:** While intentionality is important, so too are spontaneity and playfulness. The Creative Self thrives when given the space to experiment and explore new possibilities without fear of judgment or failure. Allowing yourself to play and explore, whether through creative hobbies, brainstorming sessions, or unstructured time, opens up new pathways for expression that can lead to unexpected and innovative outcomes.

- **Creative flow:** One of the ultimate goals of nurturing your Creative Self is to enter a state of creative flow—a mental state in which you are fully immersed in the process of creation, where time seems to disappear, and your skills are perfectly matched with the challenge at hand. Achieving flow requires practice and the right balance between focus and openness, as well as structure and flexibility. Regular engagement with your Creative Self helps you tap into this state more frequently, allowing for deeper and more fulfilling creative experiences.

Cultivating an Authentic Creative Voice

Central to the Creative Self is the cultivation of an authentic creative voice. Your Creative Self Expression is a reflection of your unique perspective, experiences, and values. Authentic creative expression is not about conforming to external standards or expectations; it's about discovering and honing what makes your voice distinct and using that to influence the world around you.

- **Discovering your creative voice:** The process of discovering your creative voice begins with self-awareness and introspection. It involves exploring your interests, passions, and the messages you wish to communicate through your creative work. Your voice is shaped by your personal journey, and as you grow and evolve, so too does your creative expression. The more in tune you are with your Creative Self, the more confident and authentic your creative output becomes.
- **Honoring your unique perspective:** Part of nurturing your Creative Self is learning to embrace and celebrate your uniqueness. This involves resisting the urge to compare yourself to others or to follow trends that do not resonate with your true self. Authentic creative expression comes from a place of inner conviction and self-trust, allowing you to share your unique perspective without fear of rejection or criticism.
- **Consistency in expression:** While discovering your authentic creative voice is important, consistency is equally vital. Your Creative Self thrives when it is regularly expressed, whether through writing, speaking, designing, or problem-solving. Developing a consistent practice of creative expression allows you to build upon your previous work and refine your skills over time. This consistency also deepens your connection to your Creative Self, reinforcing your ability to channel creative energy in meaningful ways.

Overcoming Creative Blocks

As a conduit for creative expression, your Creative Self is also responsible for navigating and overcoming creative blocks. These blocks may arise due to fear of failure, self-doubt, external pressures, or simply a lack of inspiration. The key to overcoming these blocks lies in cultivating resilience, curiosity, and a willingness to engage with the creative process, even when it feels difficult.

- **Resilience in the face of challenges:** Creative blocks are a natural part of the creative process, but they can be overcome by developing resilience. This means learning to see challenges as opportunities for growth rather than as insurmountable obstacles. Resilience also involves being kind to yourself during moments of struggle, recognizing that creativity ebbs and flows, and trusting that inspiration will return with time and patience.
- **Reigniting inspiration:** When inspiration wanes, your Creative Self can help reignite the spark by seeking out new experiences, perspectives, and challenges. This could involve stepping away from your current project to engage in a different activity, exploring a new creative medium, or simply spending time in nature. Sometimes, taking a break is exactly what your Creative Self needs to recharge and come back with fresh ideas and renewed energy.
- **Staying open to possibilities:** Perhaps the most important skill your Creative Self can cultivate is the ability to stay open to possibilities. Even when faced with uncertainty or ambiguity, the Creative Self remains curious and willing to explore new paths. This openness allows you to find creative solutions that others may overlook and to navigate complex problems with grace and ingenuity.

Summing Up: The Creative Self as Your Guide

Your Creative Self is an active guide helping you navigate your journey of creative expression. It enables you to transform ideas into reality, cultivate your authentic voice, collaborate meaningfully with others, and overcome the inevitable challenges of the creative process. As you develop and nurture your Creative Self, you will find that creative expression becomes not just an occasional act but an integral part of how you engage with the world.

CHAPTER 9:
WHAT IS THE CREATIVE SELF MINDSET?

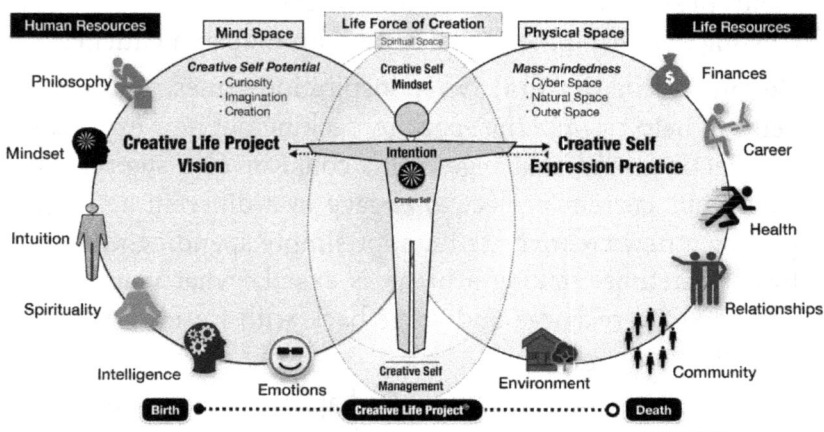

The Creative Self Mindset is an empowering set of beliefs and attitudes that guide how you harness your creative potential and engage with the world around you. It is a framework that influences your thoughts, decisions, and actions as you pursue your creative journey. More than just a static mindset, it is a fluid and evolving mental approach driven by your experiences of continuous learning and emotional growth.

This mindset helps you navigate your Creative Self by providing a conscious structure for the discovery, development, management, and expression of your creative potential. It's through this mindset that you're able to see your creative journey as one filled with opportunity, where you can turn possibilities into achievements.

Blueprint to Fingerprint Transformation

A core function of the Creative Self Mindset is its role in transforming your Creative Self Blueprint™ into your Creative Self Fingerprint™. The Creative Self Blueprint encompasses the genetic and cultural elements that define your foundation. While this blueprint provides the raw materials for your development, it is through your mindset that you can shape and transform these elements into your unique Creative Self Fingerprint, your personalized creative expression in the world.

The Creative Self Mindset empowers you to see this blueprint not as a limitation but as a starting point for growth. Through the mindset's guiding principles, you can evolve, adapt, and mold your creative potential to leave an individual imprint on the world, one that is uniquely yours.

The Role of Belief and Intention

A key component of the Creative Self Mindset is the role of belief and intention in shaping your creative journey. Belief in your capacity for creative growth and the intention to act on that belief drives your creative success. If your beliefs are limiting, you may feel constrained in your abilities; however, with a growth-oriented mindset, you can foster resilience, curiosity, and creativity.

Intention, in this case, becomes the force behind the action. Your Creative Self Mindset encourages deliberate action, where every choice and step you take is aligned with a greater creative vision. This alignment ensures that your creative efforts lead to meaningful results, helping you bridge the gap between thought and action.

Flexibility and Adaptability

In a world of constant change, the Creative Self Mindset must remain both flexible and adaptable. Flexibility allows you to adjust your approach as circumstances evolve, while adaptability ensures you can continue learning, growing, and thriving even in unpredictable environments. This mindset encourages you to view challenges not as barriers but as opportunities to innovate, problem-solve, and develop resilience.

As we move further into a future shaped by rapid technological change, environmental shifts, and new frontiers of exploration, we are increasingly called to express our creativity across a wider range of environments. The Creative Self must be equipped to navigate not only physical space but also alternative spaces—cyberspace, natural space, and even outer space—each offering distinct conditions and opportunities for Creative Self Expression. Whether communicating meaningfully in digital environments, engaging with nature as a collaborator, or imagining solutions beyond our planet, the Creative Self Mindset must remain fluid and responsive.

This adaptive mindset fosters cognitive flexibility—the ability to shift perspectives, explore diverse possibilities, and integrate knowledge across unfamiliar contexts. Guided by the principles of the Creative Self Mindset, you develop the inner agility to remain grounded in your purpose while exploring new tools, spaces, and roles. In this way, flexibility and adaptability are not just survival skills—they are essential traits for living and creating meaningfully in an ever-expanding world.

Growth-Oriented and Empowering Approach

The Creative Self Mindset is fundamentally growth-oriented, meaning it sees creative potential as something that can continually be developed and refined. Whether through formal education, life experiences, or self-directed exploration, this mindset embraces the idea that learning is a lifelong process. This attitude encourages you to expand your knowledge, skills, and creative practices, no matter the stage of life you are in. In this mindset, failure and setbacks are embraced as part of the learning process. Empowerment and resilience are key characteristics here, as they allow you to maintain progress despite the inevitable challenges encountered along the way.

Faith in Your Creative Self

A central theme of the Creative Self Mindset lies in the faith in your Creative Self. This faith is the unwavering trust that you can discover, develop, manage, and express your creative potential, regardless of external circumstances. It sustains you through the highs and lows of the creative process, providing the confidence to take risks, experiment, and innovate. This internal belief system grounds the Creative Self Mindset, enabling you to access and channel the Life Force of Creation to achieve your goals, vision, and aspirations.

Empowering Storytelling Self-Talk and the Creative Self Mindset

Our internal dialogue, or self-talk, is a powerful force that shapes our beliefs, attitudes, and behaviors. It is the constant stream of thoughts, ideas, and stories that we tell ourselves about who we are, what we are capable of, and how we relate to the world around us. This "Storytelling Self-Talk" plays a crucial role in the development of our Creative Self Mindset, which is the foundation of our ability to discover, develop, and express our creative potential in the pursuit of our best life.

The Creative Self Mindset is a set of beliefs, attitudes, and principles that empower us to embrace our creativity, take ownership of our lives, and navigate challenges with resilience and adaptability. It is the lens through which we view ourselves and the world, and it determines how we approach our CLP: the ongoing process of crafting a life that is authentic, meaningful, and aligned with our values and aspirations.

Central to the Creative Self Mindset are the stories we tell ourselves. These stories can either limit or expand our potential, depending on their content and tone. Negative or limiting self-talk, such as "I'm not creative enough" or "I'll never be able to achieve my goals," can hold us back from pursuing our dreams and expressing our unique talents. On the other hand, positive and empowering self-talk, such as "I have valuable ideas to share" or "I can overcome challenges," can motivate us to take bold action, persevere through setbacks, and unlock our full creative potential.

Cultivating a Creative Self Mindset through intentional Storytelling Self-Talk is a skill that can be developed and strengthened. It requires us to become aware of our internal narrative, challenge limiting beliefs, and consciously choose to tell ourselves stories that support our growth and well-being. This is where the Creative Self Mindset Principles™ come into play.

Fundamentals of the Creative Self Mindset

There are eight Creative Self Mindset Fundamentals.

1. Flexible/Malleable Blueprint

Each of us has our own unique genetic and cultural imprint, our blueprint, related to the structure and biology of our bodies. We have come to learn this blueprint is far more flexible and adaptive than we once thought. The science of epigenetics is an example that reveals that certain factors under our control can impact how genes are expressed in our body; we go deeper into this topic in Chapter 14. Here, we focus on how the way we think about creativity and our creative potential, our mindset toward creativity, can proactively shape our creative journey and maximize our potential.

- **Empowering growth and change:** Understanding that your genetic and neurological blueprint is flexible empowers you to seek change and growth. You recognize you can influence your creative potential by engaging in activities that foster growth, learning, and adaptation. This mindset is essential for personal transformation and is the foundation of Creative Self Development.

- **Breaking free from limiting beliefs:** One of the primary benefits of adopting a Creative Self Mindset is the ability to break free from limiting beliefs. The realization that your blueprint can change helps you overcome the notion that certain traits or limitations are permanent. Whether it's overcoming a fear of failure, pushing through creative blocks, or expanding your knowledge, this mindset enables you to push past self-imposed boundaries.

- **Cultivating new habits and skills:** Your ability to adapt to changing circumstances means you can cultivate new habits and skills at any stage in life. Whether you want to learn a new creative technique, enhance your problem-solving abilities, or simply become more open to new experiences, the Creative Self Mindset makes it possible. Every time you engage in learning, practice, or experimentation, you are impacting your thoughts and beliefs, making new creative paths more accessible.
- **Creating a feedback loop:** As you cultivate an open and adaptable mindset, the process creates a feedback loop. Engaging in creative practices strengthens neural connections, which makes it easier to engage in and develop those practices in the future. This loop, or Learning Spiral, which we explore in a later chapter, helps reinforce the development of your Creative Self, making the journey of Creative Self Development a lifelong pursuit rather than a fixed outcome.

The flexibility of your genetic and cultural makeup is both a gift and a responsibility. With an empowering Creative Self Mindset, you can constantly evolve, adapt, and grow—if you are motivated to take intentional action and willing to embrace change. By understanding that your blueprint is malleable, you can proactively shape your creative journey and maximize your potential, transforming your life through the power of mindset and intention.

2. Embodiment of Philosophy

The embodiment of philosophy refers to how your beliefs, values, and worldview are expressed through your actions and decisions. Your Creative Self is not merely an abstract concept but a living, dynamic force that manifests in the way you engage with life. This principle is key because it highlights the connection between thought and action, showing how your philosophy influences the way you approach creativity, challenges, opportunities, and relationships. The embodiment of philosophy represents the alignment between what you believe and what you do, ensuring that your Creative Self operates with authenticity and integrity.

Your philosophy serves as the foundation for your mindset, providing a framework that shapes your attitudes, decisions, and creative choices. For example, if you believe in the power of collaboration, your Creative Self will naturally seek out and foster partnerships. If you value resilience and perseverance, your actions will reflect a determination to overcome setbacks and obstacles. Embodying your philosophy in your creative process means that your beliefs guide your creative decisions, allowing you to express your creative potential in a way that is consistent with your values.

- **Creative alignment:** One of the most important aspects of embodying your philosophy is creative alignment. This occurs when your values, beliefs, and creative efforts are in harmony. Creative alignment ensures that the energy you put into your projects is authentic, meaningful, and aligned with your larger purpose. It helps avoid the dissonance that can occur when your actions do not match your beliefs. For example, if you value innovation but consistently avoid risks, there's a lack of alignment. Embodying your philosophy fosters creative integrity, allowing you to stay true to your core beliefs.

- **Authentic expression:** Embodying your philosophy is also about authentic expression. This means that your Creative Self is not performing for external validation or approval but is driven by internal conviction. Authentic expression allows your Creative Self to thrive, as it is no longer limited by fear, self-doubt, or societal expectations. Instead, your creative actions are a true reflection of your inner values and beliefs, giving you the freedom to create from a place of passion and purpose.

- **Consistency in action:** The embodiment of philosophy also requires consistency in action. It is not enough to hold certain beliefs or values; those beliefs must be reflected in the choices you make on a day-to-day basis. This consistency builds trust in your Creative Self, reinforcing your confidence and fostering a strong sense of identity as a creator. When your actions consistently align with your philosophy, you strengthen the connection between your mindset and your Creative Self, ensuring that you remain grounded in your principles even in the face of challenges.

- **Philosophy as a guide:** Your philosophy serves as a guiding light for your Creative Self, helping you navigate the uncertainties and complexities of life. Whether you're working on a creative project, solving a problem, or facing a difficult decision, your philosophy provides a reference point that keeps you grounded and focused. It ensures that your creative actions are not arbitrary but are informed by a deeper understanding of your values and purpose.
- **Long-term vision:** The embodiment of philosophy is also about sustaining a long-term vision. While creativity often involves short bursts of inspiration and action, the consistent embodiment of your philosophy ensures that your creative efforts contribute to a larger narrative or goal. This long-term vision provides clarity and motivation, helping you stay focused on what truly matters even as you navigate the day-to-day challenges of life. It allows your Creative Self to work toward a purpose that is meaningful and fulfilling, ensuring that your creative journey is guided by a clear sense of direction.

In summary, the embodiment of philosophy is about living your values through your Creative Self. It ensures that your creative actions are aligned with your beliefs, fostering authenticity, consistency, and purpose in your creative endeavors. By embodying your philosophy, you ensure that your Creative Self operates with integrity and is a true reflection of who you are as a creator. This alignment between belief and action is key to unlocking your creative potential and living a life that is rich with meaning and purpose.

3. Cultivate and Manage the Power of Intention

One of the most powerful aspects of the Creative Self Mindset is the cultivation and management of intention. Your intention represents your inner drive, motivation, and commitment to create and achieve. It is more than just a desire or wish; it is the conscious and deliberate focus on transforming your goals and ideas into reality. Intention provides a foundation for purposeful action, linking your thoughts, beliefs, and aspirations with the steps needed to bring them to fruition.

Intention is essential because it aligns your Creative Self with the Life Force of Creation, channeling that energy into meaningful and impactful outcomes. While creativity often involves spontaneous moments of inspiration, it is the intention that directs this creative energy toward your specific goals and vision for your life. Without intention, creative potential may remain dormant or underutilized, lacking the focused momentum necessary to manifest tangible results.

- **Direction and purpose:** At its core, intention provides direction and purpose to your creative pursuits. When you set clear intentions, you clarify what you want to achieve and the path you need to follow to reach your goals. This sense of purpose fuels your motivation, helping you stay focused and resilient even when obstacles arise. It transforms abstract ideas into actionable steps, giving structure to the creative process and making it easier to navigate complex challenges. For example, an artist may set the intention to explore new techniques, pushing their boundaries to grow their skills. A businessperson might establish the intention to develop a new product that meets a pressing market need. In both cases, intention provides the clarity needed to guide creative decisions and actions, ensuring that the effort is aligned with meaningful objectives.

- **Intention as a creative compass:** The power of intention also acts as a creative compass, steering your efforts toward opportunities for growth and discovery. When your intentions are aligned with your Creative Life Project Vision™, they help you navigate challenges with a sense of purpose and determination. Intention allows you to remain adaptable, adjusting your approach as necessary while staying true to your overarching goals. By setting intentional goals, you sharpen your creative focus, which in turn enhances your ability to make strategic decisions. Intention helps you filter distractions and prioritize actions that bring you closer to your desired outcomes, making your creative process more efficient and effective.

- **Aligning intention with values:** A key aspect of cultivating the power of intention is aligning your intentions with your values and long-term vision. Your Creative Self Mindset is shaped by your core beliefs about creativity, your purpose, and your aspirations. When your intentions are congruent with these values, they are more likely to lead to fulfilling and meaningful outcomes. This alignment also deepens your connection to the Life Force of Creation, enhancing your ability to channel creative energy into actions that reflect your highest self. For example, if you value innovation and discovery, setting intentions that challenge you to explore uncharted territories or experiment with new ideas will feel more authentic and energizing. Intention becomes a bridge between your internal motivations and external expressions, helping you create in ways that resonate with your deepest beliefs.
- **Overcoming resistance through intention:** One of the challenges many people face is resistance, whether it's internal doubt, fear of failure, or external pressures. Intention serves as a powerful antidote to resistance, providing the clarity and motivation to push through obstacles. When you cultivate a strong, focused intention, it empowers you to stay committed to your creative path, even in the face of adversity. In moments when you may feel disconnected from your creativity or unsure of the next step, revisiting your intention can rekindle your passion and drive. It reminds you of the bigger picture and the reasons behind your creative efforts, reinforcing your ability to move forward.
- **The habit of intentional action:** Developing the habit of setting and managing intentions is an integral part of the Creative Self Mindset. This practice allows you to align your actions with your goals regularly and to reflect on how your creative journey is unfolding. By making intention a central part of your creative process, you build the discipline necessary to stay focused, motivated, and adaptable, no matter what challenges arise.
- In summary, the cultivation and management of intention are fundamental to the Creative Self Mindset. It provides the focus, direction, and motivation necessary to transform creative po-

tential into meaningful action. By aligning your intentions with your values and goals, you can channel the Life Force of Creation more effectively and turn your vision into reality.

4. Mindset Management and Creative Potential Resource Management

Managing your creative potential is a central part of your Creative Self Development. The Creative Self Mindset enables you to not only recognize your creative potential but also to cultivate, nurture, and direct it toward meaningful outcomes. Without proper management, even the most powerful creative potential can remain dormant or underutilized. It is through intentional management that you can channel your creative energy effectively and align it with your goals, aspirations, and projects.

At the heart of mindset management is the understanding that your creative potential is not a fixed resource. Like any other skill or ability, it can be expanded, refined, and strengthened through practice and conscious effort. Your Creative Self Mindset plays a crucial role in this process, acting as the compass that guides how you allocate your mental, emotional, and physical resources toward your creative endeavors.

- **Intentional focus:** One of the key aspects of mindset management is learning how to focus your attention on the areas of creativity that matter most to you. With a clear CLP Vision, you can prioritize your creative projects and allocate your resources accordingly. This requires cultivating mindfulness, understanding your personal rhythms, and setting boundaries to protect your creative energy. When managed well, your creative potential becomes a wellspring of innovation and fulfillment.
- **Emotional regulation and resilience:** Managing creative potential also involves emotional regulation. The creative process can be fraught with uncertainty, self-doubt, and setbacks. Your ability to manage your emotions in response to these challenges is vital to sustaining creative momentum. The Creative Self Mindset supports emotional resilience, helping you stay grounded and focused even in the face of adversity. By managing your

emotions, you protect your creative energy and ensure it remains available for productive use.

- **Cultivating a growth mindset:** A crucial aspect of mindset management is the cultivation of a growth mindset. This involves embracing challenges as opportunities for learning and growth rather than obstacles. By developing this mindset, you unlock your ability to expand your creative potential continuously. The belief that your creative abilities can improve over time through effort and learning empowers you to take risks, experiment, and push beyond your current limitations.

- **Sustainable creative practice:** A well-managed creative mindset ensures that your creative efforts are sustainable over time. This involves balancing intense periods of focus with necessary breaks for rest and rejuvenation. Sustainable creative practice prevents burnout and allows you to maintain a steady flow of creative output over the long term. Through proper management of your mindset and resources, you can ensure that your creative potential is continually nurtured and replenished.

- **Leveraging creative potential for problem-solving:** Mindset management also involves understanding how to use your creative potential strategically. Whether you're working on personal projects or collaborating with others, knowing how to harness your creative energy for problem-solving can unlock innovative solutions. This requires both confidence in your abilities and the discipline to apply your creativity in structured, intentional ways.

In summary, mindset management and creative potential resource management are interwoven elements of the Creative Self Mindset. By developing your capacity to manage your creative potential, you create the conditions for consistent, meaningful creative output. This management requires emotional intelligence, intentional focus, and a commitment to growth. When applied effectively, it allows you to maximize your creative potential and align it with your goals, helping you to build and live your best life.

5. Role Management and Problem-Solving

Your Creative Self Mindset empowers you to navigate the complexities of life by managing the different roles you take on daily. Whether you are a creator, collaborator, leader, or learner, each role demands its own set of skills and approaches. The flexibility and adaptability of your mindset are key to shifting between these roles smoothly and effectively. At its core, role management is about understanding the interconnectedness of your various identities and responsibilities. As you become more adept at this, you develop an intuitive sense of when to apply creative thinking, when to focus on logic, and when to lead with empathy.

Every role, whether personal or professional, involves problem-solving in some form. Problems, challenges, and opportunities arise in different contexts, and your ability to engage with them creatively is directly influenced by how well you manage your roles. Problem-solving requires a balanced mindset that combines analytical skills with creative imagination. By developing your role management abilities, you enhance your capability to tackle problems from multiple perspectives, leading to more comprehensive solutions.

- **Creative flexibility in role management:** A crucial aspect of creative thinking is the ability to remain flexible, especially when transitioning between roles. Whether you are switching from a problem-solving mindset to a leadership role or shifting from personal introspection to collaborative teamwork, flexibility allows you to maintain a steady creative flow without becoming rigid or resistant to change. The more adaptable your mindset is, the better you can approach each role with a fresh perspective, bringing innovation to both routine and novel challenges.
- **Balancing priorities and responsibilities:** In life, you constantly juggle priorities, whether personal, professional, or creative. Role management allows you to balance these various responsibilities without becoming overwhelmed. It involves knowing when to delegate, when to collaborate, and when to take ownership of a task. By applying your Creative Self Mindset, you can navigate these priorities with a sense of purpose, ensuring that each role you play is aligned with your overall vision for your life.

- **Problem-solving as a creative act:** Every problem presents an opportunity for creativity. From minor daily challenges to significant life decisions, problem-solving is an integral part of being creative. A mindset that embraces curiosity, experimentation, and strategic thinking is essential for resolving issues efficiently and innovatively. With role management, you can approach problems from different angles, applying the appropriate mindset based on the context, whether it's a collaborative challenge requiring teamwork or a personal issue demanding deep introspection.
- **Decision-making in problem-solving:** At the heart of every solution lies a decision. The Creative Self Mindset enhances your decision-making capabilities by integrating both creative intuition and logical reasoning. Whether you are deciding on a career path, solving a family issue, or working on a creative project, your ability to make sound decisions is influenced by your role at the time. By cultivating an open and empowering mindset, you learn to trust your instincts while also weighing the practical aspects of each decision.
- **Creativity in conflict resolution:** Conflict is a natural part of life and often arises in professional or personal relationships. The Creative Self Mindset equips you with the tools to navigate conflicts with empathy, creativity, and resilience. Whether it's mediating a disagreement or finding common ground in a negotiation, problem-solving in conflict resolution requires creative thinking. By applying creative strategies to resolve disputes, you can turn conflicts into opportunities for growth and collaboration.
- **Innovation through role exploration:** One of the most exciting aspects of role management is the potential for innovation. As you explore different roles in your life, you can uncover new approaches to creativity. Whether it's through collaboration, leadership, or personal development, each role opens up new avenues for creative expression. The more you embrace the diversity of roles, the more innovative and multifaceted your creative solutions become.

By mastering role management and problem-solving, your Creative Self Mindset becomes a powerful tool for navigating the complexities of life. It enhances your ability to shift perspectives, tackle challenges, and make decisions that align with your vision for your best life. Each role you play offers a new opportunity for creativity, allowing you to adapt, innovate, and grow as you continue your journey of Creative Self Development.

6. Problem-Solving and Decision-Making

Problem-solving and decision-making are fundamental aspects of the Creative Self Mindset. These skills allow you to navigate the complexities of life with creativity and resilience. When you adopt a Creative Self Mindset, you approach problems as opportunities for growth, viewing challenges not as obstacles but as gateways to innovative solutions. This fundamental requires not only critical thinking but also the ability to use creative thinking techniques to reframe problems and discover unconventional solutions.

The fundamentals of problem-solving involve identifying the root cause of an issue and developing multiple strategies to address it. The Creative Self Mindset expands this process by encouraging openness to new possibilities and promoting a mindset of experimentation. This means being willing to try different approaches, even if they seem unconventional, and learning from both successes and failures along the way.

- **Reframing problems:** One of the core strategies within a Creative Self Mindset is the ability to reframe problems. This means looking at an issue from multiple perspectives to find new ways of understanding it. Instead of focusing on limitations, the Creative Self Mindset encourages you to focus on possibilities. Reframing a problem often leads to a shift in perception, revealing opportunities that were not initially visible.
- **Divergent thinking:** A hallmark of the Creative Self Mindset is the ability to engage in divergent thinking. This involves generating a wide range of possible solutions to a problem rather than focusing on a single "correct" answer. Divergent thinking fosters creativity by expanding the range of possibilities and allowing

you to explore unconventional ideas. This process is essential for problem-solving in complex and uncertain environments where traditional solutions may not apply.

- **Convergent thinking:** After generating multiple possible solutions through divergent thinking, convergent thinking comes into play. This is the process of narrowing down options and selecting the best solution based on the available information. In the Creative Self Mindset, convergent thinking is guided by creativity and practicality, ensuring that the chosen solution is both innovative and feasible.
- **Decision-making:** Decision-making is a key component of problem-solving. It involves evaluating different options, assessing risks and rewards, and ultimately making a choice. The Creative Self Mindset emphasizes that decision-making should be a thoughtful and intentional process. It encourages you to weigh not only the immediate consequences of a decision but also its long-term impact on your goals and overall life vision.
- **Learning from failures:** Failure is an inevitable part of problem-solving and decision-making, but it is also a powerful teacher. The Creative Self Mindset encourages you to view failures as valuable learning experiences rather than as setbacks. By analyzing what went wrong and why, you can gain insights that will improve your future decision-making and problem-solving abilities.

Incorporating problem-solving and decision-making into your Creative Self Mindset empowers you to approach life's challenges with confidence and creativity. These skills are essential for building resilience, navigating uncertainties, and turning obstacles into opportunities. They enable you to take control of your life's direction, making intentional choices that align with your creative vision and values.

With these tools in place, you are better equipped to build your best life, transforming problems and challenges into stepping stones toward growth and success.

7. Creative Expression Management

Creative expression management refers to the intentional cultivation and channeling of your creative energy into meaningful actions and outputs. This fundamental involves not only how you express your creativity but also how you manage the resources, energy, focus, and materials necessary to bring your creative ideas to life. Creative expression is one of the most visible manifestations of your Creative Self, as it transforms your thoughts, emotions, and imagination into tangible results.

At the core of creative expression management is the understanding that creativity is not a random process but one that can be directed and nurtured. It requires structure, discipline, and an ongoing commitment to refining and expanding your ability to express yourself creatively in all aspects of life. Whether it's through art, problem-solving, or innovation, managing your creative expression ensures that you can maximize your potential and achieve your creative vision.

- **Balancing spontaneity with structure:** A critical aspect of creative expression management is finding the balance between spontaneity and structure. While creativity often thrives on freedom and spontaneity, there's also a need for discipline and organization to ensure that your creative efforts are sustained and productive. This balance allows you to maintain a steady flow of creative output while also giving yourself the freedom to explore new ideas and approaches.

- **Channeling creativity across domains:** Creativity is not limited to a single medium or field; it's a versatile resource that can be applied across various domains of life, from personal relationships to professional endeavors. Creative expression management involves recognizing and harnessing your creativity in different contexts and adapting your approach to fit the unique demands of each situation. This flexibility allows you to expand your creative influence and make meaningful contributions in multiple areas of your life.

- **Managing resources for optimal expression:** Creativity, like any other endeavor, requires resources, energy, materials, and mental focus. Effective creative expression management involves assessing and optimizing how you allocate these resources to ensure that your creative projects are completed efficiently and effectively. It also involves recognizing when to take breaks, recharge, and prevent burnout, ensuring that your creative energy remains sustainable in the long term.
- **Developing creative routines:** One of the most effective ways to manage creative expression is by establishing creative routines. Routines provide the structure needed to support regular creative output, helping you build momentum and stay on track with your creative goals. Whether it's setting aside dedicated time for brainstorming, practicing a craft, or working on a project, routines help ensure that creative expression becomes an integral part of your daily life.
- **Overcoming creative blocks:** Managing your creative expression also means addressing and overcoming the challenges that can hinder your creative process. Creative blocks, whether they stem from fear, doubt, or external obstacles, are a natural part of the creative journey. By developing strategies to work through these blocks, such as changing your environment, seeking inspiration from new sources, or collaborating with others, you can maintain a steady flow of creative output even when obstacles arise.
- **Aligning creative expression with personal and collective goals:** Lastly, creative expression management is about ensuring that your creative actions are aligned with your personal values and collective goals. This means not only expressing yourself in ways that are personally fulfilling but also contributing to the well-being of others. Creativity has the power to inspire, heal, and connect people, and by aligning your creative expression with these larger purposes, you can make a positive impact on the world around you.

In summary, creative expression management is about taking control of how you channel and direct your creative energy. It involves building structures, routines, and practices that allow you to express yourself in ways that are both personally meaningful and beneficial to others. By effectively managing your creative expression, you can maximize your potential and make your unique contribution to the world.

8. Resilience and Adaptability

Resilience and adaptability are key components of the Creative Self Mindset, especially in the face of the inevitable challenges and uncertainties that arise in the creative process. Creativity, by its nature, often involves experimentation, risk, and failure, all of which can test your resolve and ability to adapt. The ability to bounce back from setbacks and adjust to new circumstances or obstacles is essential to maintaining your creative flow and continuing to make progress toward your goals.

At its core, resilience is the capacity to recover from difficulties or disruptions, while adaptability is the ability to adjust and evolve in response to new conditions. These traits work hand in hand with the creative process. When you encounter obstacles, resilience helps you to persist through adversity, while adaptability enables you to shift your approach or perspective in order to overcome challenges and seize new opportunities. Together, they empower you to keep moving forward, no matter the external circumstances.

- **Building emotional resilience:** Creative endeavors often require emotional resilience, as they can be deeply personal and subject to criticism or rejection. Developing emotional resilience means being able to manage and process emotions like frustration, disappointment, or fear of failure while still remaining committed to your creative journey. This involves cultivating self-compassion, learning to detach from external validation, and viewing challenges as opportunities for growth rather than as setbacks.
- **Flexibility in creative approaches:** Adaptability in creativity means being open to change and willing to experiment with different methods, ideas, or perspectives when your initial approach isn't working. It's about maintaining a flexible mindset

and embracing uncertainty as part of the creative process. Instead of being rigidly attached to a specific outcome or method, adaptable creators are willing to pivot, explore new avenues, and learn from unexpected results. This flexibility allows for continuous innovation and growth, as well as the ability to navigate creative roadblocks with greater ease.

- **Learning from failure:** Resilience and adaptability are closely linked to how you perceive and respond to failure. Failure is an inevitable part of the creative process, but it doesn't have to be a roadblock. Instead, it can be a valuable learning experience that strengthens your resilience and sharpens your adaptability. By viewing failures as opportunities to learn and grow, you can develop the mindset that every setback is a stepping stone toward eventual success. This shift in perspective reduces the fear of failure and fosters a more experimental, open approach to creativity.

- **Resilience in collaborative settings:** Creative collaboration also requires resilience and adaptability, particularly when working with others who may have different perspectives, ideas, or ways of working. Maintaining resilience in collaborative settings means being able to navigate interpersonal dynamics, manage conflicts or misunderstandings, and remain open to the contributions of others. Adaptability, in this context, involves being willing to adjust your own creative vision or methods to accommodate the input of others, resulting in a more harmonious and effective collaborative process.

- **Strengthening adaptability through lifelong learning:** One of the most effective ways to build adaptability is through a commitment to lifelong learning. The more you expose yourself to new knowledge, experiences, and perspectives, the more adaptable you become in your creative thinking. Lifelong learning keeps your mind flexible and open to new possibilities, enabling you to respond more effectively to changes in your creative environment. Whether through formal education, self-directed exploration, or creative experimentation, learning is a key driver of adaptability.

In conclusion, resilience and adaptability are essential traits for navigating the uncertainties and challenges of the creative process. By cultivating emotional resilience, maintaining flexibility in your creative approaches, learning from failure, and committing to lifelong learning, you strengthen your ability to persevere and adapt in the face of adversity. These qualities not only enhance your personal creative journey but also contribute to a more dynamic, innovative, and collaborative creative environment.

CHAPTER 10:
CREATIVE SELF MINDSET PRINCIPLES

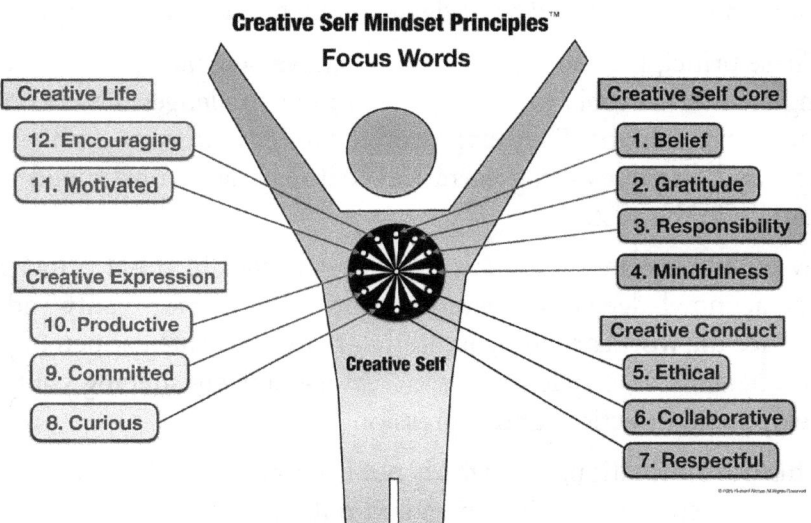

Building on an understanding of the Creative Self and the Creative Self Mindset, we now shift from how we think and believe about creativity to how we live it. The Creative Self Mindset Principles serve as a practical bridge between belief and behavior—a set of guiding values that inform how we show up in the world as creative individuals. These principles give structure and clarity to an empowering mindset, helping us align our inner perspective with outward creative action while resisting the disempowering forces of societal pressure, conformity, and external validation.

The Creative Self Mindset Principles are organized into four domains, and each principle is associated with a focus word, which appears at the beginning of the explanation for each principle.

- **Creative Self Core**
- **Creative Conduct**
- **Creative Expression**
- **Creative Life**

Together, these twelve principles form the foundation of the Creative Self Mindset, and they are intentionally integrated into the CLP logo. This visual symbol appears throughout the guide as a reminder that the mindset principles are present and active whenever creativity is intentionally expressed to navigate, build, and live a meaningful life.

These principles also support your Creative Self Navigation™—serving as internal tools to guide you through challenges, choices, and moments of doubt. They empower you to move beyond limiting beliefs and disempowering narratives that may have constrained your growth in the past.

By embracing an empowering mindset rooted in these principles, you acknowledge your inherent power to shape your reality and influence the world around you. Rather than letting life happen to you, you become a participant and a creator—actively shaping your development, direction, and expression.

This transformation, however, is not instantaneous. Adopting a new mindset requires ongoing effort and reflection. It involves challenging deeply held assumptions, re-patterning your thinking, and consistently aligning your behavior with your values. With time and dedication, you can rewire limiting thought patterns and fully activate the potential of your Creative Self. This is not about becoming someone new but about reclaiming the creative agency you've always had—and learning to use it with intention.

The Creative Self Mindset Principles are flexible and adaptive. They are not rigid rules but living ideas that you can explore, test, and shape in a way that fits your life and creative journey. As you engage with each principle, reflect on how it resonates with your experiences and how it might help you reclaim agency, develop confidence, and navigate life more intentionally.

In the chapters ahead, you will explore each principle in depth. Allow them to serve as catalysts for growth, reminders of your power, and anchors to your creative identity as you continue your path of Creative Self Development.

Creative Core (Principles 1–4): Building Your Foundation

The creative core principles establish the fundamental attitudes and beliefs that serve as the foundation of your Creative Self Mindset. These principles address your personal relationship with creativity, how you value and care for your creative capacities, and your responsibility for developing your creative potential. By embracing these core principles, you create a solid foundation from which all other aspects of your creative life can flourish.

Principle 1—Belief: I'm a creative person, and I intend to develop and express my Creative Self throughout my life.

Creativity is a fundamental human trait, and being creative is essential to living my best life. I share the life force that fuels my curiosity, imagination, and creativity and allows me to express it throughout my life however I choose. My Creative Self Mindset keeps me open to new ideas and gives me the power to overcome mass-mildness, the counterforce of creativity.

Recognizing and having faith in your inherent creativity is the first step toward unlocking your creative potential and living your best life. Your Creative Self extends beyond artistic pursuits; it informs all aspects of your existence, including your work, relationships, personal growth, and self-expression. By cultivating a Creative Self Mindset, you remain receptive to new ideas, perspectives, and experiences that can enrich your life and help you overcome the limitations of conformity and mass-mindedness.

Developing and expressing your Creative Self is a lifelong journey that requires intention, commitment, and practice. It means taking responsibility for your own creative growth and being willing to explore, experiment, and take risks. By affirming your creative potential and dedicating yourself to nurturing it throughout your life, you can build a life that is authentic, meaningful, and fulfilling.

Principle 2—Gratitude: I treasure my body because it's my most valuable creative asset and the instrument of my creative expression.

I understand the importance of using my brain for creative thinking and reasoning, yet I also understand the importance of incorporating all of my intuitive and emotional capabilities into my creative process. Taking advantage of my whole body, including any and all of the physical and nonphysical components of my being, helps me be more creative. To sustain my lifelong creativity, I respect and take good care of my whole body, which includes, among other aspects, my mental, physical, emotional, spiritual, and creative health.

Your body is not merely a physical vessel but a complex and interconnected system that encompasses your mind, emotions, intuition, and spirit. It is the instrument through which you experience the world and express your creativity. While the brain plays a crucial role in creative thinking and problem-solving, true creativity involves the integration of all aspects of your being. Your emotions, intuition, and physical sensations all contribute to your creative process and can provide valuable insights and inspiration.

To fully harness your creative potential, it is essential to cultivate a deep appreciation and respect for your body as a whole. This means taking care of your physical health through proper nutrition, exercise, and rest, as well as nurturing your mental and emotional well-being through practices such as mindfulness, self-reflection, and self-care. By treating your body as a precious creative asset and attending to its needs, you create the conditions for optimal creative expression. When you are well-rested, nourished, and emotionally balanced, you are better able to access your creativity and bring your ideas to life. By honoring and caring for your body, you lay the foundation for a lifetime of creative exploration and growth.

Principle 3—Responsibility: I'm responsible for discovering, developing, and expressing my creative potential in ways that are meaningful to me.

I free myself of dependent and mass-minded thinking to declare my creative independence so I can pursue my Creative Life Project Vision. I intend to do the best I can with what I've got and encourage others to do the same.

While we all possess creative potential, it is up to each of us to take responsibility for discovering, developing, and expressing it in ways that align with our unique talents, interests, and values. This requires a willingness to break free from dependent thinking and the expectations of others and to embrace our own creative autonomy.

Discovering your creative potential means being curious, exploratory, and open to new experiences. It means paying attention to what sparks your interest, ignites your passion, and gives you a sense of purpose. By taking the time to reflect on your strengths, aspirations, and values, you can identify the areas where you have the greatest potential for creative expression.

Developing your creative potential requires dedication, discipline, and a commitment to lifelong learning. It means actively seeking opportunities to acquire new skills, knowledge, and perspectives that can enhance your creative abilities. It also means being willing to experiment, take risks, and learn from your mistakes.

Expressing your creative potential in meaningful ways means aligning your creative pursuits with your values and using your talents to make a positive impact on the world around you. It means being true to yourself and creating work that is authentic, purposeful, and reflective of your unique voice and vision.

By taking responsibility for your own creative development and expression, you liberate yourself from the limitations of mass-minded thinking and create the conditions for a fulfilling and purposeful life. You become the architect of your own creative destiny, capable of shaping your life and work in ways that are deeply meaningful to you. Doing the best you can with what you've got and encouraging others to do the same fosters a supportive and empowering environment for creative growth and expression.

Principle 4—Mindfulness: I develop the awareness required to honor, protect, and nurture my Creative Self as I discover, develop, and express my creative potential.

I am mindful and open to life experiences that stimulate my curiosity and imagination and ignite creative possibilities. I am also mindful of protecting my curiosity, imagination, and creativity from destructive internal or external influences. I only accept constructive feedback that guides my Creative Self Development while rejecting any that may dampen or destroy it. Additionally, I support the right of Creative Self Expression by endorsing people and proposals that protect it, regardless of how it's framed.

Developing awareness is crucial for honoring, protecting, and nurturing your Creative Self as you embark on the journey of discovering, developing, and expressing your creative potential. Being mindful and open to life experiences that stimulate your curiosity and imagination allows you to recognize and seize creative opportunities when they arise. These experiences can come from various sources, such as travel, reading, conversations, or trying new things, and they serve as catalysts for igniting creative possibilities. However, it is equally important to be mindful of protecting your curiosity, imagination, and creativity from destructive influences, both internal and external. Internal influences may include self-doubt, negative self-talk, or limiting beliefs, while external influences may come in the form of criticism, discouragement, or societal pressures. By cultivating awareness, you can identify and shield yourself from these detrimental factors, ensuring that your Creative Self remains vibrant and uninhibited.

When it comes to feedback, it is essential to discern between constructive criticism that guides your Creative Self Development and feedback that may dampen or destroy your creativity. Constructive feedback provides valuable insights and suggestions for improvement, helping you refine your skills and grow as a creative individual. Destructive feedback, often rooted in negativity or personal biases, can undermine your confidence and hinder your creative progress. By developing the awareness to distinguish between the two, you can embrace feedback that supports your growth while rejecting that which threatens to stifle your creativity.

Furthermore, as a creative person, it is important to support the right of Creative Self Expression for yourself and others. This means endorsing people and proposals that protect and promote creative freedom, regardless of how it is being framed or presented. By advocating for the rights of creative individuals and standing up against censorship or speech suppression, you contribute to fostering an environment that values and nurtures creativity in all its forms.

Creative Conduct (Principles 5–7): Engaging with Integrity

The creative conduct principles focus on the ethical dimensions of creativity and how you interact with others in your creative journey. These principles recognize that creativity doesn't exist in isolation—it thrives through ethical practice, connection, collaboration, and mutual respect. By practicing these principles, you create enriching relationships that enhance your creative growth while honoring the creative expression of others with integrity and responsibility.

Principle 5—Ethical: I'm an ethical, honest, creative person.

Creativity is neutral. It's neither good nor evil but can accomplish either. I use my creativity for good to enrich my life and the lives of others. Although the work of others may inform, influence, or inspire me, I don't copy or claim it as my own.

As a creative person, it is essential to recognize that creativity itself is neutral. It is neither inherently good nor evil. However, the application of creativity can have profound consequences, both positive and negative. As an ethical, honest, creative individual, you have the responsibility to use your creativity for good, intending to enrich your own life and the lives of those around you.

Using your creativity for good means leveraging your skills and talents to create something that adds value, inspires others, or addresses a problem meaningfully. It means considering the potential impact of your creations and ensuring that they align with your values and moral principles. By channeling your creativity toward positive ends, you not only fulfill your own sense of purpose but also contribute to the betterment of society as a whole.

Honesty and integrity are fundamental aspects of being an ethical, creative person. While it is natural to be informed, influenced, or inspired by the work of others, it is crucial to maintain your own creative authenticity and avoid copying or claiming others' work as your own. Plagiarism and intellectual property infringement not only undermine your own credibility but also show a lack of respect for the efforts and rights of fellow creatives.

Instead, use the work of others as a source of inspiration, learning from their techniques, styles, or ideas to inform your own creative process. Give credit where credit is due, acknowledging the influence of others on your work while ensuring that your creations remain distinctly your own. By upholding the principles of honesty and integrity in your creative endeavors, you build trust with your audience, peers, and collaborators, fostering a culture of respect and authenticity within the creative community.

Principle 6—Collaborative: I'm prepared to share my creative knowledge, skills, and experience as a collaborator.

Because of my Creative Self Mindset, I'm ready to work with others committed to delivering successful projects. I understand that, unlike my individual projects, which I start and am responsible for, my collaborative success depends on blending my expertise with others to achieve a common goal with shared responsibility.

Collaboration is a powerful tool for amplifying creativity and achieving results that may be beyond the reach of any single individual. Embracing your Creative Self Mindset positions you as a valuable collaborator who is ready to share your creative knowledge, skills, and experience with others equally committed to successful projects.

Collaborative projects differ from individual projects in several key ways. In individual projects, you have full control over the creative process, from ideation to execution, and bear sole responsibility for the outcome. In contrast, collaborative projects involve working with others toward a common goal, blending your expertise and ideas with those of your collaborators. Success in collaborative projects depends on effective communication, mutual respect, and a willingness to compromise and adapt to the needs of the team.

As a collaborator, it is essential to approach projects with an open mind, ready to learn from and contribute to the collective knowledge and skills of the group. This means being receptive to new ideas, perspectives, and approaches, even if they differ from your own. It also means being willing to share your own insights and expertise, contributing to the overall success of the project.

Effective collaboration requires a shared sense of responsibility and accountability. Unlike individual projects, where you are solely responsible for the outcome, collaborative projects involve a distribution of tasks and responsibilities among team members. Each collaborator must commit to fulfilling their role and contributing their best, supporting and relying on others' efforts. By fostering a sense of shared ownership and investment in the project, collaborators can create a synergistic environment that maximizes creativity and productivity.

Successful collaboration also demands strong communication skills, both to express your own ideas and to actively listen to the ideas of others. Clear, respectful, and open communication ensures all collaborators understand the project goals, timelines, and expectations. Regular check-ins, feedback sessions, and progress updates help maintain transparency and keep the project on track.

By embracing your role as a collaborator and leveraging your Creative Self Mindset, you can contribute to the creation of something greater than the sum of its parts. Through the sharing of knowledge, skills, and experience, collaborators can push the boundaries of what is possible, generating innovative solutions and achieving remarkable results. By being prepared to collaborate effectively, you open yourself up to new opportunities for growth, learning, and creative expression while also building valuable relationships and networks within your creative community.

Principle 7—Respectful: I respect the Creative Self Expression rights of others.

I acknowledge the rights of others to express themselves in responsibly creative ways, regardless of my approval or disapproval. I honor creative freedom as personal freedom.

Respecting the creative expression rights of others is a cornerstone of fostering a thriving and diverse creative community. Just as you have the right to express yourself creatively, so do others, even if their ideas, opinions, or methods differ from your own. Acknowledging and respecting this right is essential for promoting an environment that values and encourages creativity in all its forms.

Creative expression is a deeply personal and fundamental aspect of human freedom. It allows individuals to share their unique perspectives, experiences, and emotions with the world, contributing to the richness and diversity of our collective cultural tapestry. By honoring creative freedom as personal freedom, you recognize the inherent value and dignity of every creative individual, regardless of their background, beliefs, or artistic style.

Respecting the creative expression rights of others does not mean agreeing with or endorsing every creative work or idea. It is natural to have personal preferences, opinions, and even disapproval of certain forms of creative expression. However, it is important to separate your personal tastes from the fundamental right of others to express themselves creatively.

This principle calls for a mindset of openness, tolerance, and respect. It means being willing to engage with creative works that challenge your preconceptions or push the boundaries of your comfort zone. It means approaching creative expression with curiosity and a desire to understand rather than immediately judging or dismissing that which is unfamiliar or unconventional.

Respecting creative expression rights also entails supporting and defending the rights of others to express themselves freely and responsibly. This may involve speaking out against censorship, discrimination, or attempts to stifle creative voices. It may also involve advocating for policies and practices that protect and promote creative freedom, such as fair use, intellectual property rights, and freedom of speech.

By embracing the principle of respecting the Creative Self Expression rights of others, you contribute to a diverse culture and mutual respect within the creative community. You create space for a wide range of voices and perspectives to be heard, enriching the creative landscape and fostering a more vibrant and innovative society.

Creative Expression (Principles 8–9): Nurturing the Creative Process

The creative expression principles focus on the dynamic process of generating ideas and persevering through creative challenges. These principles recognize that creative expression requires both the curiosity to explore new possibilities and the commitment to overcome obstacles. By practicing these principles, you develop the resilience and resourcefulness needed to express your unique creative voice.

Principle 8—Curious: I use my curiosity and imagination to generate lots of creative ideas.

I intentionally practice using my curiosity and imagination to stimulate creative ideas.

My ideas evolve by embracing new perspectives and using my ability to make new connections between my curiosity, imagination, knowledge, and experiences.

Curiosity and imagination are the twin engines of creativity, propelling you to generate a wealth of innovative ideas and solutions. By intentionally harnessing these powerful tools, you can tap into an endless source of creative inspiration and potential.

Curiosity is the driving force behind your desire to explore, learn, and discover. It is the spark that ignites your interest in the world around you, prompting you to ask questions, seek answers, and venture into uncharted territories. By cultivating and nurturing your curiosity, you open yourself up to new experiences, perspectives, and possibilities, all of which serve as fodder for your creative ideation process.

Imagination is the ability to envision and create mental images, concepts, and scenarios that transcend the boundaries of reality. It allows you to see beyond what is and imagine what could be, to combine and recombine elements in novel and unexpected ways, and to bring your creative ideas to life in vivid detail.

Maximizing your creative output requires intentionally practicing the use of your curiosity and imagination regularly. This may involve setting aside dedicated time for creative exploration, engaging in activities that stimulate your mind and senses, or exposing yourself to new and diverse sources of inspiration. By making curiosity and imagination a habitual part of your creative process, you train your brain to generate ideas more freely and fluently.

As you generate creative ideas, it is important to embrace new perspectives and make connections between seemingly unrelated concepts. This means being open to seeing things from different angles, considering alternative viewpoints, and challenging your assumptions and biases. It also means actively seeking knowledge and experiences that broaden your horizons and deepen your understanding of the world.

By combining your curiosity, imagination, knowledge, and experiences in novel ways, you create a fertile ground for creative ideas to take root and flourish. Each new piece of information or insight you gain becomes a building block for your creative process, allowing you to make unexpected connections and generate ideas that are both original and meaningful. Remember that the creative ideation process is iterative and growing. Your initial ideas may be rough or incomplete, but by continually refining, combining, and expanding upon them, you can transform them into fully fledged creative solutions. Embrace the fluidity and flexibility of your creative thoughts, allowing them to grow and change as you explore new possibilities and incorporate fresh insights.

By intentionally leveraging your curiosity and imagination to generate creative ideas, you tap into a limitless source of inspiration and innovation. You empower yourself to see the world in new and exciting ways, to find creative solutions to problems, and to bring your unique vision to life. Embrace the power of your curious and imaginative mind, and let it guide you on a journey of endless creative discovery.

Principle 9—Committed: I commit to overcoming and learning from the problems, challenges, and opportunities I'll face throughout my creative journey.

Although expressing my creative vision is enriching and exciting, it can also be frustrating, messy, and scary. I overcome and learn from the obstacles and resistance I'll face by exercising my creative independence. I also remember to celebrate my progress and successes along the way.

Embarking on a creative journey is a courageous and rewarding endeavor, but it is not without its challenges and obstacles. As you strive to express your creative vision, you will inevitably encounter problems, setbacks, and moments of doubt or fear. However, by committing to overcoming and learning from these experiences, you develop the resilience and adaptability necessary to thrive as a creative individual.

Creative expression is a deeply personal and often vulnerable process. It requires you to put your ideas, emotions, and unique perspective out into the world, which can be both exhilarating and terrifying. You may face criticism, rejection, or misunderstanding from others or struggle with your own inner resistance and self-doubt. These challenges are a natural part of the creative process, and it is essential to approach them with your empowering Creative Self Mindset, supporting a willingness to learn and adapt.

When faced with problems or obstacles, exercise your creative independence by taking ownership of your creative journey and finding innovative solutions. This may involve looking for new resources, skills, or collaborators, or experimenting with different approaches and techniques. It may also require you to reframe challenges as opportunities for growth and learning and to view failures as valuable lessons that can inform and strengthen your future efforts.

Overcoming creative challenges also demands a certain level of persistence and determination. It means staying committed to your vision even in the face of setbacks or discouragement and continuing to show up and do the work even when it feels difficult or uncomfortable. By cultivating a sense of grit, resilience, and resourcefulness, you develop the mental and emotional stamina necessary to weather the difficulties of the creative process.

At the same time, it is important to remember to celebrate your progress and successes along the way. Creative journeys are often long and winding, and it's easy to get caught up in the challenges and forget to acknowledge the milestones and achievements you have already accomplished. Take the time to reflect on your growth, savor the moments of breakthrough or inspiration, and appreciate the courage and dedication you have shown in pursuing your creative vision.

Celebrating your successes not only boosts your motivation and confidence but also helps to counterbalance the inevitable frustrations and setbacks you will face. It serves as a reminder of why you embarked on this creative journey in the first place and of the inherent value and meaning in the process of creative expression itself. By committing to overcoming and learning from the problems, challenges, and opportunities you encounter throughout your creative journey, you develop the resilience, adaptability, and empowering mindset necessary to thrive as a creative individual. You learn to view obstacles as stepping stones rather than barriers and to find joy and meaning in the process of creative expression itself. Embrace the messy, challenging, and ultimately rewarding nature of the creative journey, and trust in your ability to navigate it with courage, curiosity, and a commitment to lifelong learning.

Creative Life (Principles 10–12): Sustaining Your Creative Journey

The creative life principles address how you integrate creativity into your daily existence and sustain it as a lifelong practice. These principles emphasize turning ideas into action, maintaining internal motivation, and contributing to the broader creative culture. By embracing these principles, you transform creativity from an occasional activity into a consistent, fulfilling way of life.

Principle 10—Productive: I transform my creative thoughts into things through my creative projects.

Turning my creative thoughts into things, regardless of the medium, requires me to use the Life Skill of Being Creative. Through planning and completing a project, I show my creative skills by delivering real-world representations of my imaginary ideas.

Transforming creative thoughts into tangible outcomes is the essence of the creative process. It is the act of bringing your ideas to life, making them real and accessible to others. Through your creative projects, you bridge the gap between the imaginary world of your mind and the physical world around you.

The process of turning creative thoughts into things requires the use of your Creative Self Management™ skills. These skills encompass a wide range of abilities, from ideation and problem-solving to planning, execution, and project management. By leveraging these skills, you can navigate the complexities of the creative process and bring your vision to fruition.

Creative projects can take many forms, depending on your interests, skills, and medium of choice. They may involve writing a story, composing a piece of music, designing a product, or developing a new business idea. Regardless of the specific project, the common thread is the use of your creative abilities to translate abstract concepts into concrete realities.

The process of planning and completing a creative project is a testament to your creative skills and commitment. It requires you to break down your ideas into actionable steps, set goals and deadlines, and manage your time and resources effectively. It also demands that you embrace the iterative nature of the creative process, being willing to experiment, revise, and refine your work as you go.

As you work through your creative projects, you will encounter challenges and obstacles that test your creative problem-solving abilities. You may need to find innovative solutions to technical difficulties, navigate creative blocks, or adapt to changing circumstances. By persevering through these challenges and overcoming them, you strengthen your creative skills and develop a greater sense of confidence and resilience.

Ultimately, the completion of a creative project is a powerful demonstration of your ability to transform intangible ideas into tangible realities. It is a validation of your creative skills and a recognition of the power of your imagination. By delivering real-world representations of your creative thoughts, you not only bring your own vision to life but also inspire and engage others with your unique perspective and voice.

Remember that transforming creative thoughts into things is not always linear or predictable. It may involve false starts, detours, and moments of doubt or frustration. However, by staying committed to your creative vision and trusting in your creative abilities, you can navigate the difficulties of the creative journey and ultimately bring your ideas to life in meaningful and impactful ways.

Principle 11—Motivated: I'm internally motivated to live a creative life by committing to a daily practice of creative intent, childlike curiosity, lifelong learning, and whole-body health.

This Creative Self Expression Practice™ energizes my creativity, makes me a valuable collaborator, and contributes to my happiness and well-being.

Living a creative life is not just about the end products or outcomes of your creative endeavors. It is a way of being, a mindset, and a daily practice that permeates every aspect of your existence. By committing to a daily practice of creative intent, childlike curiosity, lifelong learning, and whole-body health, you cultivate the internal motivation and energy necessary to sustain and enhance your creativity over the long term.

Creative intent is the conscious choice to approach life with a Creative Self Mindset, to see the world through the lens of possibility and potential. It means setting the intention to infuse creativity into your daily thoughts, actions, and interactions and to find opportunities for active creative expression and exploration. By bringing a sense of creative purpose and intentionality to your daily life, you open yourself up to new ideas, insights, and inspirations.

Childlike curiosity is the ability to approach the world with a sense of wonder, openness, and eagerness to learn. It means maintaining a beginner's mind, even in areas where you have expertise, and being willing to ask questions, explore new ideas, and challenge assumptions. By nurturing your natural curiosity and sense of play, you keep your creative mind fresh, flexible, and receptive to new possibilities.

Lifelong learning is the commitment to continuous growth and development, both personally and professionally. Lifelong learning acknowledges that creativity is a skill that can be learned, practiced, and refined over time and that there is always more to discover and explore. By actively searching out new knowledge, skills, and experiences, you expand your creative toolkit and broaden your perspective, enabling you to approach creative challenges with greater insight and adaptability.

Whole-body health is the recognition that creativity is not just a mental or intellectual pursuit but one that involves your entire being, as described in Principle 2. It means taking care of your physical, emotional, and spiritual well-being and recognizing the interconnectedness of these aspects of yourself. By attending to your overall health and wellness, you create a firm foundation for your creative practice, ensuring that you have the energy, clarity, resilience, and resourcefulness necessary to engage fully in the creative process.

This daily practice contributes to your overall happiness and well-being. By living a creative life, you tap into a deep sense of purpose, meaning, and fulfillment. You experience the joy of self-expression, the satisfaction of learning and growth, and the sense of connection and contribution that comes from sharing your creativity with others. In this way, your creative practice becomes not just a means to an end but an end in itself, a source of ongoing vitality, happiness, and well-being.

Principle 12—Encouraging: I support the development of creative individuals and creative cultures to help make the world a better place to live for everyone.

I practice and share the Creative Self principles to enrich my life and the lives of others. Practicing, sharing, and protecting these principles reinforces them within me and reminds me to encourage others as they develop and express their own creative potential.

As a creative individual, you have the power to make a positive impact on the world around you. By supporting the development of other creative individuals and contributing to the growth of creative cultures, you help to create a ripple effect of positive change, making the world a better place with one creative act at a time.

The Creative Self principles provide a framework for nurturing and expressing your own creativity, but they are also a powerful tool for empowering and inspiring others. By practicing these principles, you not only enrich your own life but also contribute to the creative growth and well-being of those around you.

As you share the fruits of your creative practice through your interaction with others, you help to create a culture of creativity, one that values and nurtures the unique talents and perspectives of every individual. You contribute to a sense of community and connection, fostering an environment of mutual support, inspiration, and collaboration. In this way, you help to build a world that is more innovative, compassionate, and resilient, one that is better equipped to face the challenges and opportunities of the future.

Practicing the Creative Self principles also serves to reinforce and deepen your own commitment to creative living. By regularly engaging with these principles, you remind yourself of the value and importance of creativity in your own life, and you stay accountable for your own creative goals and aspirations.

By supporting the development of creative individuals and cultures, you also help protect and preserve the Creative Self principles themselves. You become an advocate for the value and importance of creativity in all its forms, and you help to create a world that is more receptive and supportive of creative expression and innovation.

Ultimately, practicing these principles is an act of generosity and service, one that has the power to transform lives and communities. By enriching your own life and the lives of others through creativity, you become a force for positive change in the world, helping to build a future that is more vibrant, connected, and alive with possibility.

Keep in mind that supporting the development of creative individuals and cultures is not a one-time event but an ongoing commitment and practice. It requires patience, persistence, and a willingness to lead by example, even in the face of challenges or resistance. But by staying true to your creative principles and values and by consistently showing up as a champion for creativity in your own life and in the lives of others, you can make a profound and lasting impact on the world around you.

PART 04

CATEGORY—CREATIVE LIFE PROJECT VISION

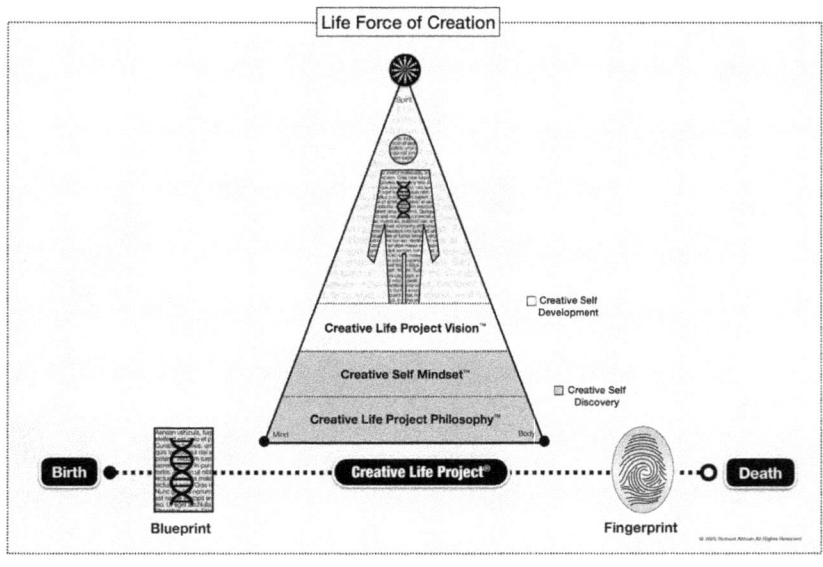

The Creative Life Project Vision is the next category of the Creative Self Development Framework we explore.

Armed with an expanded understanding of creativity and its essential role in building and living what we consider to be our best lives, we are ready to apply these insights to the actual crafting of our vision.

A vision is not a rigid plan or a fixed project—it's a flexible, evolving sense of direction shaped by learning, experience, and aspiration.

It may begin as a feeling, a mental image, or an inner knowing of the life you want to create. You might interpret it through vision boards, journal entries, or moments of insight, but it isn't bound to one form. A vision doesn't dictate every step—it illuminates the general path you want to follow, as well as the directions you want to avoid. It energizes and motivates, offering meaning and momentum while allowing space for discovery and growth along the way.

Vision serves as both motivation and magnet—fueling our momentum while attracting and drawing us toward opportunities, resources, and connections that align with our aspirations. This vision becomes the foundation for meaningful development and authentic creative expression.

While many tools exist to support the vision-crafting process—mood boards, mind mapping, journaling, and guided visualization exercises—our focus here is not on specific tools. Instead, we concentrate on the more crucial aspect: how to prepare yourself to fully leverage your fresh perspective on creativity as you craft your vision. The tools you choose should align with your personal preferences and working style. What matters most is the mindset and approach you bring to the process.

In the chapters that follow, we explore how to create a vision that is both inspiring and actionable, serving as both a source of motivation and a practical reference for decision-making. Like much of the Creative Self Development Process™, crafting your CLP Vision is an ongoing journey of discovery, refinement, and growth. As you develop and gain new experiences, your vision may shift and expand.

This flexibility reflects your growing self-awareness and willingness to adapt to new insights and opportunities.

Remember, this process is deeply personal and unique to you. The key is to remain open, curious, and willing to explore the full range of your creative potential. You're not just planning for the future; you're actively engaging in the creative act of designing your best life. This vision will become the cornerstone of your CLP, informing your choices and inspiring your actions as you move through your creative journey.

CHAPTER 11:
PREPARING TO CRAFT YOUR VISION

Creating a vision marks an important shift from creating a foundation for Creative Self Development to building upon it, starting with the following two elements:

1. Creating a clear CLP Vision of what you consider to be your best life.
2. Developing the capacity to navigate intentionally through life in pursuit of that vision.

These challenges aren't separate; they are deeply interconnected. Your vision is your aspirational direction and purpose. Creative Self Navigation is the process and practice of moving effectively through the problems, challenges, and opportunities you will face as you work toward realizing your vision.

The Transformative Value of Having a Vision

As you begin to craft your CLP Vision, realize this vision does far more than simply describe a desired future—it becomes a powerful catalyst for personal growth, achievement, and fulfillment while providing essential direction for your Creative Self Navigation practice.

Understanding the transformative value of your CLP Vision helps you appreciate why this work is so essential to your development. When thoughtfully crafted and regularly engaged with, your vision becomes both a source of motivation and a practical guide informing decision-making and action.

Your vision serves multiple vital functions in your Creative Self Development Process:

- **Internal motivation:** Your CLP Vision acts as a powerful internal motivator, providing compelling reasons to persist through challenges and setbacks. This motivation, rooted in your deepest values and aspirations, proves far more sustainable than external rewards or pressures. It fuels your daily actions with purpose and enthusiasm, making the journey itself rewarding and meaningful.
- **Clarity and focus:** A clear vision helps you discern which opportunities, relationships, and pursuits align with your ultimate goals. This clarity enables you to focus your energy and resources more effectively, reducing distractions and increasing your chances of success in areas that truly matter to you. Your vision becomes an essential reference point for your Creative Self Navigation practice.
- **Enhanced decision-making:** With a well-crafted vision in place, decision-making becomes more straightforward and confident. Your vision provides clear criteria for evaluating choices based on how well they align with your long-term aspirations. This alignment leads to more consistent and purposeful decisions across all areas of life.
- **Increased resilience:** A compelling vision provides the emotional fortitude to weather life's inevitable challenges. When faced with obstacles or setbacks, your vision reminds you of the bigger picture, helping you maintain perspective and bounce back more quickly. This resilience is crucial for long-term success and personal growth.
- **Attraction of resources:** Your vision naturally draws people, opportunities, and resources that resonate with your goals. When you clearly articulate and pursue your vision, you're more likely to connect with like-minded individuals, mentors, and collaborators who can support and enhance your journey. Your vision helps create conditions that support its own realization.
- **Personal growth and self-discovery:** Crafting and pursuing your vision is inherently transformative. It challenges you to step out of your comfort zone, develop new capabilities, and continually evolve. This journey of self-discovery leads to greater

self-awareness and personal growth, expanding your creative potential along the way.
- **Sense of purpose and fulfillment:** A vision that aligns with your values and passions infuses your life with a deep sense of purpose. This alignment brings a level of fulfillment and satisfaction that goes beyond mere achievement, contributing to overall well-being and life satisfaction. Your vision helps ensure that your efforts create a meaningful impact.
- **Improved time management:** With a clear vision, you're better equipped to prioritize your time and energy. You're more likely to invest in activities that contribute to your long-term goals, leading to a more productive and satisfying use of your resources. Your vision helps you make intentional choices about how you spend your time.
- **Legacy and impact:** Your CLP Vision often extends beyond personal success to how you want to impact the world. This broader perspective allows you to create a meaningful legacy, contributing to causes larger than yourself and leaving a positive mark on your community or field.
- **Flexibility and adaptability:** Rather than being rigid, your vision provides a framework for adapting to change while staying true to your core values. This balance of stability and flexibility is crucial in navigating our rapidly changing world, allowing you to adjust your approach while maintaining your direction.

Understanding these benefits helps you appreciate why crafting your CLP Vision is such a crucial step in your creative development. This vision becomes both your inspiration and your practical guide, enabling you to navigate life's complexities with intention and create a life that truly reflects your Creative Self.

As you prepare to craft your vision, remember that this work lays the foundation for all the creative development that follows. The time and effort you invest in creating a clear, compelling vision will serve you throughout your journey of discovering, developing, and expressing your creative potential.

The Downside of Not Having a Vision

While understanding the transformative value of a CLP Vision is important, it's equally crucial to recognize what happens when this essential component of Creative Self Development is missing. Without a clear vision, your creative development process lacks a crucial reference point for decision-making and direction.

- **Lack of directional clarity:** Without a CLP Vision, individuals often find themselves adrift in their creative development journey. This lack of direction can lead to a sense of purposelessness, making it difficult to make meaningful decisions or take actions that align with their authentic, Creative Self. You may find yourself constantly reacting to circumstances rather than proactively shaping your path through intentional Creative Self Navigation.

- **Vulnerability to external influences:** In the absence of a personal vision, you become more susceptible to being swayed by external pressures, societal expectations, and others' opinions. This vulnerability can lead to pursuing paths that don't truly resonate with your creative potential or authentic desires, potentially resulting in a sense of disconnection from your Creative Self.

- **Limited motivation and resilience:** A clear CLP Vision serves as a powerful source of motivation, especially during challenging times. Without it, you may struggle to find the drive to persevere through obstacles or setbacks in your creative development. The absence of a compelling "why" can make it difficult to bounce back from failures or stay committed to long-term growth.

- **Missed development opportunities:** Your vision acts as a filter, helping you identify opportunities that align with your creative development goals and values. Without this filter, you may overlook valuable chances for personal and professional growth simply because you lack the context to recognize their potential significance for your creative journey.

- **Difficulty achieving fulfillment:** True fulfillment often comes from pursuing development paths that align with our deepest values and aspirations. Without a vision, you may achieve success by external standards but still feel a sense of emptiness or lack of purpose. This disconnect can lead to a perpetual search for meaning and satisfaction in your creative expression.

- **Ineffective resource allocation:** Your time, energy, and creative resources are finite. A vision helps you prioritize and allocate these resources effectively in your development journey. Without it, you may find yourself spreading too thin or investing in pursuits that don't ultimately contribute to your creative growth and expression.
- **Reduced adaptability:** In our rapidly changing world, adaptability is crucial. A clear CLP Vision provides a framework for adapting to change while staying true to your core creative values and goals. Without this anchor, you may struggle to navigate shifts in your personal or professional life, leading to increased stress and uncertainty.
- **Diminished self-awareness:** The process of crafting a vision requires deep self-reflection and understanding. Without engaging in this process, you may have a less developed sense of your own creative values, strengths, and aspirations, limiting your ability to make authentic choices in your development journey.
- **Limited legacy impact:** A vision often extends beyond personal achievement to how you want to impact others through your creative expression. Without this broader perspective, you may miss opportunities to create a lasting positive influence through your creative development and sharing.

Understanding these effects reinforces why crafting your CLP Vision is essential to your creative development journey. Rather than viewing these potential consequences as threats, see them as compelling reasons to engage fully in the vision-crafting process.

The good news is that by engaging in this work now, you're already taking steps to avoid these limitations. Your commitment to developing a clear vision shows your readiness to take an active role in shaping your creative journey and maximizing your potential for meaningful impact.

Where to Begin: Embracing Passion, Purpose, Meaning, and Mission

As we begin, it's essential to start with the core personal considerations that will inform and shape your vision. These fundamental elements—passion, purpose, meaning, and mission—serve as the building blocks for a vision that truly resonates with your authentic Creative Self.

The following are the core personal considerations:

- **Passion—the source of energy and enthusiasm:** Passion represents your deep emotional connection to activities, ideas, or causes that energize and inspire you. It's the internal fire that fuels sustained engagement and perseverance. When considering passion in relation to your vision, look beyond surface-level interests to identify what truly moves you at your core. What activities or pursuits make you lose track of time? What topics or challenges light up your mind with possibilities? Understanding your authentic passions helps ensure your vision will continually energize and motivate you.

- **Purpose—the reason behind your actions:** Purpose provides the foundational "why" that gives direction to your life's journey. It's more than just having goals—it's understanding the deeper reason those goals matter to you. Purpose connects your individual actions to something larger than yourself, giving weight and significance to your daily choices. When considering purpose, reflect on how you want your life to matter. What difference do you want to make? How do you want your presence in the world to be meaningful? Your sense of purpose helps anchor your vision in what truly matters to you.

- **Meaning—the personal significance:** While closely related to purpose, meaning focuses on the personal significance you derive from your life experiences and choices. It's about how you make sense of your journey and what gives your life its unique value and importance. Meaning often emerges from the intersection of your personal values, relationships, and the impact you have on others. When considering meaning, explore what makes life feel rich and worthwhile to you. What experiences give you a sense of fulfillment? What creates a feeling of genuine satisfaction? Understanding what creates meaning for you helps ensure your vision will lead to authentic fulfillment.

- **Mission—the path of action:** Mission transforms purpose and meaning into a defined path of action. It's the specific way you choose to express your passion and pursue your purpose in the world. Your mission might evolve over time, but it provides a concrete direction for your efforts and helps you evaluate opportunities. When considering a mission, think about the specific ways you want to contribute to and act in the world. What form will your purpose take? How will you translate your passions into a tangible impact? A clear sense of mission helps your vision become actionable and achievable.

Integration of Core Considerations

These core considerations don't exist in isolation—they interact and reinforce each other to create a robust foundation for your vision. Your passions fuel the energy needed to pursue your purpose. Your sense of purpose helps you find meaning in your experiences. Your understanding of what creates meaning shapes your mission. And your mission provides a concrete way to express your passions.

As you prepare, take time to reflect on each of these considerations. How do they currently manifest in your life? How might they evolve? What aspects feel clear, and what areas need exploration? Your thoughtful engagement with these core elements will help ensure your vision emerges from your deepest truths rather than surface-level aspirations.

This understanding creates the foundation for exploring specific approaches to vision-crafting and answering the core questions that will shape your vision. With these considerations in mind, you'll be better prepared to create a vision that truly represents your best life and supports your ongoing creative development.

Core Questions for Vision Development

A starting point for this vision-building process is four fundamental questions that help you program your Creative Self Mindset for real-world Creative Self Navigation. These questions aren't merely planning tools—they're prompts for deep reflection that help you integrate your philosophical foundation with the practicalities of developing a vision for your best life.

Take time with each question, allowing your responses to emerge naturally. Your answers will evolve as you progress in your creative development, providing increasingly clear direction for your journey.

1. Who am I now, and who do I want to become?

- **Your current identity, values, and strengths:** Take a thorough inventory of who you are today. What fundamental qualities define you? Which aspects of your current self provide solid ground for growth? What values consistently guide your choices? This assessment creates a strong foundation for your vision development.

- **The qualities and capabilities you wish to develop:** Look beyond your present abilities to envision your potential. Which new capabilities would enhance your creative expression? What qualities would help you navigate more effectively toward your goals? How might developing these attributes support your vision?

- **The gap between your present and potential self:** Honestly, assess the distance between who you are and who you want to become. What specific areas of growth will bridge this gap? Which transformations would most significantly affect your ability to realize your vision? How will developing these areas enhance your creative expression?

- **The character traits you want to embody:** Consider the qualities that would characterize your best self. What traits would make you most effective in pursuing your vision? How would these characteristics support your creative development? What aspects of character would help you navigate life's challenges more effectively?

2. How do I want to live my life, and what values do I want to embody?

- **Daily rhythms and experiences you desire:** Examine what constitutes a fulfilling day in your envisioned life. What activities would engage your creativity most meaningfully? How would you balance various aspects of life to support your creative expression? What experiences would contribute most to your development?
- **Principles that will guide your decisions:** Identify the core values that will inform your choices. What beliefs will help you navigate complex situations? Which principles, when followed, would lead to authentic creative expression? How will these values support your vision realization?
- **How you'll allocate your time and energy:** Plan thoughtfully for investing your vital resources. What priorities deserve your primary focus? How can you align your time with activities that support your creative development? What balance would best serve your vision?
- **The environment and relationships you want to cultivate:** Envision the context that would best support your creative growth. What kind of spaces inspire your best work? Which relationships would nurture your development? How would your surroundings enhance your creative expression?

3. Why do I want to pursue certain paths and not others?

- **Sources of genuine passion and meaning:** Explore what truly ignites your enthusiasm and sense of purpose. Which activities connect you most deeply with your creative potential? What work feels naturally aligned with your authentic self? Where do you find flow and natural motivation?
- **Activities that bring you alive:** Identify pursuits that energize rather than deplete you. What kinds of work engage your creativity most fully? Which activities give you a sense of mean-

ingful contribution? How do these activities relate to your larger vision?

- **Causes that matter deeply to you:** Consider what issues or challenges move you to action. Where could your creative contributions make the most difference? What changes would you like to help create? How might your vision serve larger purposes?
- **Reasons behind your chosen direction:** Examine your motivations carefully to ensure they spring from authentic desires. What paths resonate with your core values? How do your choices align with your creative development goals? What evidence suggests these directions will serve your vision?

4. How do I want to *be* in life—emotionally, spiritually, and relationally?

- **Desired emotional states and well-being:** Reflect on the emotional qualities you want to cultivate. What feelings would characterize your best creative work? How would you like to handle challenges and celebrate successes? What emotional maturity would support your vision?
- **Spiritual growth and connection:** Consider your relationship with life's deeper dimensions. How would you like to grow in wisdom and awareness? What practices would nurture your creative spirit? How might spiritual development enhance your vision realization?
- **Quality of relationships:** Envision the connections that would enrich your creative life. How would you like to show up in your relationships? What qualities would you bring to your interactions? How would these relationships support your vision?
- **Impact on community and world:** Think about your broader influence. How would you like your creative work to affect others? What legacy would you like to create? How might your presence make a positive difference?
- **Personal fulfillment and satisfaction:** Imagine what true fulfillment means for you. What would give you a deep sense of

accomplishment? How would you measure the success of your creative expression? What would make you feel your life was well-lived?

Having invested time and energy in considering these core questions, we can move on to the personal challenge of crafting your vision, which is the topic of the next chapter.

CHAPTER 12:
CRAFTING YOUR VISION

When crafting your vision, you'll inevitably confront the challenges of integrating passion, purpose, mission, and meaning. These concepts are fundamental to creating a fulfilling life and are programmed into your Creative Self Mindset. Let's explore a few different strategies for incorporating these elements into your vision.

Follow Your Passion

This strategy, exemplified by Joseph Campbell's quote, "Follow your bliss and the universe will open doors where there were only walls," suggests that pursuing your passions is the key to a fulfilling life. This philosophy encourages individuals to identify what truly excites and motivates them and to build their lives around these passions.

Proponents of this view argue that when you're passionate about what you do, you're more likely to persist through challenges, produce high-quality work, and find deep satisfaction in your daily activities. They believe that passion fuels creativity, innovation, and personal growth, providing essential energy for creative development and expression.

However, this approach isn't without its critics. Some argue that blindly following passion can lead to impractical career choices, financial instability, or disappointment if passion doesn't translate into success. Additionally, this perspective might not account for the reality that many people's passions may not align with viable career options or societal needs.

Bring Your Passion

On the other end of the spectrum is the pragmatic approach, represented by Mike Rowe's "Dirty Jobs" strategy: "Don't follow your passion, but always bring it with you." This view emphasizes practicality, skill development, and adaptability over the pursuit of passion alone.

Advocates of this approach argue that success and satisfaction often come from becoming very good at something valuable rather than pursuing an idealized passion. They suggest that by focusing on developing useful skills and meeting market demands, individuals can build successful careers and find fulfillment through mastery and contribution. This perspective encourages people to remain open to opportunities, even if they don't align perfectly with preconceived passions. This perspective suggests that proficiency and recognizing the value of one's work cultivate passion over time.

Critics of this view, however, worry that it might lead people to settle for unfulfilling work or suppress their authentic desires and talents. There's also concern that this approach might not fully leverage an individual's unique gifts and interests.

Integrate Your Passion

As you craft your CLP Vision, it's worth considering a more nuanced strategy that combines elements from both of the previous strategies. The Japanese concept of Ikigai (pronounced "eye-ka-guy") offers a valuable perspective. Roughly translated as "a reason for being," Ikigai emerges at the intersection of four key considerations:

- **What you love:** This consideration focuses on your passions and interests. It's about identifying the activities, topics, and pursuits that ignite your enthusiasm and bring you joy. Crafting your vision requires reflecting on what you love; this alignment with your inner desires and passions fuels your creative development.
- **What you are good at:** This pillar emphasizes your skills and talents. It involves recognizing your strengths and the areas where you naturally excel. Integrating your abilities into your vision ensures that you are leveraging your natural gifts and

competencies, making your journey more effective and fulfilling. This understanding becomes an essential part of your Creative Self Mindset development.

- **What the world needs:** This consideration addresses the external impact of your actions. It involves understanding the needs and challenges of the world around you and identifying how you can contribute meaningfully. By considering what the world needs, your CLP Vision becomes more purposeful and aligned with broader societal goals, creating opportunities for meaningful creative expression.

- **What you can be paid for:** The last consideration focuses on the practical aspect of sustainability. It includes evaluating if your potential pursuit will provide the stability you desire. When your CLP Vision aligns with avenues for compensation, it becomes more sustainable and realistic, allowing you to maintain and expand your creative development over time.

At the intersection of these four considerations lies your Ikigai—your sweet spot. This is where you find the deepest sense of fulfillment and purpose. It's the place where your creative endeavors resonate with your true self, meet the needs of the world, and use your unique talents while providing the means to sustain your journey. This intersection becomes a vital reference point for your CLP Vision.

Your vision emerges from this intersection, reflecting both practical reality and authentic aspiration. It's here that your creative expression finds its most powerful and sustainable form, contributing to your ongoing development while serving genuine needs. This balanced approach helps ensure that your vision remains both inspiring and achievable.

Applying Ikigai to Your Creative Life Project Vision

When crafting your vision, the concept of Ikigai provides valuable guidance to ensure your vision is holistic and aligned with your true meaning and purpose. Here's how these elements relate to your vision development:

- **Aligning passions and talents:** By reflecting on what you love and what you are good at, you ensure that your vision is not only fulfilling but also achievable. It becomes a realistic plan grounded in your unique abilities and interests, supporting sustained creative development.
- **Connecting with the world's needs:** Understanding what the world needs allows you to shape a vision that is impactful and relevant. It encourages you to look beyond personal gain and consider how your creativity can contribute to societal well-being, creating meaningful opportunities for creative expression.
- **Considering personal compensation:** To work toward sustainability, incorporate potential compensation into your vision, which helps direct your creative pursuits toward sustainable endeavors. This consideration ensures you can dedicate time and resources to your development without undue stress, supporting continuous growth and expression.

While you create your vision, remember that you're not bound to follow any single strategy. Your approach to passion, purpose, and meaning can be as unique as you are.

As this vision evolves, it becomes imprinted into your Creative Self Mindset and provides both inspiration and intention for Creative Self Navigation throughout your CLP journey. Remember that this isn't about creating rigid plans or systems but about developing natural ways to express your creative potential in the service of your best life. Your vision should feel like an authentic expression of who you are and who you're becoming, supporting your continuous creative growth and expression.

Be thoughtful as you use these vision-crafting strategies to ensure they honor your passions while embracing the practical realities of building a satisfying and impactful life. Your vision should inspire you to navigate, build, and live what you consider to be your best life, integrating your unique blend of passions, skills, and aspirations with the needs of the world around you.

Guidelines for Crafting Your Vision

As you work through creating your vision, consider these ideas to guide you along the way. As a group, these nine guidelines help you keep this process within the perspective of your CLP and underline the importance of seeking an appropriate outlet for your individual Creative Self Expression.

1. Remember, This is the Vision for *Your* Best Life

Embrace the idea that you have the power to create your own future. The best way to predict your future is to create it for yourself. Your CLP Vision is a deeply personal and unique representation of what you consider to be your best life. It is essential to recognize that external expectations or mass-mindedness do not dictate this vision—it emerges from your own authentic desires, values, and aspirations. Embracing the idea that you have the power to create your own future is a fundamental aspect of crafting a meaningful and empowering vision.

When you accept that you are the architect of your own life, you understand that your future is not predetermined or limited by your current circumstances. Instead, you have the agency and ability to shape your path and create the life you truly desire. This realization can be both liberating and daunting, as it places the responsibility for your life's direction squarely in your own hands.

Remember to give yourself permission to dream big and imagine possibilities that may seem beyond your current reality. This is not about creating fantasy or an unattainable ideal but about tapping into your innermost desires and aspirations and allowing them to guide your vision. By doing so, you create a powerful source of motivation and direction, which can help you overcome obstacles and make decisions that align with your Creative Self.

2. Transforming Your Genetic and Cultural Blueprint into Your Fingerprint

Acknowledge the influence of your genetic and cultural blueprint, but recognize your ability to shape your own unique identity and path. Your genetic and cultural background undoubtedly shaped your experiences, opportunities, and perspectives. However, it is equally important to understand that these influences do not determine your destiny.

While your genetic and cultural imprint may provide a starting point, including possibilities and limitations, you have the power to shape your own unique identity and path through the choices you make and the actions you take. This process of transformation involves a deep exploration of your own beliefs, priorities, and goals. It requires asking yourself what truly matters to you, what kind of person you want to be, and what impact you want to have on the world.

By engaging in this self-reflection and using your insights to inform your vision, you create an idea for your life that is uniquely your own. As you navigate the journey of bringing your vision to life, you will undoubtedly encounter challenges and obstacles that are rooted in your genetic and cultural imprint. However, by staying true to your vision and continually making choices that align with your Creative Self, you gradually transform these influences into a source of strength and uniqueness.

3. Listen to Your Whole Body

Pay attention to your intuition, emotions, and physical sensations as you develop your vision. Your body can provide valuable insights and guidance in this process. Your intuition is the inner knowing that comes from a place of deep wisdom and understanding. It's the quiet voice inside you that guides you toward what feels right for you, even if it doesn't always make logical sense.

When you tune into your intuition, you tap into a powerful source of guidance that can help you clarify your values, priorities, and goals. Your emotions and physical sensations can also offer important insights as you craft your vision. Notice how your body feels as you explore different ideas and possibilities. Do you feel energized, expansive, and open? Or do you feel tense, constricted, and closed off?

Your body's responses can help you discern between what aligns with your Creative Self and what may come from fear, doubt, or external pressure. Listen to your whole body as you seek a deep sense of self-awareness and self-trust. Learn to tune into the subtle cues and messages that your intuition, emotions, and physical sensations are sending you, and use this information to guide your choices and actions.

4. Vision as Both a Motivation and a Magnet

Your CLP Vision is a powerful force that can propel you forward and shape the course of your life in profound ways. When crafted effectively, your vision serves two crucial functions: it acts as a source of motivation, inspiring you to take action toward your goals, and it functions as a magnet attracting you toward the people, opportunities, and resources that align with your values and aspirations.

As a source of motivation, your vision provides a clear and interesting picture of the life you want to create. It taps into your deepest desires and aspirations, creating a sense of excitement and purpose that drives you to take consistent action toward your goals. When you have a powerful vision that resonates with your Creative Self, you are more likely to persist through challenges and setbacks.

Your vision also functions as a magnet attracting the people, opportunities, and resources that can help you bring your envisioned future to life and serve as a powerful energy that draws you forward in challenging times.

5. Empowering vs. Disempowering Visions

Focus on what you want to achieve and who you want to become rather than dwelling on limitations or obstacles. When crafting your vision, it is crucial to ensure it is empowering and uplifting rather than disempowering or limiting. The way you frame your vision can have a profound impact on your mindset, motivation, and ability to take action toward your goals.

An empowering vision focuses on the positive outcomes you want to achieve and the person you want to become. This vision emphasizes possibilities, growth, and potential instead of limitations or obstacles.

When your vision is empowering, it creates a sense of excitement, hope, and inspiration that fuels your motivation and resilience.

To create an empowering vision, start by focusing on what you want. Instead of dwelling on your fears, doubts, or perceived shortcomings, direct your attention toward the qualities, experiences, and achievements that you desire. Use positive, affirmative language that reflects your aspirations and values, and paint a vivid picture of the life you want to create.

6. Your Vision is Both the Script and Storyboard for the Story of Your Life

Treat your vision as the narrative framework for your life story. It serves as both the script, outlining the key themes and events, and the storyboard, providing a vision representing your desired future. Your vision goes beyond being just a set of goals or aspirations; it's the narrative framework for the story of your life.

As the script for your life story, your vision defines the central plot, conflicts, and resolution of your journey. It identifies the major themes and values that will guide your choices and actions, as well as the key events and milestones that will mark your progress along the way. Just like a good script, your vision should have a clear beginning, middle, and end, with an empowering arc that draws you forward toward your desired outcome.

As the storyboard for your life story, your vision provides a vivid, sensory-rich picture of the future you want to create. It engages your imagination and emotions, allowing you to see, feel, and experience your desired reality as if it were already happening. Your vision should be clearly sketched, depicting the people, places, and experiences that will comprise your ideal life, just like a storyboard for a film or graphic novel.

7. As You Evolve, So Does Your Vision

As you begin the journey of bringing your CLP Vision to life, it's important to recognize that your vision is not a fixed or static destination but a dynamic process that will grow and change along with you. Just as you are a work in progress, constantly learning, growing, and adapting to new experiences and insights, so too is your vision a living, breathing entity that grows over time.

As you take action toward your goals, you will inevitably encounter new information, challenges, and opportunities that will shape your understanding of what's possible and desirable for your life. You may discover new passions or priorities, develop new skills or insights, or face unexpected obstacles or setbacks that require you to adapt and pivot in new directions.

Rather than seeing this evolution as a failure or a sign that your original vision was flawed, embrace it as an opportunity for growth and refinement. Recognize that your vision is not a rigid blueprint but a flexible framework that you can and should update and expand as you learn and grow.

8. Patience is a Virtue

As you embark on the journey of building your vision, it's essential to cultivate a set of qualities that will help you navigate the inevitable challenges and setbacks you will face along the way. These qualities include patience, faith, resourcefulness, and resilience.

Patience is the ability to remain calm, focused, and persistent in the face of delays, obstacles, or frustrations. It's the understanding that meaningful change and growth often take time, and rushing the process can lead to burnout, stress, or suboptimal outcomes. When you cultivate patience as you pursue your vision, you develop the ability to stay committed to your goals for the long haul, even when progress feels slow or difficult.

Faith is the belief in yourself, your vision, and the universe's ability to support you in manifesting your dreams. It's the trust that, even when things feel uncertain or challenging, you have the strength, wisdom, and resources within you to overcome any obstacle and create the life you envision.

9. The Idea of a Thing vs. the Reality of It

Recognize the difference between the idea of a thing and the reality of it, or you may find yourself getting what you asked for but not what you really want.

This wisdom applies to two distinct but equally important considerations as you craft your vision: the reality of what it takes to achieve your vision and the reality of living that vision once achieved.

The Reality of Achievement

The path to realizing your vision often differs significantly from how you might imagine it. While it's essential to dream big and envision inspiring possibilities, it's equally important to understand what genuine achievement requires.

The idea of achievement often appears pristine and straightforward in our minds—a clear, direct path from where we are to where we want to be. However, the reality of achievement involves developing new skills and capabilities you might not initially recognize as necessary. These might include not just technical skills related to your goals but also emotional resilience, relationship building, and adaptability. The journey typically demands investing more time, energy, and resources than first expected, requiring careful planning and sustained commitment.

Facing unexpected challenges and necessary detours becomes an integral part of the journey. These obstacles aren't just roadblocks; they're opportunities for growth and learning that ultimately strengthen your capacity to achieve and maintain your vision. The path often requires making sacrifices or tradeoffs you hadn't considered, whether in terms of time, relationships, or other pursuits. Understanding these potential tradeoffs helps you make conscious choices about what you're willing to invest in your vision.

Building support systems and relationships crucial for success often proves essential, though it might not be apparent at first. Few significant achievements happen in isolation—you'll likely need mentors, collaborators, supporters, and various forms of help along the way.

Understanding this reality helps you cultivate these relationships early in your journey.

The Reality of Living Your Vision

Perhaps even more crucial is understanding the difference between how you imagine living your vision and what that life actually entails. The external appearance of an achieved goal or life circumstance might seem appealing, while the day-to-day reality could be quite different from what you truly desire.

Consider the experience of a well-known performer whose fame brings unwanted intrusions into private life. While the spotlight might seem attractive from afar, the constant scrutiny, loss of privacy, and pressure to maintain a public image can significantly impact personal well-being and relationships. Similarly, a successful executive might discover that their position demands sacrificing personal relationships and life balance in ways they hadn't anticipated. The role might bring prestige and financial rewards, but at the cost of time with family, personal interests, or peace of mind.

An acclaimed artist might find that commercial success requires compromising creative freedom in unexpected ways. The pressure to produce work that sells rather than work that inspires can create internal conflict and diminish the joy of creation. A wealthy entrepreneur might discover their lifestyle creates unexpected personal pressures, from managing complex financial decisions to navigating changes in relationships and dealing with constant demands on their time and attention.

Bridging the Gap

Creating a meaningful vision requires balancing these two realities—both the journey and the destination. To achieve this balance, several key elements must be considered.

Being honest about what achievement requires while maintaining inspiration and motivation is essential. This means acknowledging the full scope of effort, resources, and commitment needed while not letting this reality diminish your enthusiasm. It's about finding ways to stay inspired by your vision while developing practical strategies to overcome obstacles. When you maintain this balance, challenges become opportunities for growth rather than discouraging setbacks.

Looking deeply into how living your vision aligns with your authentic desires and values requires careful reflection and honesty. Take time to imagine not just the highlights of your envisioned future but the day-to-day reality. Consider how this reality meshes with your personal values, preferred lifestyle, and what truly matters to you. This deep examination helps ensure your vision leads to genuine fulfillment rather than just external success.

Adjusting your vision as you gain a clearer understanding of both realities is a natural and necessary part of the process. As you learn more about what achievement requires and what living your vision truly means, you may need to refine or revise aspects of your vision. This isn't compromise—it's wisdom gained through deeper understanding. Your vision should evolve as your awareness grows, becoming more aligned with both practical reality and your authentic desires.

Ensuring your path and destination truly serve your best life, not just an idealized image, requires ongoing attention and reflection. Regular check-ins with yourself about both the journey and the destination help maintain this alignment. Ask whether the steps you're taking and the future you're creating genuinely reflect what you want for your life, not just what looks appealing from the outside. This continuous awareness helps keep your vision authentic and meaningful.

By understanding both the reality of achievement and the reality of living your vision, you can craft aspirations that are both inspiring and genuinely fulfilling. This dual awareness helps ensure that your CLP Vision leads not just to achievement but to authentic satisfaction and well-being.

Creative Self Navigation

By working to establish your CLP Vision, you have already begun programming it into your Creative Self Mindset to support Creative Self Navigation. This helps cultivate a natural way to translate your vision into daily reality by developing and strengthening your Creative Self Mindset.

Beyond Traditional Approaches

In content related to creativity and personal development, you've likely encountered various ways to think about moving toward goals. While these approaches can offer valuable insights, they often fall short of providing a comprehensive, actionable framework and are overly simplistic, failing to capture the complex, dynamic nature of Creative Self Development.

Creative Self Navigation represents something different. It emerges as part of the ongoing development of your Creative Self Mindset, integrating your meaning and purpose with intentional action. It's not a one-size-fits-all solution but a deeply personal approach supporting your lifelong Creative Self Development and Expression vision.

What Makes Creative Self Navigation Distinct

Your creative potential and your philosophy, mindset, and vision influence the unique development of your Creative Self Navigation abilities. This personalization ensures that your navigation practice remains specific to your CLP journey.

As you progress in your development, your navigation abilities grow with you, helping you move more effectively toward your vision. This dynamic adaptation means your ability to navigate life's complexities increases alongside the development of your Creative Self Potential™.

Your navigation practice integrates with and relies upon all the categories of the Creative Self Development Framework, translating your knowledge, attitudes, aspirations, and beliefs into practical, day-to-day guidance for problem-solving and decision-making. Rather than following external rules or systems, you learn to navigate from an internal understanding that grows more refined through experience into Creative Self independence.

Developing Your Navigation Practice

The development of Creative Self Navigation happens naturally as you do the following:

- **Assess your current reality:** Begin by honestly evaluating your present circumstances. Understanding your strengths, challenges, and available resources forms your point of departure for effective navigation.
- **Engage with your vision:** Your CLP Vision becomes your primary reference point, helping you evaluate opportunities and make choices that align with the future you envision.
- **Identify key inflection points:** Determine significant milestones that will mark your progress from your current reality to your envisioned future. These inflection points help you track your development while maintaining flexibility in your approach.
- **Establish decision-making criteria:** Using your philosophy, mindset, and vision, develop principles that guide your choices along your journey. These criteria help you navigate complex situations while staying true to your vision.
- **Create feedback mechanisms:** Develop ways to measure your progress and receive feedback, allowing you to make necessary course corrections while maintaining momentum toward your vision.
- **Build in adaptability:** Foster flexibility in your navigation practice, allowing it to evolve as your environment, circumstances, and context change. This adaptability ensures your practice remains relevant and effective throughout your journey.

Moving Forward with Vision and Navigation

As you continue your Creative Self Development journey, remember that vision and Creative Self Navigation abilities work together, each enhancing the other. Your vision provides direction and purpose, while navigation abilities help you think, feel, and act to move effectively toward that vision.

This interdependence supports both practical success and personal fulfillment while maintaining alignment with your expanding Creative Self Mindset. As you engage with subsequent categories of the Creative Self Development Framework, your vision and navigation abilities will continue to grow, supporting your ongoing Creative Self Development and Expression.

The journey ahead involves discovering more about your Creative Self Potential, developing practical skills, and finding meaningful ways to express your Creative Self.

PART 05

CATEGORY—THE LIFE SKILL OF BEING CREATIVE

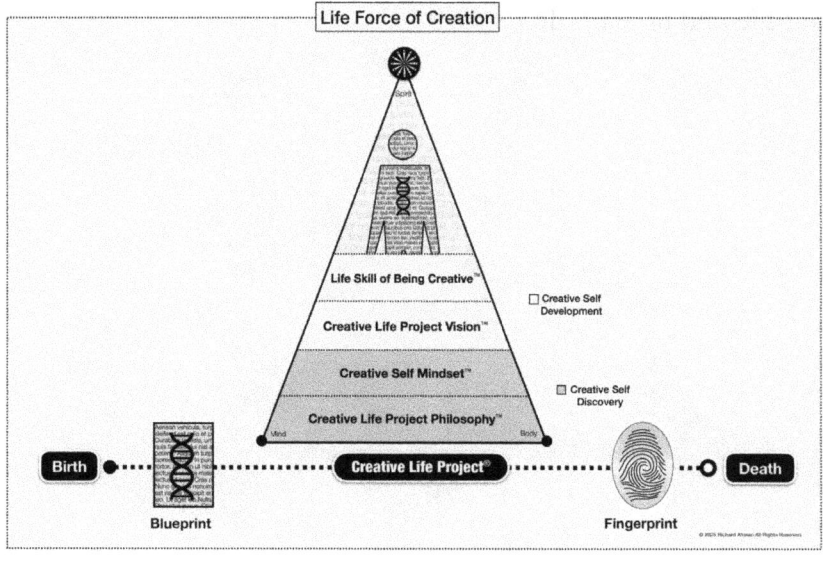

The Life Skill of Being Creative is the practical, intentional, action-based skill for transforming our aspirational thoughts from our mind space into the realities of physical space.

The current, most common understanding of creativity comes from viewing it through a tactical lens, emphasizing brainstorming techniques, innovation exercises, and problem-solving methods. While all this has value, it represents only a fraction of what it means to live a truly creative life. The CLP represents a fresh perspective—one that views being creative as a strategic life skill rather than a special talent possessed by a select few. This perspective is integral to the CLP's philosophy, process, and practice.

The Life Skill of Being Creative is a web of interconnected competencies that empowers our Creative Self Mindset to seek out and reinforce purposeful living. It serves as the strategic foundation for managing, applying, and expanding creative potential, ensuring that creativity is not something we access occasionally but something we intentionally develop through lifelong learning and practice.

In the chapters that follow, we will explore the strategic considerations that support lifelong Creative Self Development. By developing and practicing the Life Skill of Being Creative, you transform yourself from someone who occasionally practices creativity to someone who strategically lives creatively—becoming the creator in your life and of your life.

CHAPTER 13:
THE STRATEGIC LIFE SKILL OF BEING CREATIVE

At first, the idea of developing creativity as a strategic life skill may seem overwhelming. After all, how do you commit to something so broad and dynamic? The answer lies in understanding that the strategic Life Skill of Being Creative is fundamentally built on the principle of lifelong learning and practice. This foundation distinguishes it from tactical approaches to creativity and transforms creative potential into a sustainable capacity for navigating life's challenges.

Consider learning to ride a bike. At first, the process feels complex—balancing, pedaling, steering, and braking all at once can seem like too much to manage. However, with practice and repeated effort, these once-challenging tasks become second nature. Over time, riding a bike requires little conscious effort, allowing for greater focus on the experience—exploring alternative routes, increasing speed, or even performing advanced maneuvers.

Creativity follows a similar trajectory. In the beginning, developing creative skills may require intentional effort—learning to approach problems differently, training yourself to ask new questions, and engaging in unfamiliar forms of expression. However, as these patterns take root through consistent lifelong learning and practice, creativity becomes second nature, running in the background as a natural way of thinking and interacting with the world. Just as a musician no longer consciously considers every note played or a driver no longer fixates on every motion involved in steering, creativity becomes an integrated, automatic part of how we live, work, and solve problems.

This process of gradual integration through lifelong learning and practice ensures that creativity does not remain an external pursuit or something to be turned on and off as needed. It transforms into a constantly improving, strategic life skill—refined through experience, practice, and adaptation. In this way, the Life Skill of Being Creative is about reaching a state where creativity becomes an undercurrent, flowing naturally and available whenever we choose to engage it.

The Difference Between Strategic and Tactical Approaches to Being Creative

To understand the strategic nature of this life skill, let's examine the contrast between tactical and strategic approaches to being creative. Here is a list of the most frequent recommendations that appear in articles, blogs, and creativity websites when searching for ways to improve creativity:

- Practice brainstorming techniques regularly.
- Keep a journal or sketchbook for ideas.
- Learn a new hobby or skill.
- Change your environment/workspace regularly.
- Try mind mapping for problem-solving.
- Take regular walks in nature.
- Practice meditation or mindfulness.
- Read books outside your usual genres.
- Collaborate with others/join creative communities.
- Use the "yes and" technique from improvisation.
- Set aside dedicated time for creative activities.
- Challenge assumptions by asking "what if" questions.
- Take art or music classes.
- Travel to new places.
- Write morning pages (stream-of-consciousness writing).

Each of these tactics has value, yet their actual power emerges when we understand how to use them within a more comprehensive strategy. Tactical tools provide concrete ways to apply our creative capacity, while the strategic approach ensures our creative potential continues growing stronger and more refined. Without this strategic foundation, we risk limiting ourselves to momentary creative spurts or blocks rather than developing the sustained creative fluency that can transform our lives. This integration of approaches mirrors the CLP's comprehensive view of creativity as an innate human trait that is developable into a strategic life skill.

The distinction between tactical and strategic approaches becomes clear when we consider their impact on long-term creative development. You can, for example, learn individual moves in chess without understanding the strategic principles that guide a master player. In contrast, a strategic approach to a chess match embraces the specific tactical moves in harmony with a game strategy, guiding the selection and timing of the moves during a game.

This strategic perspective aligns perfectly with our understanding of creativity as fundamental to surviving, thriving, and flourishing. Just as our ancestors needed sustained creative capabilities to navigate life's challenges, we, too, require more than occasional creative moments to thrive in our rapidly changing technological world.

The focused cultivation of creativity as a life skill requires understanding both the why and how of Creative Self Development. Through this lens, creativity becomes a strategic resource that we intentionally develop and apply across all aspects of our experience, from everyday problem-solving to our most ambitious personal aspirations.

Integrating lifelong learning and practice into Creative Self Development mirrors the natural way humans gain and refine capabilities. Just as we learn language through constant exposure and practice, creative capabilities develop through ongoing engagement with creative challenges and opportunities. This natural development process, when approached with intention and awareness, accelerates our growth and deepens our creative understanding.

Exploring the Foundations of Lifelong Learning and Practice

Let's look at the fundamental components of lifelong learning and practice on which the strategic Life Skill of Being Creative is built. These components provide insight into how lifelong learning and practice fuel creative development. In the next chapter, we'll build upon this foundation by exploring the meta-skill of learning to learn—the essential capability that maximizes our creative potential and makes the most efficient use of our precious resources of time and energy.

Maslow: Motivation and the Need to Be Creative

In the mid-20th century, Abraham Maslow revolutionized our understanding of human motivation and development by examining what drives humans to grow, develop, and achieve their potential. As a pioneering humanistic psychologist, he studied highly successful individuals rather than focusing on psychological dysfunction, as was common in his era. This approach led to his influential contribution, the Hierarchy of Needs, which presents human development as a progression from basic survival needs to self-actualization.

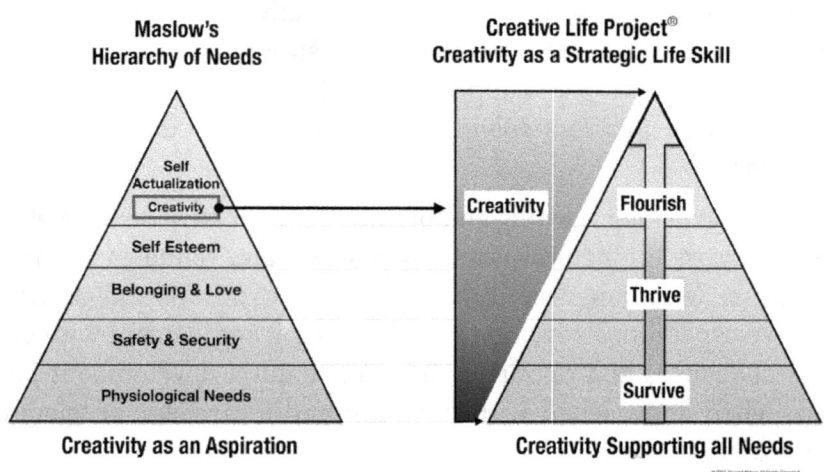

Traditional interpretations of Maslow's hierarchy place creativity at the peak of human development—positioning it as a component of self-actualization that can only occur after satisfying more basic requirements for survival, safety, belonging, and esteem. This view implies that creativity is a privilege for those who have overcome their fundamental life challenges, suggesting that creative development must await the fulfillment of other needs.

However, the CLP perspective challenges this conventional interpretation, while honoring Maslow's insights about human potential. Our understanding recognizes that creativity isn't merely a high-level achievement—it is a fundamental resource that supports us at every stage of life, from basic survival to self-actualization. This shift in perspective aligns perfectly with our understanding of creativity's role in human adaptation and development throughout history.

Consider how our earliest ancestors used creativity not as a luxury but as an essential tool for survival. They needed creativity, along with resourcefulness, to solve immediate challenges of finding food, creating shelter, and protecting their communities with whatever was available to them, doing the best with what they had. This historical perspective reveals creativity as a fundamental capability that has always supported human survival and growth rather than an advanced skill reserved for those who have satisfied all other needs.

The CLP's reframing of creativity's role in human development has profound implications for how we approach Creative Self Development. When we recognize creativity as essential rather than optional, we understand why continuous learning and practice are crucial. Creativity becomes a vital resource we must cultivate throughout life, not a distant goal to pursue only after achieving stability.

This insight transforms how we think about Creative Self Development in three key ways:

- It validates the importance of developing our foundational elements—curiosity, imagination, and creation—at every stage of life. These capabilities support not just our highest aspirations but also our daily navigation of life's challenges and opportunities. They become essential tools for addressing needs at every level of Maslow's hierarchy.

- It emphasizes why waiting to develop creative capabilities until life is "settled" or "stable" misses crucial opportunities for using it for growth and development. Our creative capacities serve us best when developed continuously, allowing us to use them to address challenges and seize opportunities at every stage of life.
- It highlights how creativity supports both immediate problem-solving and long-term development. Rather than seeing creativity as relevant only to self-actualization, we recognize its role in everything from managing daily challenges to pursuing our highest aspirations.

With this understanding of the value of being creative, we can begin to explore other components of lifelong learning and practice.

The Creative Life Project Creative Continuum

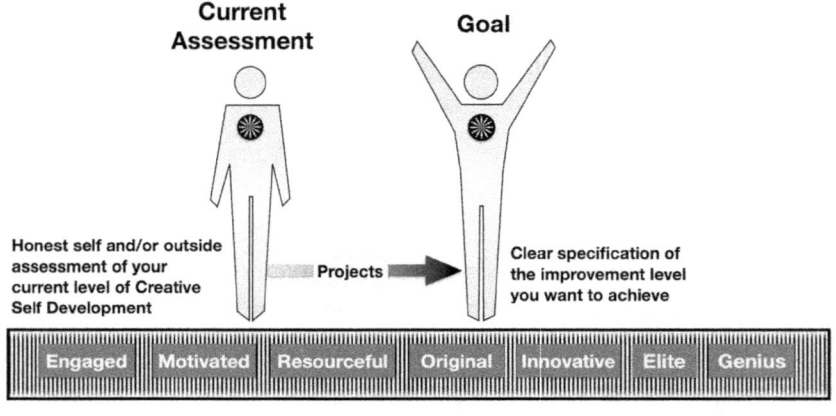

To support the Life Skill of Being Creative and the commitment to lifelong learning and practice, the CLP uses a *continuum* as a transformative way to understand and assess creative development throughout life. This model represents a fundamental shift from traditional binary thinking about creativity to a more nuanced and realistic understanding of how creative capabilities evolve over time.

Unlike models that divide people into creative or not creative, or segment creativity into fixed types—such as the Four C Model of

Creativity (mini-c, little-c, Pro-c, Big-C)—the CLP Creative Continuum recognizes that creativity is not fixed, categorical, or confined. It exists on a dynamic continuum of continuous development and engagement.

For context, the Four C Model organizes creativity into levels:

- **Mini-c**: personal insights and everyday learning moments (like a child discovering something new);
- **Little-c**: everyday problem-solving and creative expression (like cooking a meal or writing a poem);
- **Pro-c**: expert-level creativity developed over time in a specific domain (like a skilled designer or teacher); and
- **Big-C**: legendary contributions that change a field or society (like Einstein or Leonardo da Vinci).

While this model is useful for understanding how creative contributions can vary, the CLP approach emphasizes that creativity is always in motion—developing through curiosity, practice, and purpose, no matter where you begin. It's not about fitting into a category—it's about engaging your Creative Self and growing from where you are.

The Creative Continuum encourages honest self-assessment as well as outside input to evaluate your current relationship with creativity. It also emphasizes identifying a meaningful direction for growth. Between where you are now and where you want to go lies the practical work of Creative Self Development—represented by the projects, practices, and challenges that support movement along the continuum. These projects become the bridge between aspiration and actualization.

The diagram above illustrates this progression visually. On the left, a figure represents your current state of creative development—grounded in a candid assessment of how you currently relate to your creative potential. On the right stands a version of you who has grown into a more fully realized Creative Self. The arrow in between is marked "Projects," signifying the process of transformation fueled by learning, experimentation, and expression. This movement is not just about becoming more skilled but about becoming more engaged, more aligned, and more expressive, in your own unique way.

The terms beneath the figures—Engaged, Motivated, Resourceful, Original, Innovative, Elite, Genius—represent a general developmental progression of creative capabilities. These are not ranks or rigid stages but a continuum of deepening creative identity and contribution. Each term offers a reference point for reflection, providing language to describe different phases of creative growth. Here's a closer look at what these stages represent:

- **Engaged**: You've moved from passive acceptance of life's default modes to becoming aware of your own creative potential. This stage marks the spark of curiosity and the willingness to begin exploring who you are, what you're capable of, and how creativity might play a meaningful role in your life.
- **Motivated**: You've begun to sense the value of your creative potential and have developed a growing desire to nurture it. Learning becomes more intentional, and you begin actively seeking new insights, skills, and experiences to support your development.
- **Resourceful**: You start to embody the principle of "doing the best with what you have, when, where, and however you are." At this stage, creativity becomes more pragmatic—you experiment, problem-solve, adapt, and stretch your resources across different contexts. You begin to see challenges as opportunities for creative engagement.
- **Original:** Your voice, style, or approach begins to emerge with distinction. Whether in personal expression or professional pursuits, you are developing your own lens for interacting with your domain(s) of interest, shaped by personal values, insights, and aesthetics. The focus shifts from imitation to intentional originality.
- **Innovative**: Your creative efforts begin to shift or influence the domain itself. You offer new perspectives, combinations, or systems that others recognize as valuable. Innovation emerges from sustained learning, reflection, and applied action—pushing boundaries while remaining grounded in purpose.

- **Elite:** You are recognized within your domain as a person of consequence—someone whose work demonstrates excellence, leadership, and consistent creative contribution. Your knowledge, skill, and insight position you to mentor others, shape the field, or influence creative culture.
- **Genius:** The rare individual whose creativity transcends mastery and leaves an indelible mark on human culture. Genius integrates curiosity, imagination, and application at extraordinary levels, often pioneering new fields or paradigms. Think Da Vinci. While few reach this level, it serves as a symbolic north star for lifelong creative potential.

This progression is not about external achievement or prestige—it's about expanding your capacity to live, work, and contribute creatively in a way that feels authentic and meaningful. By identifying your current position and imagining where you want to go, you can begin selecting or designing projects that challenge you just enough to spark growth. The Creative Continuum provides a framework for that process—a dynamic way to engage with your aspirations and move forward with purpose.

As you navigate this continuum, it is important to remember that progress is rarely linear. Growth often unfolds in successive approximations—gradual refinements and repeated attempts that bring you closer to your creative potential over time. The next section explores how the concept of successive approximations supports this developmental journey, reinforcing the idea that Creative Self Development is a continuous, adaptive process of learning, doing, and becoming.

Successive Approximations: The Power of Incremental Growth

As we continue exploring the Life Skill of Being Creative, having established the Creative Continuum as our framework for understanding development progression, we encounter a powerful concept that explains how we actually move along this continuum: successive approximations. This concept provides a more authentic and empowering framework for skill development than the common but potentially misleading notion of "fake it till you make it."

Beyond "Fake It till You Make It"

The popular phrase "fake it till you make it" suggests pretending to have skills or knowledge until you actually acquire them. While this concept contains a kernel of truth about building confidence through action, it carries problematic connotations of inauthenticity and misrepresentation. It implies that learning requires a form of deception—both of others and perhaps of ourselves.

The CLP offers a more nuanced and honest approach: successive approximations. Rather than "faking" anything, this perspective recognizes that mastery develops through a series of increasingly refined attempts—each one a genuine expression of your current capability, each one bringing you closer to your desired level of skill. This process explains how we actually progress along the Creative Continuum we've just explored.

Understanding Successive Approximations

Successive approximations is a concept with roots in behavioral psychology and learning theory, representing a process where complex behaviors are developed through the reinforcement of increasingly accurate steps toward a target behavior. In the context of Creative Self Development, this translates to the gradual refinement of skills through consistent practice and progressive challenges.

Unlike the binary thinking implied by "faking it," successive approximations acknowledge that creative development exists on a continuum—precisely as we've established. Each attempt you make, each project you complete, and each skill you practice is not a fake version of some idealized end state—it is a legitimate step in your ongoing journey along the continuum. Every approximation holds value as both an authentic expression of your current abilities and a necessary building block toward greater mastery.

When you engage in successive approximations, you're not pretending; you're actively building the architecture of skill that will eventually support fluid, natural performance. This reality reinforces that there is no "faking" involved—just the natural, incremental process of growth that moves you along the Creative Continuum from novice to mastery.

Applying Successive Approximations to Creative Self Development

The framework of successive approximations offers several advantages for your CLP:

- **Authenticity**: You can embrace where you are on the Creative Continuum without pretense, recognizing that your current attempts are genuine expressions of your learning journey, not inadequate imitations.
- **Reduced pressure**: By focusing on incremental progress rather than perfect execution, you lower the psychological barriers to beginning and continuing your creative work.
- **Meaningful feedback**: Each approximation provides concrete information about what's working and what needs refinement, creating a natural feedback loop that guides your development.
- **Sustainable motivation**: Celebrating small improvements keeps motivation high, as you recognize the value in each step rather than fixating solely on distant end goals.
- **Adaptability**: The framework encourages flexibility in your approach, allowing you to adjust your path based on what you learn through each approximation.

Embracing the Wisdom of Small Steps

Viewing your creative development through the lens of successive approximations invites a profound shift in perspective. Instead of seeing your current work as somehow lacking or inauthentic compared to an imagined ideal, you can appreciate it as a necessary and valuable step in your evolution. Each approximation contains wisdom and represents genuine growth, worthy of both honest assessment and sincere appreciation.

This perspective aligns perfectly with the CLP Philosophy's emphasis on transforming your blueprint into your fingerprint. This transformation doesn't happen in one dramatic moment but through countless successive approximations, each one bringing your unique creative expression into sharper focus.

As you progress in your Creative Self Development journey, embrace the power of successive approximations. Recognize that each step you take, however small it might seem, is not a pretense or a false representation but an authentic marker on your path to mastery. By honoring these incremental steps, you cultivate both the technical skills and the patient, empowering mindset essential for sustainable creative development.

Rather than faking it until you make it, you are quite simply and powerfully making it—one approximation at a time.

The Creative Life Project Learning Spiral

The concept of successive approximations provides the mechanism for how we progress in our creative development, but it doesn't yet address the structure of this progress. In this section, we'll explore how these approximations organize into a Learning Spiral™—a cyclical pattern of growth that carries us forward in our creative journey.

Building on successive approximations and the Creative Continuum concept, the CLP frames this gradual learning process along the continuum as a Learning Spiral to illustrate how creative development actually unfolds. This model demonstrates that creative growth isn't linear but a spiral in nature, with each cycle of learning to build upon previous experiences to take on new challenges and opportunities for growth.

Creative Continuum + Learning Spiral

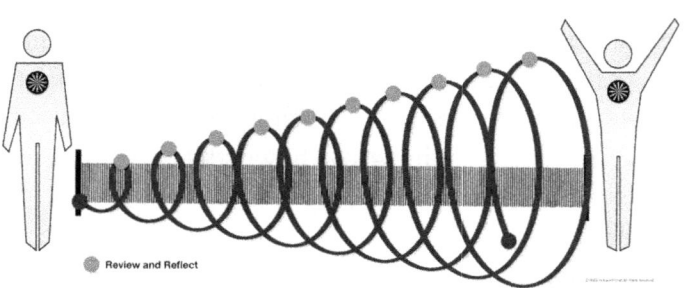

The spiral nature of this development reflects how learning in creative domains involves revisiting fundamental concepts with increasingly sophisticated understanding and application. As we progress through each cycle, our perspective expands, allowing us to see connections and possibilities that weren't visible before. This progression creates a dynamic learning environment where each experience enriches our understanding and capabilities.

The Learning Spiral provides a structured perspective on how skill development unfolds over time while recognizing that how individuals move through these stages varies based on their unique learning strengths. Not everyone learns in the same way or at the same pace—some may require extensive engagement with fundamentals, while others may grasp concepts more intuitively and move forward quickly.

There are four stages of the Learning Spiral:

1. **Fundamentals:** The foundation of any creative skill or discipline. Learning starts with core principles, techniques, and essential knowledge that provide a baseline for future development.

2. **Practice and coaching:** Skill-building requires deliberate practice, feedback, and mentorship. Whether guided by a teacher, mentor, peer, or self-directed inquiry, coaching plays a vital role in accelerating learning and overcoming challenges.

3. **Performance assessment:** Distinguishing between practice and performance is critical. Performance is the real-world application of creative skills, requiring self and external assessment to gauge effectiveness, identify areas for improvement, and refine one's abilities. Each performance provides new insights that shape the next cycle of learning. Assessments may come from the following places:

    Self-reflection (personal evaluation of strengths and weaknesses)

    Coaches, mentors, and teachers (structured feedback and guidance)

    Peers and collaborators (insight from those engaged in similar creative pursuits)

Managers or audiences (real-world reception and impact of creative work)

4. **Skill progression and self-assessment:** As learning continues, skills evolve in complexity, depth, and integration. Through ongoing cycles of practice, performance, and reflection, we move along the Creative Continuum, gradually refining our expertise and ability to self-assess both our performance and progress.

Although self-assessment is ongoing throughout the process, the dots appearing along the spiral represent milestones as we advance through the spirals of learning, providing opportunities for review and reflection that will be addressed when we reach Part VIII: Category—Creative Self Expression Practice.

The Learning Spiral illustrates how we progressively build not just knowledge and experience but also wisdom throughout our creative journey. Each cycle adds new layers of understanding, deepening our insights and expanding our capabilities. This accumulation of wisdom—the ability to apply what we've learned in increasingly sophisticated ways—becomes a crucial element in our Creative Self Development.

Summary

Creativity as a resource to support human survival, thriving, and flourishing that exists along a Creative Continuum, and through lifelong learning and practice, it provides the foundation for the Life Skill of Being Creative.

With such importance placed on learning, we stand to benefit by learning how to optimize how we learn. This brings us to meta-skills in creative development: learning to learn. This capability—understanding how we gain and apply knowledge—transforms us from passive recipients of information into active architects of our own development, empowering us to take control of our creative growth with purpose and intention.

With all this emphasis on learning now and in the future, we turn our attention to how to optimize our learning ability by looking more closely at what learning to learn is all about.

CHAPTER 14:
LEARNING TO LEARN

Advancing from our understanding of the foundations of lifelong learning and practice that support the strategic Life Skill of Being Creative, we now turn our attention to a fundamental meta-skill that amplifies this development: learning to learn.

Learning to learn includes a set of considerations that underpin how you learn. It is the ability to understand, adapt, and optimize your own learning process, ensuring that you can acquire new knowledge, skills, and wisdom effectively and efficiently throughout your life. By developing this meta-skill, you can become a more adaptable, resilient, and self-directed person, capable of navigating the complexities of personal and creative growth.

Learning to learn involves understanding how you learn best, identifying your strengths and weaknesses, and developing strategies to enhance your learning process. This includes enriching and cultivating your empowering Creative Self Mindset, embracing challenges as opportunities for growth, and seeking experiences that push you beyond your comfort zone.

In today's rapidly changing world, the ability to learn continuously and adapt quickly has become more valuable than ever before. As new technologies emerge, industries transform, and societal challenges evolve, those who can learn effectively will be best positioned to thrive. Learning to learn is not just about academic or professional development; it's about equipping yourself with the tools to navigate life's ever-changing landscape with creativity, confidence, and purpose.

Let's explore various aspects of learning to learn that support the strategic Life Skill of Being Creative.

Why We Learn

*"Those who have a 'why' to live
can bear with almost any how."*

Viktor Frankl (1905–1997), an Austrian neurologist, psychiatrist, and Holocaust survivor, profoundly influenced our understanding of human motivation and purpose. Through his experiences in concentration camps and his subsequent work developing logotherapy, Frankl demonstrated that finding meaning is fundamental to human resilience and growth. His insights, particularly relevant to creative development, emerged from observing how individuals who maintained a sense of purpose could overcome even the most devastating circumstances.

At the heart of learning to learn is the fundamental question: why do we learn? Frankl's work emphasizes that learning is not just about knowledge accumulation—it is about meaning and purpose. He observed that individuals who had a clear sense of purpose and who understood why they needed to persist and grow were more likely to overcome even the most difficult circumstances.

A powerful illustration of this principle appears in Frankl's observation: "When we are no longer able to change a situation, we are challenged to change ourselves." This insight embodies the essence of learning to learn—we may not always control what happens to us, but we do control how we respond, adapt, and grow. Learning to learn is about developing this resilience, using knowledge, creativity, and self-direction to navigate challenges and reshape our perspective and actions.

For Creative Self Development, this means learning transcends the mere acquisition of information. Instead, it becomes a purposeful journey of using knowledge to develop our creative potential and ability to shape our lives. This understanding of why we learn sets the foundation for exploring what we need to learn through Benjamin Bloom's comprehensive model of learning domains, which we'll explore next.

What We Learn

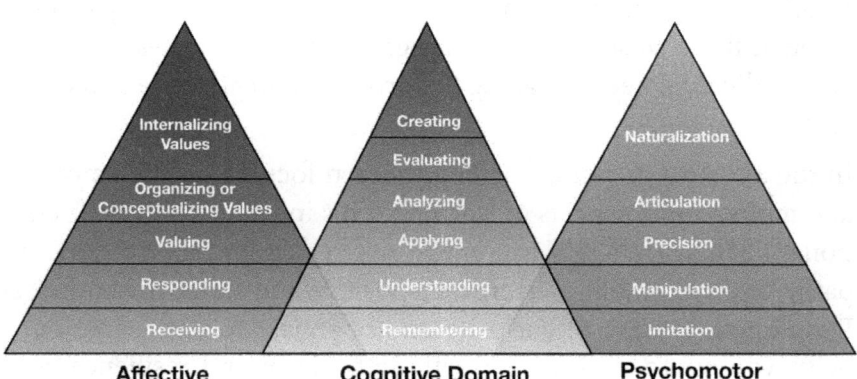

Bloom's Taxonomy of Learning

One helpful tool in this learning-to-learn process is *Bloom's Taxonomy*, a framework often used in education to structure and assess learning. It identifies three main domains of learning:

1. **Cognitive (knowledge):** Focuses on mental skills like understanding, analyzing, and applying information.
2. **Affective (attitudes and emotions):** Centers on feelings, values, and emotional development in learning.
3. **Psychomotor (physical skills):** Involves hands-on skills and coordination.

By understanding these domains, you can better discover, develop, and express your creative potential. Each domain presents unique challenges and opportunities, making Bloom's Taxonomy a valuable reference for aligning your learning objectives with your personal growth.

In the cognitive domain, learning to learn involves developing strategies for acquiring, processing, and applying information effectively. As you progress through the levels of learning in this domain—remembering, understanding, applying, analyzing, evaluating, and creating—you enhance your ability to think critically and creatively. These higher-order cognitive skills enable you to synthesize information, generate innovative ideas, and solve complex problems. For example, you might begin by learning the foundational principles of a concept (remembering and understanding) and then apply this knowledge to a real-world scenario. As you practice analyzing and evaluating outcomes, you develop the capacity to create unique solutions and adapt them to new challenges. By consciously working through these stages, you can design learning strategies tailored to your individual needs, making the process both effective and enjoyable.

In the affective domain, learning to learn focuses on the emotional and motivational aspects of learning. This includes cultivating emotional intelligence—self-awareness, self-regulation, motivation, empathy, and social skills—to create a positive and supportive mindset. Developing a sense of curiosity and openness to new experiences helps you approach learning with enthusiasm and resilience, even when faced with challenges. For example, reflecting on how your values influence your goals can deepen your connection to the learning process, while recognizing the emotional barriers to learning—like fear of failure—can help you develop strategies to overcome them. By aligning your attitudes and values with your learning objectives, you create an environment conducive to creative growth and personal fulfillment.

In the psychomotor domain, learning to learn involves mastering physical skills through practice and refinement. This may include breaking down complex tasks into smaller, manageable components, seeking feedback from mentors, and using deliberate practice to improve precision and efficiency. For example, if your creative expression involves drawing, you might focus on mastering shading techniques before moving on to complex compositions. Similarly, for skills like public speaking or playing an instrument, consistent practice and performance opportunities build confidence and proficiency. By intentionally engaging with the psychomotor domain, you develop the technical abilities needed for creative expression, turning practice into mastery.

How We Learn

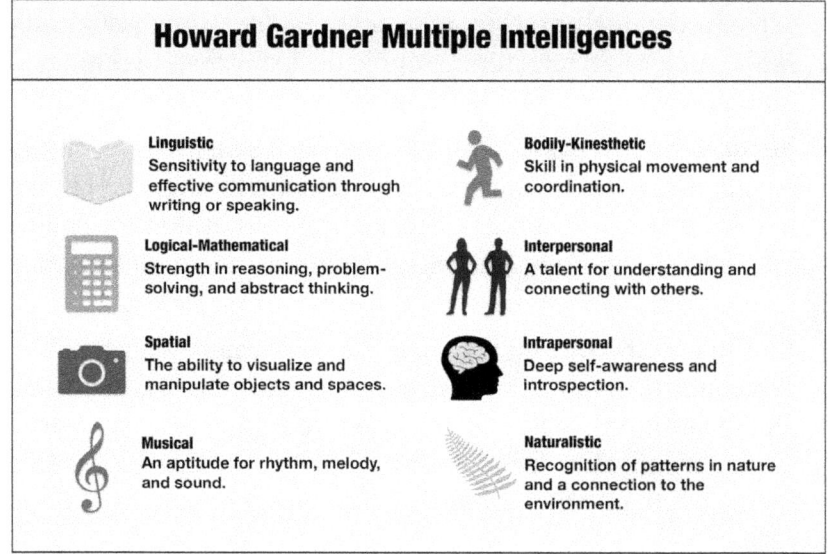

Beyond Bloom's Taxonomy, Howard Gardner's theory of *multiple intelligences* adds another dimension to understanding your learning style. This theory suggests that intelligence is diverse and multidimensional, with individuals possessing varying degrees of abilities across eight areas. Incorporating Howard Gardner's theory of multiple intelligences adds a valuable dimension to learning to learn.

- **Linguistic intelligence** impacts learning by favoring activities that involve reading, writing, and verbal communication. Individuals with this intelligence often excel when lessons include storytelling, discussion, or written assignments. In terms of career alignment, these strengths naturally guide them toward fields such as writing, journalism, law, public relations, or teaching.
- **Logical-mathematical intelligence** enables learners to thrive in structured environments that emphasize problem-solving and abstract reasoning. They enjoy puzzles, experiments, and logical exercises. Careers in science, engineering, finance, data analysis, and programming often provide fulfilling paths for those with this intelligence.

- *Spatial intelligence* is clear in learners who think visually and often use diagrams, maps, or illustrations to understand concepts. These individuals excel in fields that require strong visualization skills, such as architecture, graphic design, urban planning, and filmmaking.
- *Musical intelligence* is characterized by a sensitivity to rhythm, sound, and melody. Learners with this intelligence benefit from lessons that incorporate music, auditory repetition, or rhythm-based activities. They are well-suited to careers in music composition, performance, sound engineering, or music therapy.
- *Bodily-kinesthetic intelligence* shines in learners who grasp concepts best through hands-on activities and physical interaction. Demonstrations, role-playing, and movement-based learning are highly effective for them. This intelligence often leads to careers in acting, athletics, physical therapy, construction, or surgery.
- *Interpersonal intelligence* involves a natural ability to connect with others, making collaborative and group-based learning environments ideal. These learners excel in understanding emotions and fostering connections, which align with careers in counseling, sales, social work, leadership, or event planning.
- *Intrapersonal intelligence* is reflected in learners who excel at self-reflection and prefer independent, introspective approaches to learning. They thrive in environments that allow for self-paced study and personal exploration. Careers in psychology, philosophy, writing, or entrepreneurship often resonate with individuals who have this intelligence.
- *Naturalistic intelligence* is evident in learners who connect deeply with nature and patterns in the environment. Fieldwork, real-world examples, and nature-based activities enhance their learning experience. This intelligence often aligns with careers in biology, environmental science, farming, or conservation.

While individuals may have stronger orientations toward certain types of intelligence, creative development often engages multiple intelligences simultaneously. A sculptor might employ spatial intelligence for visualization, bodily-kinesthetic intelligence for physical creation, and intrapersonal intelligence for artistic expression.

Understanding these different pathways to learning helps us recognize and leverage our natural strengths while developing capabilities across multiple intelligences. This insight transforms our approach to creative development, showing us that there are many valid ways to learn, grow, and express creativity.

This perspective on multiple pathways to learning is illustrated in Sir Ken Robinson's legendary TED Talk "Do Schools Kill Creativity?"—currently the most viewed TED Talk of all time. (TED Talks are influential presentations shared globally through the TED organization's platform. TED stands for technology, entertainment, and design.)

Robinson illustrated his point with the story of Gillian Lynne, who was struggling in school until a doctor recognized her natural tendency to learn through movement. Rather than treating her constant motion as a problem, she was enrolled in a dance school, where her kinesthetic intelligence flourished. Lynne became a renowned choreographer for productions like *Cats* and *Phantom of the Opera*. His message reinforces our understanding that creative development must honor diverse ways of learning, thinking, and expressing.

Understanding multiple intelligences can help you tailor your learning and development strategies to your unique strengths. Start by identifying the intelligences that resonate most with you. For example, if you are musically inclined, incorporate rhythms or melodies into your learning process. If you have strong spatial intelligence, use diagrams or visual aids to understand concepts.

You can also use this knowledge to address challenges in areas where you feel less confident. For instance, if logical-mathematical tasks seem daunting, pair them with your natural strengths, like working collaboratively if you excel interpersonally. Recognizing your preferred learning styles not only makes learning more enjoyable but also helps you set career and life goals aligned with your abilities.

How Well We Learn

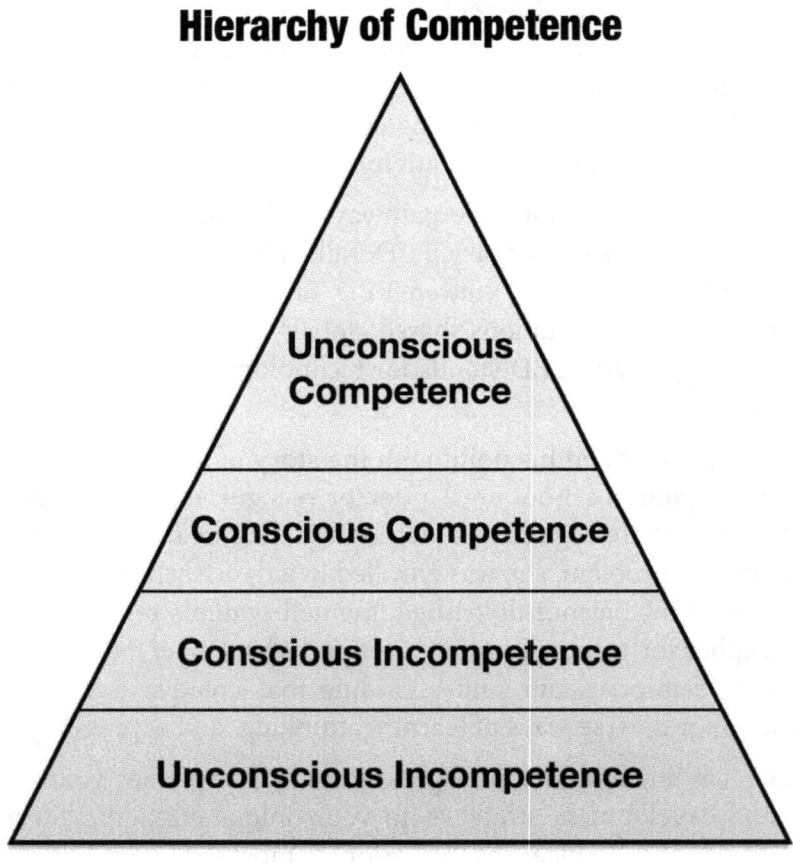

Competence is the ability to apply what we've learned effectively, transforming knowledge and practice into real-world execution. It ensures that we are not just absorbing information but developing the skills necessary to create, solve problems, and express ourselves with fluency and confidence.

As part of the learning-to-learn process, competence plays a key role in how we progress along the Creative Continuum. Although people often consider creativity spontaneous, structured learning, experience, and refinement over time build creative fluency.

- **Unconscious incompetence—"I don't know what I don't know":** At this stage, we are unaware of our skill gaps—we don't yet recognize what we lack or what is required to develop competence. In creative development, someone may struggle with problem-solving but not recognize creativity as a tool for solutions.
- **Conscious incompetence—"I know what I don't know":** Here, we realize our gaps in knowledge or ability. While this stage can be frustrating, it is also where intentional learning begins. We recognize our creative potential but struggle to apply it effectively.
- **Conscious competence—"I can do it, but I have to think about it":** At this stage, we have developed the skills, but execution requires focus and effort. With practice, these skills become more fluid and intuitive. We can generate ideas and express creativity intentionally, but it still feels structured and deliberate.
- **Unconscious competence—"It comes naturally":** Here, competence becomes second nature—skills are executed fluidly, without conscious thought. This level allows for true creative fluency and innovation. At this level, we can apply creative thinking and problem-solving instinctively.

How We Assess and Develop Competence

Competence is measured differently depending on the skill, domain, and context. In some cases, it is formally tested, while in others, it is demonstrated through application.

- **Accredited and certified competence:** Some fields assess competence through formal exams, certifications, or credentialing (e.g., professional licenses and academic degrees).
- **Performance-based competence:** In creative disciplines, competence is often demonstrated rather than tested. Apprenticeships, portfolios, and live performances provide proof of ability (e.g., an artist's portfolio or a musician's recital).

- **Real-world settings:** Evaluators assess many competencies, judging success by results, industry recognition, or audience reception (e.g., an entrepreneur proving their business model).
- **Self-assessed competence:** Some individuals determine their own readiness to advance, especially in self-directed learning. Often, marketplace reactions or personal reflection serve as feedback for progression.

Often, competence is about giving ourselves permission to take the next step in our creative journey.

The Life Skill of Being Creative in Action

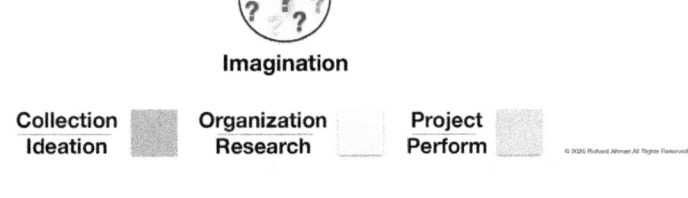

The Life Skill of Being Creative process integrates awareness, exploration, refinement, and execution into a structured approach to Creative Self Development. The components illustrated in the above diagram outline how this process unfolds within the Creative Self

Development Framework, ultimately guiding individuals in navigating, building, and living their best lives through creativity.

Intention (! Icon): The Decision to Engage Creatively

Intention is the conscious decision to embrace creativity as a guiding force in life. It represents the commitment to exploring, developing, and applying creative potential with purpose. Without intention, creative potential remains dormant. When we set an intention to create, we establish a foundation for meaningful engagement, signaling our readiness to observe, learn, and act. Intention guides all other aspects of the creative process, ensuring creativity becomes integral to how we shape our lives, not merely a matter of chance.

Attention (! →? Icon): Mindfulness and Awareness

Attention is the practice of being present and aware of the details in our environment. Creativity begins with what we notice—the colors, sounds, emotions, and patterns that capture our awareness and stimulate a response of "interesting" without judgment. By training our attention, we develop a heightened sensitivity to inspiration, recognizing creative opportunities in everyday life. Attention is not passive; it requires mindfulness and active engagement with the world, making us more receptive to unexpected insights from the people, places, things, and experiences of daily life.

Curiosity (? Icon): The Catalyst for Exploration

Attention triggers an "interesting" response, while curiosity challenges us with the "why," "what," and "how" of our interest. When something catches our attention, we explore its meaning and significance, expanding our perspective. Curiosity is the catalyst that transforms passive observation into active exploration. It leads us to investigate, question assumptions, and uncover new possibilities. Without curiosity, creativity remains stagnant. By nurturing a mindset of curiosity, we continuously open ourselves to new ideas and experiences that challenge and inspire us.

Imagination (Cluster of Question Marks): The 'What If' Factor

With imagination, we explore the "what if" of the object of our attention. Creativity requires imaginative thinking, where ideas and associations take shape. This is where connections form between ideas, leading to insights, speculations, and creative possibilities. The open-ended nature of imagination allows us to see things not just as they are but as they could be. Imagination enables us to mentally experiment with concepts, visualize solutions, and explore alternative perspectives before acting. It is a playground for ideas, and the only boundaries regulating our visions are the ones we place upon ourselves.

Notation (My Ideas Icon): Capturing Ideas for Future Use

Notation is the process of documenting creative insights, thoughts, and inspirations to preserve them for future exploration. Whether through sketching, journaling, voice recording, or digital tools, notation serves as a crucial bridge between imagination and action. Ideas are fleeting, and without capturing them in some form, they risk being lost. Habitual notation builds a personal reservoir of creative material that we can revisit, refine, and expand upon when the time is right.

Research (Magnifying Glass Icon): Expanding Knowledge and Understanding

Research and other forms of exploration help us deepen our understanding of our area of interest and begin to provide organization, context, validation, and inspiration. It allows us to explore existing knowledge, learn from the experiences of others, and build upon established ideas. Research extends beyond traditional study. Whether gathering information on a subject, testing a hypothesis, or seeking diverse perspectives, research transforms raw curiosity into the potential for creative action.

Synthesis (Overlapping Ideas): Connecting and Combining Ideas into New Forms

Synthesis is the stage where disparate pieces of information, experiences, and ideas come together to form something new. It is blending elements in unique ways, creating original concepts, and refining them into cohesive expressions. Synthesis often involves iteration—trial and error, restructuring, and improvement. It is where creativity becomes tangible, where abstract thoughts take form, and where innovation emerges through the recombination of existing elements.

Project (A → B Icon): Turning Ideas into Action

A project is the structured execution of creative ideas. It represents the transition from conceptualization to reality, requiring planning, effort, and persistence. Whether an artistic endeavor, a business initiative, or a personal goal, a project transforms creative potential into real-world impact. The project phase involves problem-solving, adaptation, and resilience as we bring our ideas to fruition. It is the culmination of all preceding steps, requiring us to commit, refine, and follow through with our creative vision.

The Learning Spiral (Background Arrow): The Continuous Cycle of Growth

The arrowhead represents the Learning Spiral and reminds us that creativity is not a linear process but an ongoing cycle of learning, practice, and refinement. Each stage in the creative process feeds into the next, and as we gain experience, we revisit earlier steps with new perspectives and deeper understanding. This cyclical nature ensures continuous growth, allowing us to refine skills, build knowledge, and evolve our Creative Self Expression. By embracing the Learning Spiral, we are engaging with lifelong learning and practice, ensuring that our creative potential development remains a priority throughout our lives.

The Creative Self (Central Figure): Creative Self Development as the Central Focus

At the center of the entire process is the Creative Self—the individual actively engaging in the discovery, development, management, and expression of their creative potential. The Creative Self synthesizes all elements of the process, guiding them toward meaningful expression. By engaging with the Creative Self intentionally, we turn our creative potential into action, shaping our lives and contributing to the world around us.

The Color-Coded Background and Dotted Lines: A Non-Linear, Dynamic Process

Distinct color-coded sections, representing general categories and the supporting actions of the creative process, divide the background. The sections include Idea Collection and Ideation, Organization and Research, and Project and Performance, showing how creativity moves from inspiration to execution. The dotted lines emphasize that this process is not strictly linear—curiosity, for example, could lead directly to research, or imagination might spark an immediate experimental project. Creativity flows in multiple directions, allowing for flexibility in how ideas grow.

Blueprint to Fingerprint Transformation

Again, we return to the "Blueprint to Fingerprint" analogy; it's the transformation of our inherited genetic and cultural blueprint—our traits, knowledge, and experiences—into our unique fingerprint: the creative life we build and the impact we leave on the world. Through our commitment to lifelong learning and practice of the Life Skill of Being Creative, we shape a life that reflects our deepest aspirations, talents, and contributions.

This is the essence of the CLP—not just to develop creativity in isolation but to cultivate it as a guiding force in how we think, learn, and build a fulfilling life. As we move forward in our journey, we will explore how to further manage, refine, and apply this skill in real-world contexts, ensuring that creativity remains a sustainable and growing resource throughout our lives.

By choosing to develop and express our creative potential, we take an active role in shaping not only our individual journeys but also the creative cultures we contribute to—at home, in our communities, and in the world. This is the power of the Life Skill of Being Creative, and it is yours to cultivate and express.

CHAPTER 15:
THE BIOLOGY OF BEING CREATIVE

The human body is not merely a vessel for carrying our brain; it is an intricate, highly evolved system specifically designed to help us survive, thrive, and flourish in a constantly changing world. Every aspect of our physical being—from our brain's neural networks to our hormonal systems, from our sensory organs to our capacity for movement—contributes to our ability to imagine and craft clever and strategic solutions to life's challenges and opportunities.

When we truly recognize our body as our most valuable creative asset and the instrument of our creative expression, we unlock new dimensions of creative potential. This understanding is practical wisdom that transforms how we approach creativity in our daily lives. By working with our biological systems rather than against them, we can enhance our creative capabilities and sustain our creative practice over time.

In this chapter, we explore the biological foundations of creativity—not through complex scientific terminology but through accessible insights that you can immediately apply to your CLP. We'll discover how your thinking about creativity affects your biology, how various systems in your body support different aspects of the creative process, and how to use these systems for optimal creative expression.

This exploration directly supports our Creative Self Mindset Principle #2: "I treasure my body because it's my most valuable creative asset and the instrument of my creative expression." By understanding the biological resources you already possess, you'll develop a deeper appreciation for your body's role in creativity and learn to use these resources more intentionally as you transform your genetic and cultural blueprint into your unique creative fingerprint.

How We're Designed for Creativity

The human body has been engineered through millions of years of evolution to survive, thrive, and flourish in a constantly changing world. This evolutionary journey has equipped us with a remarkable set of biological resources that make creativity possible. Unlike other species whose survival strategies are primarily instinctual, humans have developed extraordinary capacities for curiosity, imagination, and creation—the foundational elements of being creative.

Our biology supports creativity in ways that are both obvious and subtle. The human brain, with its hundred billion neurons forming trillions of connections, gives us unparalleled abilities to recognize patterns, make novel associations, and envision possibilities that don't yet exist. Our opposable thumbs and upright posture free our hands for manipulation and creation. Our extended childhood development allows for prolonged periods of play and exploration, which is essential for developing creative capacities.

All of these adaptations serve a crucial purpose: they enable us to overcome obstacles and adapt to new circumstances through creative problem-solving rather than through specialized physical adaptations. Where other species evolved specific physical traits for particular environments, humans evolved general-purpose creativity abilities that allow us to thrive in virtually any environment.

This biological legacy means that creativity isn't a special talent possessed by a lucky few—it's a fundamental human trait encoded in our very being. The Life Force of Creation, which we've explored philosophically, has a biological reality; it manifests through the complex and interconnected systems of our bodies.

From the perspective of Creative Self Development, this means that you already possess all the biological resources necessary for creative expression. Your task is to discover, develop, and express the creative potential already within you; by understanding how these biological systems function, you can learn to work with them more intentionally, optimizing your creative practice and enhancing your ability to transform your inherent blueprint into your unique fingerprint.

All the individual systems in your body work together for the purpose of navigating, building, and living your best life. You can choose to what degree you want to guide this process—whether to engage your creative capacities unconsciously and reactively or to develop them intentionally and strategically. The biology of creativity provides the background for helping you make this choice, offering an overview of resources that you can draw upon for Creative Self Development throughout your creative journey.

The first capacity we explored was fundamental to establishing your philosophy and mindset toward creativity at the beginning of this guide, which encouraged us to think about… how we think about creativity, which is metacognition in action.

Metacognition: How You Think About Your Creative Self

Metacognition is the ability to think about how you think—and specifically here, how you think about creativity and your creative potential—can shape your biology. This process of metacognition—thinking about thinking—is a uniquely human capacity that allows us to observe, reflect on, and intentionally direct our own mental processes. It's a key element in the Creative Self Development Process, making possible the journey from unconscious creativity to intentional creative practice.

Recall the "Before We Begin" chapter at the beginning of this guide. Your answers to the questions go beyond just your opinions; they actually influence your biology and determine how your creative potential manifests.

Metacognition in action looks like this: think about how you think about creativity and your creative potential and realize that this is how you think about yourself as a creator in your life and of your life—your Creative Self. When you become aware of these thoughts, you begin the lifelong practice of Creative Self Discovery, Development, Management, and Expression.

This awareness has a biological impact. When you think about yourself as inherently creative, your brain forms neural pathways that support creative thinking and behavior. When you doubt your creative abilities, your brain forms pathways that inhibit creative expression. This is why the Creative Self Mindset you are developing is so powerful—it literally reshapes the way you think about creativity and the biology supporting rather than inhibiting your ability to be creative.

Through the process of Creative Self cognition, you recognize several key insights:

- *The Life Force of Creation* is not just a philosophical concept but a biological reality—the energy of life embedded in our bodies to support surviving, thriving, and flourishing. This fundamental energy is the source of all creation, from microscopic biological processes to grand expressions of human innovation. When our bodies are alive, we are connected to this life force, enabling creative expression in countless ways.

- *Your Creative Self* functions as the conscious conduit for this life force, enabling you to become the creator in your life and of your life by cultivating and managing all the innate resources of your body. These biological resources form what we might call your "creative life system." Through Creative Self Discovery, Development, and Expression, you learn to work intentionally with these resources to transform your inherited blueprint into your unique creative fingerprint.

- *Your Creative Life Project* represents your commitment to this transformative process—your lifelong dedication to discovering and developing your creative potential and expressing it daily. This commitment empowers you to navigate, build, and live what you consider to be your best life while encouraging others to do the same, ultimately helping make the world a better place for everyone.

Intentional Creative Self Development relies upon the ongoing interaction with the biological resources of our body, influenced by how we think about ourselves, our lives, and our world. By cultivating awareness of how your thinking shapes your biology, you can begin to harness your biological resources more effectively in service of your creative vision.

As we move forward, remember that your body is not separate from your creative mind—it is the physical manifestation of your creative potential. By treasuring your body as your most valuable creative asset, you align with the Life Force of Creation and unlock your capacity to transform your genetic and cultural blueprint into a unique creative fingerprint that leaves your mark on the world.

Key Biological Systems Supporting Creativity

Now that we understand how metacognition influences our creative biology, let's explore the other biological systems that support creativity. These systems aren't separate entities but integrated components of your creative life system—the biological foundation that enables you to discover, develop, and express your creative potential.

Rather than viewing these systems as complex scientific phenomena, think of them as natural resources already at your disposal. By understanding how they work, you can engage them more intentionally in your creative practice, enhancing your ability to navigate life's challenges and opportunities with creativity and resilience.

Epigenetics: How Environment and Mindset Shape Your Creative Potential

Epigenetics reveals a fascinating truth: your genetic blueprint is more flexible than once believed. While your DNA provides the basic instructions for your development, epigenetics determines which genes are activated or suppressed. This process is influenced by both your physical environment and your internal environment—your thoughts, emotions, and beliefs.

This means that your Creative Self Mindset directly impacts which aspects of your creative potential come to life. When you engage in positive Storytelling Self-Talk about your creative abilities, when you immerse yourself in environments that stimulate creative thinking, and when you practice creativity regularly, you're not just changing your habits—you're influencing the very expression of your genes.

Consider the implications for Creative Self Development: the stories you tell yourself about your creativity—whether empowering or limiting—can actually influence your biology at a fundamental level. Your mindset doesn't just change how you feel about creativity; it can change how your body expresses creativity.

This doesn't mean you can completely rewrite your genetic code, but it does mean you have more influence over your creative potential than you might have thought. By consciously cultivating a Creative Self Mindset that embraces and values creativity, you create biological conditions that support creative expression.

In practical terms, this means that when you declare, "I'm a creative person, and I intend to develop and express my Creative Self throughout my life" (Creative Self Mindset Principle #1), you're not just making an affirmation—you're sending signals throughout your body that influence genetic expression in ways that support creativity. Your mindset becomes a powerful tool for activating your inherent creative potential.

Neuroplasticity: Your Brain's Creative Adaptability

Your brain is not a static organ but a dynamic, constantly evolving network that changes in response to experience. This quality—neuroplasticity—is the biological foundation for lifelong creative development. It means that, in general, no matter your age or background, your brain can form new connections, strengthen existing pathways, and even grow new neurons in response to learning and practice.

Every time you engage in creative thinking or problem-solving, you're physically reshaping your brain. The neural pathways involved in creativity become stronger and more efficient with use, making creative thinking increasingly natural and accessible. Conversely, when you avoid creative challenges or succumb to self-doubt or mass-mindedness, these creative pathways can weaken over time.

This biological reality reinforces the importance of consistent creative practice. The Creative Self Expression Practice, the final category of the framework, is a practical strategy for strengthening the neural networks that support creativity. When you engage in the cycle of Restart, Discover/Develop/Express, and Reset, you support the building of a more creative brain.

Neuroplasticity also explains why learning diverse skills and exploring new experiences enhances creativity. Each new skill or experience creates new neural connections, providing more material for creative combinations and associations. The broader your knowledge and experience base, the more connections your brain can make, leading to more innovative and original ideas.

By understanding neuroplasticity, you can approach creative development with confidence, knowing that your brain and creative body will physically adapt to support your creative growth. This isn't just a hopeful idea—it's a biological reality. Your brain is designed to become increasingly creative with practice, regardless of your starting point.

Embodied Cognition: Your Whole Body Thinks Creatively

Creativity is more than a brain function—it's a whole-body experience. Embodied cognition recognizes that thinking, including creative thinking, involves your entire physical being. Your posture, movements, gestures, and sensations all influence how you think and create.

This biological capacity helps explain why physical activities like walking, dancing, or working with your hands can stimulate creative thinking. These movements engage different neural networks and trigger different biochemical processes than sitting still, often leading to new insights and ideas. It's why many creative thinkers report breakthroughs while taking a walk or engaging in physical activities.

Your sensory experiences—what you see, hear, touch, taste, and smell—also play a crucial role in creativity. These sensory inputs become the raw material for creative combinations and associations. The richer and more diverse your sensory experiences, the more material you have to work with creatively.

Even your emotions, which have distinct physical signatures in your body, influence creativity. Certain emotional states can either enhance or inhibit creative thinking. Joy, curiosity, and even mild anxiety can stimulate creative thinking, while intense fear, rigid perfectionism, or deep depression can block it.

For Creative Self Development, this means engaging your whole body in the creative process. Notice how your physical state affects your creativity. Experiment with different postures, movements, environments, and sensory experiences to find what enhances your creative thinking. Remember that getting stuck in your head—thinking about creativity without engaging your body—limits your creative potential.

This biological perspective again reinforces the Creative Self Mindset Principle #2: "I treasure my body because it's my most valuable creative asset and the instrument of my creative expression." Your body isn't just carrying your creative mind around—it's an active participant in the creative process, providing both the biological machinery and sensory experiences that make creativity possible.

The Reticular Activating System: Your Creative Attention Filter

Located at the base of your brain, the reticular activating system (RAS) acts as a filtering mechanism that determines what information from your environment reaches your conscious awareness. Out of the millions of sensory inputs bombarding you at any moment, your RAS allows only a small fraction to enter your conscious mind.

What makes this system particularly relevant to creativity is that it can be trained. Your RAS tends to prioritize information that relates to your goals, values, and beliefs. When you cultivate a Creative Self Mindset, your RAS begins to filter the world differently, allowing in more information that supports creative thinking and problem-solving.

This explains why, when you're working on a creative project, you suddenly notice relevant ideas, information, and inspiration everywhere—your RAS is actively filtering for these inputs. It also explains why two people can experience the same environment yet notice completely different things; their RAS systems are filtering based on different priorities.

For Creative Self Development, this means that by consistently focusing on creativity and training yourself to notice creative opportunities, you literally change what you perceive in the world around you. Your environment doesn't change, but your perception of it does. You begin to see possibilities where others see only problems, and potential where others see limitations. This is what the phrase "learning to see" is all about.

This biological insight reinforces the importance of intention in the creative process. When you set a clear creative intention—whether for a specific project or for your broader CLP—you're programming your RAS to filter for information, ideas, and opportunities that support that intention. Your attention naturally gravitates toward what's relevant to your creative goals.

In practical terms, this means that the more you focus on being creative, the more your brain will help you notice creative opportunities in your environment. By declaring, "I'm a creative person," you train your RAS to present you with evidence that supports this belief, creating a powerful feedback loop that enhances your creative confidence and capabilities.

Prefrontal Cortex: The Mind's Creative Navigator

The prefrontal cortex (PFC) is one of the most uniquely human parts of the brain—and one of the most essential to Creative Self Development. Located at the front of the brain, the PFC is responsible for many of the higher-order functions that distinguish us as conscious creators: self-awareness, imagination, reflection, planning, and complex decision-making.

When you visualize a future project, consider multiple possible outcomes, or reflect on your personal values and goals, you are engaging the prefrontal cortex. It enables you to bridge the gap between vision and action—between imagining what could be and guiding yourself toward making it real. It is deeply involved in metacognition and intentional living, both of which are foundational to the CLP Philosophy.

In Creative Self Development, the prefrontal cortex is your internal navigator. It allows you to monitor your own mindset, override limiting beliefs, shift perspectives, and act in alignment with your creative values. However, it is also the region associated with self-judgment and perfectionism. Overactivation of the PFC can trigger hesitation or fear of failure, especially in the early stages of creative expression.

This is why the Creative Self Mindset Principles are so powerful—they help train the prefrontal cortex to support rather than suppress your creative intentions. They give your brain a script to follow when uncertainty arises, allowing the PFC to be a wise leader rather than a harsh critic.

For Creative Self Development, strengthening the prefrontal cortex means actively practicing reflection, reframing, goal-setting, and visualization. These activities stimulate this region of the brain and improve its ability to manage your creative energy with purpose and agility.

The Default Mode Network: Your Creative Insight System

Have you ever noticed that your best ideas often come when you're not actively trying to be creative—perhaps in the shower, while taking a walk, or just before falling asleep? This phenomenon has a biological explanation: your default mode network (DMN).

The DMN is a network of brain regions that becomes active when you're not focused on external tasks—when your mind is wandering, daydreaming, or reflecting. Unlike your focused attention networks (which help you concentrate on specific tasks), the DMN allows your mind to make broad, sometimes unexpected connections between different ideas, memories, and concepts.

This biological system explains why creativity often requires both focused work and unfocused downtime. The focused phase allows you to gather information, define problems, and work through logical steps. The unfocused phase—where the DMN is active—allows your brain to process this information in the background, making novel connections that may lead to creative insights or "a-ha moments."

For Creative Self Development, this means recognizing the importance of both work and rest in the creative process. Pushing constantly for productivity without giving your DMN time to work can actually inhibit creativity. Conversely, idle daydreaming without focused input and effort rarely leads to meaningful creative output.

The most effective creative practice involves alternating between periods of focused attention and periods of relaxed reflection. This rhythm aligns with how your brain naturally processes information and generates insights. That's why the Creative Self Expression Practice includes elements like Reimagine and Reflect, which engage different neural networks and allow for both active and passive creative processing.

In practical terms, this means scheduling regular breaks during creative work, engaging in activities that activate the DMN (like walking, showering, or simple meditation), and paying attention to the insights that emerge during these "off" times. It also means resisting the cultural pressure to be constantly productive, recognizing that apparent "downtime" is often when your brain is doing its most creative work.

By understanding and working with your DMN, you harness a powerful biological system that specializes in making the unexpected connections that lie at the heart of creativity. This isn't lazy thinking—it's a sophisticated cognitive process that complements focused work and leads to deeper, more original creative insights.

Subsystems Support the Key Biological Systems for Creativity

While the systems we've explored form the primary biological foundation for creativity, several supporting systems also play crucial roles in your creative process. These systems might not be immediately associated with creativity, but they provide essential resources that fuel, sustain, and enhance your creative capabilities. Understanding and working with these supporting systems can significantly amplify your creative potential and sustain your creative practice.

The Emotional Resonance System: Feelings as Creative Fuel

Emotions are not just subjective experiences; they have biological foundations and serve important functions in creativity. Your emotional system provides vital information, motivation, and meaning to your creative process.

This emotional dimension of creativity connects directly to Viktor Frankl's insights about meaning as a fundamental human motivation. As Frankl observed, "Those who have a 'why' to live can bear with almost any 'how.'" In creative terms, emotionally meaningful work provides the motivation to persist through the inevitable challenges of the creative process. When you connect emotionally to your creative vision, you tap into a powerful biological resource that sustains your efforts even when faced with obstacles.

Different emotional states activate different neural networks and biochemical patterns in your body, influencing how you think, perceive, and create. Positive emotions like joy, interest, and wonder tend to broaden your attention and thinking, allowing for more creative associations and insights. They literally change your brain chemistry, releasing dopamine and other neurotransmitters that enhance neural connectivity and creative thinking.

Even challenging emotions can serve creative purposes. Mild anxiety can sharpen focus and motivate action. Sadness can deepen empathy and insight. Frustration can signal when to push harder or when to take a different approach. By developing emotional intelligence—the ability to recognize, understand, and work with your emotions—you gain access to a rich internal landscape that informs and enhances your creative expression.

For Creative Self Development, this means learning to recognize and work with your emotions as creative resources rather than obstacles. When you feel inspired, channel that energy into creative action. When you feel stuck or frustrated, use those emotions as signals that it's time to shift your approach. By integrating emotional awareness into your creative practice, you align with your body's natural motivational systems.

This emotional dimension relates directly to your position on the Creative Continuum we explored earlier. As you move along this continuum, you develop increasingly sophisticated emotional relationships with your creative work. What begins as a simple pleasure in creating evolves into deeper emotional engagement with the meaning and impact of your creative contributions.

The Biochemical Messenger Network: Your Creative Chemistry

Your body contains a sophisticated biochemical network that influences every aspect of creativity. Neurotransmitters, hormones, and other signaling molecules form a complex communication system that affects your energy, focus, mood, and cognitive capabilities.

This biochemical network explains why physical factors like nutrition, hydration, sleep, and exercise significantly impact your creative abilities. These aren't separate from creativity; they're foundational to it. When you prioritize physical well-being, you're actually optimizing your biological conditions for creative thinking, similarly to an athlete preparing for a competition or a dancer for a performance.

Several key biochemical messengers play particularly important roles in creativity:

- *Dopamine,* often called the "reward chemical," is associated with motivation, pleasure, and learning. It drives the sense of satisfaction that comes from creative insights and achievements, reinforcing creative behavior. Activities that increase dopamine—like completing manageable challenges, experiencing novelty, and receiving positive feedback—can enhance creative motivation and engagement.
- *Serotonin,* which influences mood regulation, contributes to the emotional stability needed for sustained creative work. Balanced serotonin levels help you maintain perspective during creative challenges and setbacks. Activities that support healthy serotonin levels—like exposure to natural light, positive social interactions, and certain foods—can enhance your creative resilience.
- *Endorphins,* your body's natural mood elevators, are released during physical activity, laughter, and certain foods. They create the pleasurable sensations that can accompany creative flow states, making creativity intrinsically rewarding. Regular physical activity that triggers endorphin release can enhance both creative mood and energy.

- *Cortisol*, often called the "stress hormone," has a complex relationship with creativity. Mild, temporary increases in cortisol can sharpen focus and motivation, while chronic elevation can impair creative thinking by narrowing focus and inhibiting the brain's ability to make novel connections. Learning to manage stress effectively is, therefore, essential for maintaining biological conditions conducive to creativity.

The Learning Spiral we explored earlier has a biochemical dimension. As you progress through the spiral of fundamentals, practice, performance, and skill progression, your body's biochemistry changes. Mastery of new skills and successful creative performances trigger positive biochemical responses that reinforce learning and motivation, creating an upward spiral of creative development.

For Creative Self Development, understanding this biochemical dimension means recognizing that lifestyle choices directly impact your creative capabilities. Nutrition, sleep, exercise, stress management, and social connection aren't separate from creativity—they're integral to it. By making choices that support your body's biochemical balance, you create optimal conditions for creative thinking, energy, and resilience.

The Restorative Cycle System: Renewal for Sustained Creativity

Creativity isn't meant to be a constant, uninterrupted process. Your body operates according to natural cycles of activity and rest, and honoring these cycles is essential for sustainable creative practice. The restorative cycle system includes sleep, relaxation, and various forms of renewal that replenish your creative energy and capacity.

This cyclical nature of creativity aligns with our understanding of the Learning Spiral and the Creative Self Expression Practice. Just as our practice includes phases of Reset and Restart alongside active development and expression, our biology requires periods of restoration alongside creative output.

Sleep plays a particularly crucial role in creativity. During sleep, especially during REM (rapid eye movement) periods, your brain processes information, consolidates learning, makes new connections between ideas, and clears out metabolic waste products that accumulate during waking hours. Many creative insights occur either during dreams or immediately after waking because sleep allows your brain to reorganize information in novel ways.

This explains why forcing creativity through sleep deprivation or constant work rarely leads to optimal results. You might complete a project through sheer willpower, but the quality of your thinking and the originality of your solutions will likely suffer. True creative sustainability requires rhythmic alternation between engagement and renewal.

Beyond sleep, other forms of restoration also support creativity. Brief mindfulness practices, time in nature, enjoyable social interactions, and engaging in activities that bring you joy all replenish your creative resources. These aren't indulgences or distractions from "real work"—they're biologically necessary for sustained creative performance.

For Creative Self Development, this means designing your creative practice with restorative cycles in mind. Schedule regular breaks, ensure adequate sleep, and build renewal activities into your routine. Pay attention to your body's signals of fatigue, which indicate when restoration is needed. By honoring these natural cycles, you maintain the biological conditions for creativity over the long term, avoiding burnout and sustaining your creative journey.

The Body Awareness System: Creativity Through Interoception

Interoception—your ability to sense and interpret signals from within your body—provides valuable information for the creative process. These internal sensations, sometimes called "gut feelings" or "intuition," are actually your brain interpreting complex patterns of information from your body's various systems.

This body awareness creates a bridge between conscious and unconscious processing, giving you access to insights that might not be available through logical thinking alone. Creative intuition isn't mystical; it's biological—a sophisticated system that integrates information from multiple sources within your body and presents it as feelings or sensations that can guide decision-making.

The body awareness pathway explains why physical practices like deep breathing, meditation, or body scanning can enhance creativity. These practices strengthen your interoceptive abilities, allowing you to access more of the information your body is processing. When you "listen to your body," you're actually tapping into complex pattern recognition happening below the threshold of conscious awareness.

This relates to Howard Gardner's theory of multiple intelligences, which we explored in our discussion of learning. Bodily-kinesthetic intelligence and intrapersonal intelligence both involve this capacity to sense and work with the body's signals. By developing these intelligences, you enhance your access to creative insights that emerge through embodied awareness.

For Creative Self Development, this means developing practices that enhance body awareness and learning to trust the information your body provides. Pay attention to physical sensations that arise during creative work. Notice when something feels "right" or "off" in your creative process. These bodily signals contain valuable information that can guide your creative decisions and help you navigate complex creative challenges.

By developing this pathway, you create a more integrated creative process that draws on both conscious reasoning and embodied knowing. This integration allows you to access a fuller range of your creative potential, using all the information available to you—both explicit and implicit—in service of your creative expression.

The Integrated Biology of Being Creative

The biological systems we've explored don't function in isolation—they form an integrated network that supports your creative expression. Understanding how these systems work together helps you engage your complete creative biology, maximizing your ability to transform your blueprint into a fingerprint that leaves your unique mark on the world.

This integration occurs naturally when you engage in a holistic approach to Creative Self Development. When you refresh your environment, take stock of your circumstances, and place them in context, you activate embodied cognition and interoception. When you reimagine possibilities and recalibrate your mindset, you engage your DMN and trigger positive epigenetic responses. Each element of your creative journey aligns with biological systems that support creative development and expression.

The relationship between biological systems and evolution along the Creative Continuum is particularly important. As you progress along this continuum, you're not just developing skills; you're creating increasingly sophisticated neural networks, more flexible epigenetic expression, and more integrated emotional responses. Your biology literally transforms as you develop creatively, creating an upward spiral of growth and discovery.

This biological perspective reinforces the Life Skill of Being Creative as a strategic approach to life, not just a collection of tactical techniques. When you understand the biological foundations of creativity, you recognize that being creative is about aligning your entire being—body, mind, and spirit—with the creative process. It's about living in ways that nurture and express your inherent creative nature and, over time, can cultivate wisdom.

For Creative Self Development, integration means taking a holistic approach to creativity that honors all aspects of your biology:

- Recognizing that physical well-being directly impacts creative thinking
- Understanding that emotions are integral to, not separate from, the creative process
- Appreciating how rest and renewal are as important as active creation
- Learning to work with both conscious reasoning and embodied intuition
- Creating environments that support rather than hinder your biological creative systems

By working with rather than against your creative biology, you maximize your ability to navigate life's challenges and opportunities with creativity and resilience. You develop sustainable creative practices that enhance rather than deplete your resources. Most importantly, you align with the Life Force of Creation that flows through your entire being, enabling you to express your unique creative gifts in service of your vision.

Flow State: The Ultimate Experience of Creative Biological Harmony

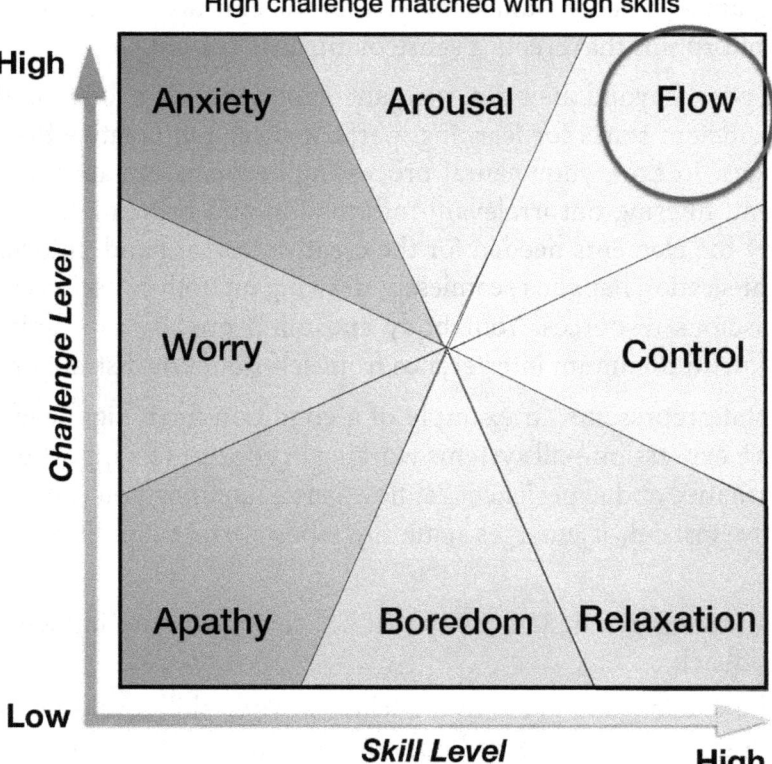

Perhaps the most profound personal experience of integrated creative biology is the experience of flow—that extraordinary state where you become completely immersed in a creative activity, losing track of time and self-consciousness while performing at your peak. First identified by psychologist Mihaly Csikszentmihalyi, flow represents a state of optimal experience where challenge and skill are perfectly balanced, attention is completely absorbed, and action and awareness merge.

From a biological perspective, flow represents a remarkable synchronization of multiple systems. During flow, your brain shifts into a pattern where the prefrontal cortex—the part responsible for self-consciousness and self-criticism—becomes less active, while neural networks involved in attention, perception, and action become highly coordinated. Your biochemistry changes too, with just the right balance of stress hormones to maintain focus without triggering anxiety, accompanied by pleasure chemicals like dopamine and endorphins that create a sense of intrinsic reward.

Flow goes beyond being a pleasant experience—it's one of the most efficient states for learning, performance, and creative breakthroughs. In flow, your neural processing becomes extraordinarily efficient, filtering out irrelevant information and bringing together exactly the elements needed for the creative task at hand. Information integration happens seamlessly, drawing on both conscious and unconscious resources. Your body and mind operate as a unified whole, with minimum interference from self-doubt or distraction.

This state represents an example of a condition for a high level of creative expression—all systems working in concert to support peak performance and experience. Yet flow isn't something you can force directly. Instead, it emerges naturally when certain conditions are met:

- You're engaged in an activity that has clear goals and immediate feedback.
- The challenge is perfectly matched to your skill level—neither too easy (leading to boredom) nor too difficult (causing anxiety).
- You can focus completely without distraction.
- You find the activity intrinsically rewarding.

For Creative Self Development, understanding flow offers powerful insights for structuring your creative activities. By creating conditions conducive to flow—clear goals, appropriate challenges, focused attention, and intrinsic motivation—you set the stage for this optimal creative state to emerge. This doesn't mean you'll experience flow every time you create, but you can increase its frequency and duration through thoughtful practice.

Flow also provides a compelling biological argument for pursuing creative activities that you find inherently meaningful and enjoyable. When you engage in activities that naturally induce flow, you're not just creating more effectively—you're experiencing one of the most rewarding states available to human consciousness. This combination of peak performance and deep satisfaction represents creativity at its most fulfilling.

The experience of flow reinforces Creative Self Mindset Principle #2 in a profound way. When you treasure your body as your most valuable creative asset, you create the conditions for these moments of extraordinary creative harmony. Your body isn't just executing your creative ideas—it's creating an experiential state that is itself a masterpiece of biological coordination and one of life's most meaningful experiences.

Treasuring Your Creative Body: Practical Applications

Now that we understand the biological systems supporting creativity, how do we put this knowledge into practice? How do we truly treasure our bodies as our most valuable creative assets?

The answer lies not in complex techniques or rigid practices but in simple, consistent actions that honor our creative biology. Next, we'll go over some practical ways to work with your biological systems to enhance your creative potential.

Work With Your Brain's Natural Rhythms

Your brain naturally alternates between focused attention (ideal for analytical thinking and execution) and diffuse attention (ideal for creative insights and connections). Rather than forcing yourself to maintain constant focus, structure your creative practice to include both:

- Work in focused sessions of 25–90 minutes, followed by short breaks.

- When stuck on a problem, switch to a different activity that doesn't require intense focus.
- Pay attention to insights that arise during "off" times, like showering or walking.
- Schedule both structured work time and unstructured thinking time.

Engage Your Whole Body in the Creative Process

Remember that your entire body contributes to creativity, not just your brain:

- Try standing or walking while thinking through creative challenges.
- Use hand gestures and movement to explore ideas physically.
- Engage multiple senses in your creative process—touch, sight, sound, even taste and smell.
- Notice how different physical positions and movements affect your thinking.
- Create with your hands regularly, regardless of your primary creative domain.

Nourish Your Creative Chemistry

Your biochemistry directly impacts your creative capabilities:

- Stay hydrated, as even mild dehydration affects cognitive function.
- Eat foods that support brain health and neurotransmitter production.
- Get regular physical activity, which enhances blood flow to the brain and triggers beneficial biochemical changes.
- Spend time in natural light and natural environments.
- Monitor how different foods and drinks affect your creative energy and clarity.

Honor Restoration as Part of Creation

Recognize that rest and renewal aren't separate from creativity but essential components of it:

- Prioritize sleep as a creative tool, not a luxury.
- Build brief restorative practices into your daily routine.
- Take longer breaks when you notice signs of creative depletion.
- Alternate between different types of creative activities to prevent fatigue.
- View restoration as productive, not as time away from productivity.

Develop Your Creative Intuition

Train yourself to access the embodied wisdom that supports creativity:

- Practice body scanning to enhance interoceptive awareness.
- Pay attention to physical sensations that arise during creative work.
- Ask yourself, "How does this feel in my body?" when evaluating creative options.
- Develop regular mindfulness practices that strengthen the connection between mind and body.
- Learn to distinguish between fear-based resistance and intuitive caution.

Create Environments That Support Your Biology

Your physical surroundings significantly impact your creative biology:

- Adjust lighting, temperature, and sound to support your creative comfort.
- Surround yourself with objects and images that stimulate creative thinking.
- Minimize distractions that force your RAS to filter irrelevant information.

- Create different spaces for different phases of the creative process.
- Notice how different environments affect your creative energy and thinking.

By implementing these simple practices, you align with your creative biology rather than working against it. You treat your body not as a vehicle that carries your creative mind but as an integrated system designed for creative expression. This alignment enhances both the quality of your creative work and the sustainability of your creative practice.

CHAPTER 16:
THE LIFE SKILL OF BEING CREATIVE FUNDAMENTALS

In this chapter, we explore the ten Fundamentals of Creativity. Like fundamentals in any domain, they represent the essential building blocks—core capacities, ways of thinking, and areas of practice that support skillful, consistent, and intentional engagement. They help us create a solid foundation from which more complex creative abilities can grow.

1. Commit to connecting with the Life Force of Creation through your Creative Self.

Connecting with the Life Force of Creation through your Creative Self is a fundamental aspect of developing your creative potential. This commitment involves recognizing and nurturing the innate creative energy that flows through all living things, including yourself.

The Life Force of Creation is the universal energy that drives growth, change, and innovation in the world around us. It's the spark that ignites new ideas, fuels artistic expression, and propels scientific discoveries. By consciously connecting with this force, you tap into a wellspring of inspiration and potential that can transform your creative practice.

Your Creative Self is the unique conduit through which this life force manifests in your individual experience. It's the aspect of your being that perceives, processes, and expresses creativity in ways that are distinctly your own. Embracing your Creative Self means acknowledging and cultivating this essential part of your identity.

Committing to this connection requires developing a heightened awareness of the creative energy that surrounds and flows through you. It involves cultivating a sense of openness and receptivity to the world, allowing yourself to be moved and inspired by the beauty, complexity, and wonder of existence. This commitment also entails regular practice and intentional effort to create a space in your life for creative expression.

By connecting with the Life Force of Creation, you align yourself with the natural creative rhythms of the universe. This alignment can lead to a sense of flow in your creative work, where ideas and inspiration seem to come effortlessly. It can also foster a deeper sense of purpose and meaning in your creative endeavors, as you recognize your role in the ongoing process of creation that shapes our world.

This commitment also involves recognizing the inherent value of the creative process, regardless of the outcome. Your unique perspective and creative evolution benefit from every creative act, regardless of whether external standards deem it successful. By focusing on the process rather than just the product, you can find joy and fulfillment in the act of creation itself.

Connecting with the Life Force of Creation through your Creative Self is not a one-time event but an ongoing practice. It requires patience, persistence, and a willingness to remain open and vulnerable. You may find that this connection ebbs and flows, with periods of intense creativity followed by quieter times of reflection and renewal. Embracing this natural rhythm is part of the commitment.

As you deepen your connection with the Life Force of Creation, you may find that your creative expression becomes more authentic and powerful. You may discover new facets of your creative abilities or uncover hidden passions. This connection can also enhance your problem-solving skills and innovative thinking as you learn to tap into the creative energy that permeates all aspects of life.

Ultimately, committing to connect with the Life Force of Creation through your Creative Self is about recognizing and honoring the creative essence that is fundamental to your being. It's a powerful affirmation of your creative potential and a gateway to a more fulfilling and expressive life.

2. Establish your own Creative Life Project to discover, develop, manage, and express your Creative Self to help you navigate, build, and live your best life.

Establishing your own CLP is a transformative journey that goes beyond mere self-improvement—it's a holistic approach to living that harnesses your creative potential to shape a fulfilling life and positively affect the world around you. This project serves as the overarching framework for your personal growth, guiding you through the processes of discovering, developing, managing, and expressing your Creative Self.

The discovery phase of your CLP involves deep self-exploration. It's about uncovering the unique talents, passions, and values that form the core of your creative identity. This process often requires you to challenge assumptions about yourself and creativity, pushing beyond societal expectations to reveal your authentic creative voice.

As you develop your Creative Self, you'll engage in continuous learning and skill-building. This might involve honing specific artistic or problem-solving techniques, but it also encompasses broader life skills like adaptability, resilience, and innovative thinking. The development process is iterative, allowing you to refine your abilities and expand your creative repertoire. Managing your Creative Self is about creating the optimal conditions for your creativity to flourish. It involves organizing your time, resources, and energy to support your creative endeavors. This management aspect also includes learning to balance your creative pursuits with other life responsibilities, setting boundaries, and making strategic decisions that align with your creative goals.

Expression is where your Creative Self comes alive in the world. It's the act of bringing your ideas, insights, and innovations into tangible form, whether through art, business ventures, community projects, or personal relationships. This expression is not just about producing creative works but about infusing creativity into every aspect of your life.

By engaging in this CLP, you develop powerful tools to navigate life's challenges and opportunities. Creativity becomes your compass, guiding you through uncertain times and helping you craft innovative solutions to personal and professional obstacles. It enables you to build a life that resonates with your deepest values and aspirations, one that feels authentic and fulfilling.

Crucially, this project extends beyond personal benefit. As you grow and thrive creatively, you naturally inspire and encourage others to embark on their own creative journeys. This ripple effect can transform communities and contribute to a more vibrant, innovative society. By openly sharing your creative process, challenges, and triumphs, you create a supportive environment that nurtures creativity in others.

Ultimately, your CLP becomes a force for positive change in the world. It's a recognition that personal growth and societal progress are interconnected. As you live your best life through Creative Self Expression, you contribute to a world that values and cultivates creativity in all its forms. This collective embrace of creativity can lead to more innovative solutions to global challenges, more empathetic and connected communities, and a richer, more diverse cultural landscape. Your CLP is thus both deeply personal and universally significant. It's a commitment to ongoing growth and a powerful way to leave a positive mark on the world, making it a better place for everyone through the transformative power of creativity.

3. Accept the paradox of creativity and being creative.

Embracing the paradoxical nature of creativity is a fundamental aspect of developing your creative skills. This acceptance opens up new perspectives and frees you from limiting beliefs about what it means to be creative.

The paradox of creativity lies in the tension between seemingly contradictory truths. On the one hand, all acts of creation stem from the Life Force of Creation, expressed through our individual creative selves. This suggests that every person has the capacity for creativity, and every creative act holds inherent value. However, external standards and societal norms don't view all creations as "creative." This dichotomy can be perplexing and sometimes disheartening for those embarking on a creative journey.

However, accepting this paradox allows you to navigate the creative process with greater ease and authenticity. It frees you from the pressure of constantly producing work that others deem creative or innovative. Instead, you can focus on the intrinsic value of engaging in creative activities, regardless of the outcome.

This paradoxical nature extends to the creative process itself. Creativity often thrives in the space between structure and chaos, between discipline and spontaneity. It requires both focused effort and the ability to allow ideas to flow freely. Recognizing and working with these apparent contradictions can enhance your creative abilities. The paradox of creativity manifests in the traits of highly creative individuals. Research has shown that creative people often exhibit opposing characteristics simultaneously. They might be both introverted and extroverted, humble and proud, playful and disciplined. These contrasting traits allow for a rich internal life and diverse experiences that fuel creativity.

Accepting the paradox of creativity also means acknowledging that creative growth often comes through failure and struggle. The process of creating something new inherently involves risk and the potential for disappointment. Yet, it's often through these challenges that the most significant breakthroughs occur.

Another aspect of this paradox is the relationship between individual creativity and collective innovation. While creativity is deeply personal and unique to each individual, it doesn't occur in a vacuum. Our creative expressions both shape and are shaped by the broader cultural and social context. Recognizing this interplay can help you appreciate both your unique creative voice and your role in the larger creative ecosystem.

The paradox of creativity extends to its impact as well. Creative acts can be simultaneously ephemeral and enduring, personal and universal. A moment of creative expression might be fleeting, yet its effects can resonate far beyond the initial creation, influencing others and sparking further creativity.

By accepting these paradoxes, you develop a more nuanced and flexible approach to creativity. You learn to hold multiple perspectives simultaneously, embrace ambiguity, and find inspiration in unexpected places. This acceptance fosters resilience in the face of creative challenges and allows for a deeper, more fulfilling creative practice. Accepting the paradox of creativity is about embracing the full spectrum of the creative experience. It's recognizing that creativity is not a linear or predictable process but a complex, multifaceted phenomenon that defies simple categorization. This acceptance liberates you to explore, experiment, and express yourself more fully, enriching your creative journey and amplifying your creative potential.

4. Be open, flexible, and adaptable to the experience of life.

Cultivating openness, flexibility, and adaptability is crucial for harnessing your creative potential and navigating life's ever-changing landscape. These qualities form a triad of resilience that enables you to thrive amidst uncertainty and complexity.

Openness involves maintaining a receptive attitude toward new ideas, experiences, and perspectives. It's about approaching life with curiosity and wonder, ready to learn from every situation. This quality allows you to absorb diverse influences, enriching your creative repertoire and broadening your understanding of the world. By remaining open, you create space for unexpected connections and innovative solutions to emerge.

Flexibility in the creative context refers to the ability to bend without breaking, to adjust your approach in response to changing circumstances. It's about being willing to let go of rigid expectations and preconceived notions. Flexible thinking allows you to see multiple angles of a problem, consider alternative solutions, and pivot when necessary. This mental agility is invaluable in creative problem-solving and artistic expression alike. Adaptability builds on openness and flexibility, enabling you not just to survive but to thrive in new environments and situations. It's capacity to change your behavior, thoughts, or emotions to suit changing conditions better. In the realm of creativity, adaptability allows you to strengthen your skills, embrace new technologies or techniques, and find fresh ways to express your ideas as the world around you shifts. These qualities interconnect and mutually reinforce one another.

Openness allows you to recognize the need for change, flexibility gives you the mental dexterity to consider various options, and adaptability empowers you to implement necessary adjustments effectively.

Embracing these qualities can transform how you approach creative challenges. Instead of viewing obstacles as roadblocks, you begin to see them as opportunities for growth and innovation. Unexpected changes become invitations to explore new creative territories. This mindset fosters resilience, enabling you to bounce back from setbacks and maintain your creative momentum even in difficult times.

In addition, openness, flexibility, and adaptability enhance your ability to collaborate with others. They allow you to appreciate diverse viewpoints, find common ground, and synthesize different ideas into novel solutions. This collaborative capacity is increasingly valuable in our interconnected world, where complex problems often require multidisciplinary approaches.

These qualities also play a crucial role in personal growth and self-discovery. By remaining open to new experiences, flexible in your self-conception, and adaptable in your personal development, you create space for continuous learning and evolution. This ongoing growth feeds directly into your creative practice, providing fresh inspiration and deeper self-awareness.

In practical terms, cultivating these qualities might involve seeking new experiences, challenging your assumptions, or deliberately placing yourself in unfamiliar situations. It could mean experimenting with different creative techniques, collaborating with people from diverse backgrounds, or reimagining your creative goals in light of changing circumstances. By embodying openness, flexibility, and adaptability, you position yourself to fully engage with the rich tapestry of life experiences. You become more attuned to the subtle nuances and hidden possibilities in everyday situations. This heightened awareness and responsiveness can spark creative insights and fuel innovative thinking.

Ultimately, these qualities enable you to navigate the complexities of modern life with grace and creativity. They empower you to turn challenges into opportunities, find beauty in unexpected places, and continually reinvent yourself and your creative expression in harmony with the ever-changing world around you.

5. Habitually practice empowering Storytelling Self-Talk.

Empowering Storytelling Self-Talk is a potent tool for shaping your creative mindset and influencing your actions. This practice involves consciously crafting and internalizing narratives that empower your creative growth and reinforce your belief in your creative abilities.

The stories we tell ourselves have a profound impact on our thoughts, emotions, and behaviors. By deliberately choosing empowering narratives, you can overcome self-doubt, boost confidence, and cultivate a resilient, creative spirit. This practice is about framing your experiences in ways that motivate and inspire you to persist in your creative endeavors. Empowering self-talk begins with awareness. Pay attention to your inner dialogue, especially when facing creative challenges or setbacks. Are you engaging in negative self-criticism, or are you encouraging yourself to learn and grow? By becoming conscious of your habitual thought patterns, you can reshape them in more constructive ways.

Crafting empowering narratives involves reframing challenges as opportunities for growth. Instead of telling yourself, "I'm not good enough," you might say, "I'm developing my skills with every attempt." This shift in perspective can transform obstacles from insurmountable barriers into stepping stones on your creative journey.

Another aspect of empowering self-talk is acknowledging your progress and celebrating small wins. By recognizing your achievements, no matter how minor they may seem, you build momentum and reinforce your creative identity. This positive reinforcement can fuel your motivation and inspire you to take on bigger creative challenges.

Empowering self-talk also involves cultivating an empowering mindset. This means believing that you can develop your creative abilities through effort, learning, and persistence. By telling yourself stories that emphasize the power of practice and the value of effort, you create a psychological environment conducive to creative risk-taking and experimentation.

It's important to note that empowering self-talk is not about toxic positivity or denying genuine difficulties. Instead, it's about approaching challenges with a constructive, solution-focused mindset. When faced with setbacks, your self-talk might acknowledge the disappointment while also emphasizing your capacity to learn and adapt.

Practicing empowering self-talk can also help you combat the influence of external negativity and mass-mindedness. By strengthening your internal narrative, you become more resilient to discouraging messages from others or societal pressures that might stifle your creativity.

As you develop this habit, you may find it helpful to create specific affirmations or mantras that resonate with your creative goals. These can serve as anchors, helping you stay focused and motivated, even when facing uncertainty or self-doubt.

Remember, the goal of empowering self-talk is not to eliminate all negative thoughts but to create a balanced, realistic, and supportive inner dialogue. It's about fostering a mindset that acknowledges challenges while maintaining faith in your ability to overcome them.

By consistently practicing empowering Storytelling Self-Talk, you create a powerful internal ally in your creative journey. This practice can help you maintain enthusiasm, overcome obstacles, and stay committed to your creative vision, even in the face of adversity. You become the author of your own creative story, crafting a narrative that propels you toward growth, innovation, and fulfillment.

6. Cultivate curiosity and imagination for inspiration, ideation, and creation.

Curiosity and imagination are the twin engines that drive creative thinking and innovation. By cultivating these qualities, you open doors to new ideas, fresh perspectives, and innovative solutions. They serve as the wellspring of inspiration and the catalyst for creative breakthroughs.

Curiosity is the insatiable desire to learn, explore, and understand. It's the willingness to ask questions, challenge assumptions, and delve into the unknown. In the creative context, curiosity fuels the discovery process, leading you to uncover new information, make unexpected connections, and see familiar things in novel ways.

To nurture curiosity, adopt an attitude of wonder toward the world around you. Approach everyday situations with a beginner's mind, as if experiencing them for the first time. Ask questions like "Why?" and "What if?" to probe deeper into subjects and challenge the status quo. Engage with diverse topics and experiences, even those outside your usual interests, to broaden your knowledge base and stimulate new thought patterns.

Imagination lets us form mental images or concepts of things not present or experienced. The mind uses imagination as a playground where new ideas are born and possibilities are explored without constraints. Imagination allows you to envision alternative realities, combine disparate elements in unique ways, and conceptualize solutions that don't yet exist.

To cultivate imagination, create space for daydreaming and unstructured thinking. Allow your mind to wander and explore ideas freely without immediate judgment or practical considerations. Engage in activities that stimulate your imagination, such as reading fiction, playing imaginative games, or practicing visualization exercises.

When combined, curiosity and imagination become powerful tools for ideation. Curiosity drives you to gather diverse information and experiences, while imagination allows you to recombine and transform this raw material into novel ideas. This synergy can lead to innovative concepts, unique artistic expressions, and creative solutions to complex problems.

In the inspiration phase, curiosity and imagination work together to help you find sparks of creativity in unexpected places. Curiosity motivates you to seek new experiences, explore different cultures, or delve into unfamiliar subjects. Imagination then helps you translate these experiences into creative inspiration, seeing potential connections and applications that others might miss.

During the creation process, curiosity keeps you open to new possibilities and willing to experiment with different approaches. It pushes you to ask, "What would happen if...?" and to explore various iterations of your ideas. Imagination, meanwhile, helps you envision the final product or solution, guiding your creative efforts toward an interesting vision.

Cultivating curiosity and imagination also involves creating an environment that supports these qualities. This might mean surrounding yourself with stimulating objects, art, or nature. It could involve joining conversations with people who have diverse perspectives and experiences. It might also mean allocating time for exploration and play, free from the pressures of productivity or immediate results. Remember that curiosity and imagination require practice. Regular practice in asking questions, exploring new ideas, and engaging in imaginative thinking can significantly enhance your creative capabilities.

By fostering curiosity and imagination, you create a rich internal landscape from which creative ideas can emerge. You become more attuned to the world around you, more adept at making unexpected connections, and more capable of envisioning innovative solutions. This not only enhances your creative output but also enriches your experience of life, infusing everyday moments with a sense of wonder and possibility.

7. Engage in Creative Self Assessment, Creative Self Management, and metacognition.

Engaging in Creative Self Assessment, Creative Self Management, and metacognition forms a powerful triad for enhancing your creative potential and output. These interrelated practices allow you to gain deeper insights into your creative process, optimize your creative efforts, and continuously refine your approach to creative work.

Creative Self Assessment involves regularly evaluating your creative strengths, weaknesses, habits, and outcomes. This practice requires honesty and objectivity as you examine your creative work and processes. It's about building a constructive analysis aimed at identifying areas for improvement and recognizing your unique creative strengths.

To conduct effective self-assessments, establish clear criteria for evaluating your creative work. These might include originality, technical skill, emotional impact, or problem-solving effectiveness, depending on your specific creative domain. Regularly review your completed projects, ongoing work, and creative ideas against these criteria. Consider seeking feedback from trusted peers or mentors to gain additional perspectives on your creative output.

Creative Self Management builds on the insights gained through self-assessment. It involves developing strategies and systems to optimize your creative process and productivity. This might include setting clear goals for your creative projects, establishing routines that support your creative work, and managing your time and resources effectively.

Effective Creative Self Management also involves understanding and working with your personal creative rhythms. Identify the times of day when you are most creatively productive, the environments that best support your creative work, and the conditions that help you enter a state of flow. Use this knowledge to structure your creative sessions for maximum effectiveness. Metacognition, often described as "thinking about thinking," is a crucial skill for creative development. In creativity, metacognition involves realizing and understanding your own thought processes during creative work. This awareness allows you to monitor your creative strategies, recognize when you're stuck in unproductive thought patterns, and consciously shift your approach when needed.

Practicing metacognition in your creative work might involve regularly reflecting on your creative process. Ask yourself questions like "What approach am I using right now?" "Is this strategy effective for the current challenge?" "What assumptions am I making, and are they limiting my thinking?" By developing this habit of self-reflection, you can become more intentional and effective in your creative problem-solving.

The interplay among these three practices, self-assessment, self-management, and metacognition, creates a powerful feedback loop for continuous creative improvement. Self-assessment provides insights into your creative strengths and areas for growth. Self-management allows you to implement strategies based on these insights. Metacognition helps you monitor the effectiveness of these strategies in real time, allowing for rapid adjustments and learning.

Engaging in these practices also fosters an empowering mindset in your creative work. By regularly assessing your skills, managing your creative process, and reflecting on your thought patterns, you build the belief that your creative abilities can be developed and refined. This mindset can help you persist through creative challenges and maintain motivation for long-term creative projects.

These practices can help you develop greater creative independence. As you become more adept at assessing your work, managing your creative process, and understanding your thought patterns, you become less reliant on external validation or direction. This independence allows you to pursue your unique creative vision with greater confidence and authenticity. By integrating Creative Self Assessment, Creative Self Management, and metacognition into your creative practice, you create a robust framework for ongoing creative growth and development. These skills empower you to take charge of your creative journey, continuously refine your approach, and unlock new levels of creative potential.

8. Learn to shift perspectives for fluid thinking and problem-solving.

Developing the ability to shift perspectives is a cornerstone of creative thinking and problem-solving. This skill allows you to view situations from multiple angles, break free from conventional thought patterns, and uncover innovative solutions that might otherwise remain hidden.

Perspective shifting involves deliberately changing your mental standpoint or frame of reference when approaching a problem or creative challenge. It's about stepping outside your habitual ways of thinking and seeing the world through different lenses. This practice can lead to breakthrough insights, novel connections, and creative solutions that transcend traditional boundaries.

One way to cultivate this skill is by practicing empathy and adopting other people's viewpoints. When faced with a problem, try to imagine how different individuals or groups might perceive and approach it. This exercise not only broadens your understanding of the issue but can also reveal additional aspects or solutions you hadn't considered from your original perspective. Another powerful technique is to change the scale at which you view a problem. Zoom out to see the bigger picture, considering how the issue fits into larger systems or contexts. Then, zoom in to examine the finer details and components. This shifting between macro and micro views can reveal new relationships and opportunities for innovation.

Temporal perspective shifting is also valuable. Consider how the problem or situation might look in the past, present, and future. How might historical context inform your approach? How could potential future developments influence your current strategy? This time-based perspective shifting can lead to more robust, forward-thinking solutions.

Interdisciplinary thinking is another form of perspective shifting. Try applying principles or methodologies from different fields to your problem. For example, how might a biologist approach a business challenge? Or how could architectural concepts inform a musical composition? These cross-domain connections often spark creative breakthroughs.

Cultivating fluid thinking goes hand in hand with perspective shifting. Fluid thinking refers to the ability to adapt your thought processes smoothly and quickly in response to changing situations or new information. It's about mental flexibility and agility, allowing you to navigate complex problems with ease.

To develop fluid thinking, practice switching between different modes of thought. For instance, alternate between divergent thinking (generating multiple ideas) and convergent thinking (evaluating and selecting ideas). Or shift between analytical and intuitive approaches to problem-solving. The goal is to become comfortable with cognitive flexibility, allowing your mind to flow between different thinking styles as needed. Embracing paradoxes and contradictions can also enhance your ability to shift perspectives and think fluidly. Instead of seeing conflicting ideas as obstacles, view them as opportunities for synthesis and innovation. This approach can lead to nuanced, multifaceted solutions that address complex problems more effectively.

Practicing mindfulness can significantly support your efforts in perspective shifting and fluid thinking. By cultivating present-moment awareness and non-judgmental observation, you can more easily notice your thought patterns and consciously shift them when needed. Mindfulness also helps maintain cognitive flexibility by reducing rigid thinking and enhancing your ability to stay open to new ideas.

Remember that perspective shifting and fluid thinking are skills that improve with practice. Regularly challenge yourself to view situations from unfamiliar angles, question your assumptions, and explore unconventional connections. Over time, this practice will become more natural, allowing you to navigate creative challenges with greater ease and effectiveness.

By mastering the art of shifting perspectives and thinking fluidly, you equip yourself with powerful tools for creative problem-solving and innovation. These skills enable you to break free from mental ruts, generate novel ideas, and approach complex issues with adaptability and insight.

9. Encourage mutually beneficial communication and collaboration for co-creation.

Fostering effective communication and collaboration is essential for amplifying creative potential and achieving innovative outcomes. This approach recognizes that creativity often flourishes in the interplay of diverse ideas, perspectives, and skills. More than just exchanging information is involved in mutually beneficial communication within creative contexts. This type of communication requires active listening, empathy, and the ability to articulate ideas clearly.

To enhance creative communication, practice articulating your ideas with precision and passion. Develop the skill of translating abstract concepts into concrete terms that others can easily grasp. Equally important is the ability to listen deeply to others, seeking to understand not just their words but the underlying thoughts and emotions driving their ideas.

Encourage an atmosphere of psychological safety where all team members feel comfortable sharing their thoughts, even if they're unconventional or still in development. This openness can lead to unexpected connections and innovations that might not emerge in a more guarded environment.

Collaboration in creative endeavors goes beyond simply working together; it's about synergizing diverse strengths and perspectives to create outcomes that surpass what any individual could achieve alone. Effective creative collaboration requires a balance of individual contribution and collective effort, where each person's unique talents can be recognized and used.

To foster productive collaboration, start by clearly defining roles and expectations while remaining flexible enough to allow for spontaneous contributions. Encourage a culture of constructive feedback, where critiques are offered and received in a spirit of mutual growth and improvement. Embrace diversity in collaborative settings. Bring together individuals with different backgrounds, skills, and thinking styles. This diversity can lead to creative friction, the productive tension that arises when different perspectives collide. When managed well, this friction can spark innovative ideas and solutions.

Develop strategies for effective brainstorming and idea generation in group settings. This might involve techniques like round-robin ideation, where each person builds on the previous person's idea, or silent brainstorming, followed by a group discussion, to ensure all voices are heard.

Use technology and tools that support remote collaboration, especially in our increasingly digital world. Virtual whiteboards, project management software, and video conferencing platforms can facilitate creative teamwork across distances, allowing for the pooling of global talent and perspectives.

Foster a collaborative mindset that values both individual creativity and collective achievement. Encourage team members to see themselves as part of a creative ecosystem where personal success and group success are intertwined.

Implement practices that nurture long-term collaborative relationships. Regular check-ins, team-building activities, and shared creative exercises can strengthen bonds and enhance collaborative efficiency over time.

Remember that successful collaboration often requires navigating conflicts and differences of opinion. Develop skills in conflict resolution and see disagreements as opportunities for deeper understanding and more robust solutions.

Celebrate collaborative achievements and learn from collaborative failures as a team. Reflect on what worked well and what could be improved in your collaborative processes, continuously refining your approach.

By prioritizing mutually beneficial communication and collaboration, you create a fertile ground for creativity to flourish. This approach not only enhances the quality and innovation of creative outputs but also contributes to a more fulfilling and enriching creative process for all involved.

10. Honor and cultivate mindfulness, flow, and creative intuition.

Honoring mindfulness, flow, and creative intuition is crucial for deepening your creative practice and unlocking your full creative potential. These interconnected concepts form a powerful triad that can elevate your creative work and enrich your creative experience.

Mindfulness, in creativity, involves cultivating a heightened awareness of the present moment without judgment. It's about fully engaging with your creative process, paying attention to your thoughts, emotions, and sensations as you work. This practice can help you notice subtle nuances in your creative work, spot new opportunities for innovation, and maintain focus despite distractions.

To incorporate mindfulness into your creative practice, start by setting aside time for focused creative sessions. During these sessions, consciously bring your attention to the task at hand. Notice the physical sensations as you work—the feel of a pencil in your hand, the texture of clay, or the sound of your fingers on a keyboard. Observe your thoughts and emotions without getting caught up in them, allowing ideas to flow freely.

Flow, the concept popularized by psychologist Mihaly Csikszentmihalyi, refers to a state of optimal experience where you're fully immersed in your creative work. In this state, time seems to fall away, self-consciousness disappears, and you're completely absorbed in the task. Flow often occurs when there's a balance between the challenge of the task and your skill level.

To encourage flow states in your creative work, set clear goals for each creative session. Choose tasks that stretch your abilities but are still within reach. Minimize distractions in your environment and give yourself uninterrupted time to work. As you engage in your creative task, focus on the process rather than the outcome, allowing yourself to become consumed in the act of creation.

Creative intuition is your inner creative voice, gut feelings, sudden insights, and unexplainable hunches that often guide creative work. It's rapid cognition that draws on your accumulated knowledge and experience, allowing you to make creative leaps without conscious reasoning.

To honor your creative intuition, learn to recognize and trust these intuitive nudges. Pay attention to sudden ideas or impulses that arise during your creative work. Even if they seem illogical at first, give them space to develop. Keep a notebook handy to jot down intuitive insights as they occur.

The interplay between mindfulness, flow, and creative intuition can be powerful. Mindfulness helps you become more aware of your intuitive insights and can facilitate entry into flow states. Flow can enhance your intuitive abilities by quieting your inner critic and allowing your subconscious mind to work freely. Creative intuition can guide you toward flow-inducing activities and provide the seeds for mindful exploration.

Practicing mindfulness outside of your creative work can also benefit your creative practice. Regular meditation or mindful walks in nature can help calm your mind, reduce stress, and increase your overall awareness—all of which can enhance your creativity. To deepen your experience of flow, reflect on past instances when you've experienced this state. What were you doing? What conditions facilitated this experience? Use these insights to create more opportunities for flow in your creative work.

To strengthen your creative intuition, expose yourself to diverse experiences and ideas. Read widely, engage with different art forms, and seek new experiences. This broadens the pool of knowledge your intuition can draw from, potentially leading to more innovative insights.

Remember that honoring mindfulness, flow, and creative intuition is an ongoing practice. Some days, you may find it easier to enter a flow state or access your intuition than others. Be patient with yourself and view each creative session as an opportunity to deepen your practice.

By integrating mindfulness, seeking flow states, and honoring your creative intuition, you can create a richer, more fulfilling creative practice. These elements can help you navigate creative challenges with greater ease, produce more authentic and innovative work, and find deeper satisfaction in your creative journey.

Embracing the Life Skill of Being Creative

Embracing creativity as a life skill transforms the way you perceive and interact with the world. It empowers you to approach challenges with resilience and innovation, to express yourself authentically, and to contribute meaningfully to your communities. By cultivating this skill, you've equipped yourself with a powerful tool for navigating the complexities of modern life and shaping a future aligned with your values and aspirations.

Creativity is not just something you do; it's a way of being. By fully embracing the Life Skill of Being Creative, you open yourself to a world of endless possibilities, deeper connections, and a more authentic, fulfilling existence. Your creative potential is limitless. Go forth and create the life and world you envision.

PART 06

CATEGORY–CREATIVE SELF MANAGEMENT

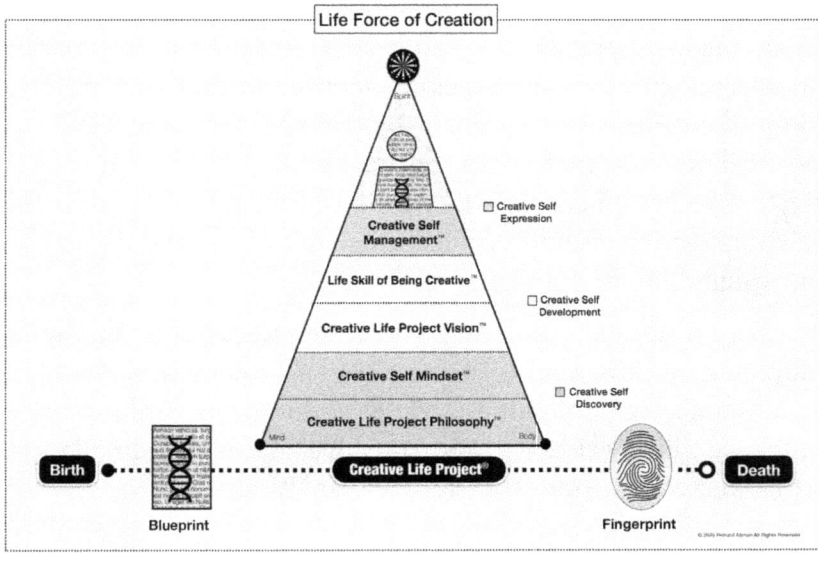

In this category of the Creative Self Development Process, you confront the reality that realizing your vision requires the masterful orchestration of the human resources available to you. This is where Creative Self Management comes into play—the operational engine that powers your creative journey.

Creative Self Management is where the transformation from Blueprint to Fingerprint becomes operationalized. While your blueprint provides the raw materials and your vision provides the destination, effective management of your creative resources creates the bridge between them. Through intentional management practices, you systematically shape your genetic and cultural imprint into your unique contribution to the world—your creative fingerprint that no one else can replicate.

Creative Self Management is the deliberate practice of taking conscious control over two essential resource domains: the rich landscape of your internal human resources (your mind, emotions, creativity, focus) and the varied external resources available to you in the physical world (time, space, relationships, tools). This crucial component serves as the vital bridge between your philosophy, mindset, and vision on one side and your life skills and practical implementation on the other.

Unlike generalized self-management approaches, Creative Self Management specifically focuses on assessing, cultivating, and deploying resources in ways that directly support the realization of your unique CLP Vision. This is where you develop the capacity to intentionally match the specific challenge or opportunity at hand with the optimal resource or combination of resources needed to address it effectively.

The key insight of Creative Self Management is this: different situations require different perspectives. To determine the most appropriate resources to use in any given moment, you must develop the ability to shift your perspective—to assume different roles and ways of thinking about your circumstances. This perspective-shifting ability allows you to select the most effective approach for each situation you encounter.

The Role-Shifting Perspective

Central to this management approach is understanding a representative set of roles you will embody throughout your creative journey. These roles aren't literal professional positions but rather different perspectives and mindsets you need to access, depending on your circumstances. Each role presented in this section represents a distinct way of thinking and acting that triggers a corresponding set of skills and responsibilities.

These roles represent different facets of how you engage with your blueprint to transform it into your fingerprint. The roles aren't separate identities but different facets of your Creative Self that you access and express depending on the needs of the moment. Being effective in these various roles requires the ability to shift perspectives fluidly while maintaining alignment with your overall vision.

No single perspective alone can create a fulfilling, creative life. It is the integration and fluid movement between these perspectives that creates a comprehensive approach to living your CLP Vision.

In the following chapter, we will explore each role perspective, examining how each contributes to effective Creative Self Management and providing insights for embodying these roles in your daily life. By mastering these different perspectives and the ability to shift between them, you'll develop a comprehensive toolkit for managing your resources and navigating the complex landscape of your creative journey.

CHAPTER 17:
THE ROLES OF CREATIVE SELF MANAGEMENT

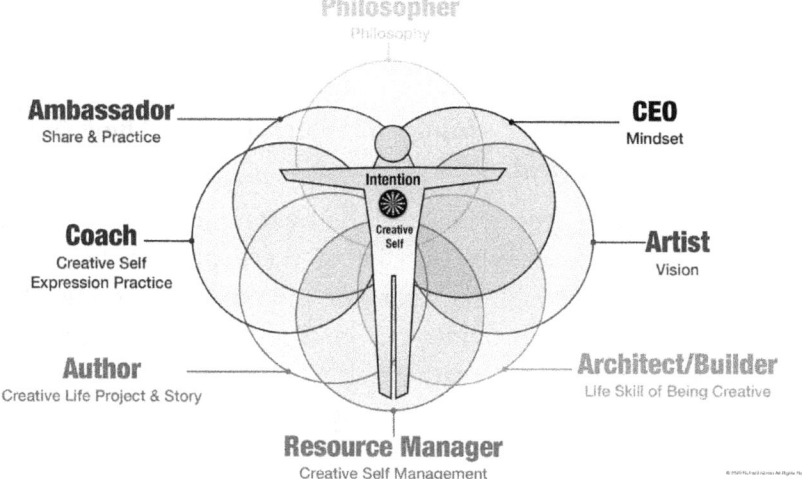

In this chapter, we explore the basic Creative Self Management roles—distinct ways to manage and deploy your human and physical resources to address any set of circumstances you face. A role, in this context, represents a persona—a name that symbolizes a specific attitude, way of thinking, or behavioral stance. These personas are not rigid identities but flexible tools you can assume to guide how you approach and act in response to a given problem, challenge, or opportunity.

These roles are introduced within the context of Creative Self Management. They provide practical strategies for applying the self-awareness, adaptability, and decision-making required to lead a creative life with intention. Each role reflects how you can actively manage how you organize and direct your efforts, shift perspectives, and navigate complexity.

Creative Self Management is the process of cultivating and deploying the beliefs, skills, and attitudes that support your ability to realize a creative vision. Each role offers a perspective on how to bring your full range of internal and external resources into alignment with your goals and values.

These roles are also directly linked to the categories of the Creative Self Development Framework. Each role corresponds to a specific category of the framework, offering guidance for how to engage with that dimension of Creative Self Development.

Creative Life Project Philosophy

You are the philosopher, deciding what you believe and how you view your life and your world.

As the philosopher, your role extends beyond establishing beliefs and worldviews to actively translating these philosophical foundations into the practical management of your creative life. While your CLP Philosophy provides the guiding principles and values, the philosopher's role in Creative Self Management focuses on applying these abstract concepts to navigate real-world decisions and challenges.

Why This Role is Essential

Your philosophical foundation determines not just what you believe but how you interpret experiences, what you value, and ultimately, how you make decisions. Without a clear philosophical perspective, your creative efforts lack coherence and deeper meaning. The philosopher ensures your actions and choices remain anchored to your core truths rather than being swayed by passing trends or others' expectations.

From a management perspective, your philosophical beliefs serve as your decision-making framework. When faced with choices or challenges, you reference your core values and principles to determine the most appropriate course of action. If authenticity is one of your guiding principles, you'll naturally make decisions that align with your true self, even when those choices prove unconventional or challenging.

The philosopher in you also actively integrates your beliefs into daily practices and routines. If your philosophy emphasizes continuous growth and learning, you naturally allocate time and resources toward knowledge acquisition and new experiences that expand your horizons. Your philosophy doesn't remain abstract—it manifests in how you structure your days and what you prioritize.

Your philosophical approach transforms how you handle setbacks and obstacles. Rather than seeing problems as barriers, you reframe them as opportunities for growth and learning. By drawing upon your philosophical foundation, you maintain perspective and adaptability when facing adversity. This philosophical grounding cultivates resilience and allows you to navigate the inevitable ups and downs of your creative journey with greater equanimity.

The philosopher role ensures alignment between your creative pursuits and your values. When selecting projects, collaborators, or opportunities, you assess them through your philosophical framework, asking whether these endeavors align with your beliefs, contribute to your growth, and bring you closer to your CLP Vision. By consistently making choices congruent with your philosophy, your creative management becomes purposeful, authentic, and fulfilling.

As the philosopher, you also recognize the interconnectedness of your creative life with the larger world. Your philosophical beliefs extend beyond personal development to consider your impact on others and your environment. You seek to manage your creative pursuits in ways that are socially responsible, ethically sound, and sustainable—ensuring your creative expression benefits not only yourself but also contributes positively to the world around you.

When to Activate This Role

Step into your philosopher perspective when you need clarity about your values, when facing ethical dilemmas, when setting fundamental priorities, or when you feel disconnected from your deeper purpose. Return to this role regularly to ensure your other creative management activities remain anchored to what truly matters to you.

The philosopher role provides the foundational perspective from which all other Creative Self Management roles operate, ensuring your creative journey remains personally meaningful and aligned with your authentic self.

Creative Self Mindset

You are the CEO, responsible for guiding your daily actions to align with your philosophy and vision as you navigate, build, and live your best life.

In the role of the CEO, you take on the responsibility of translating your CLP Philosophy and Vision into actionable strategies and daily practices that drive the growth and success of your creative endeavors. While the philosopher establishes what you believe, the CEO determines how those beliefs will be operationalized in the world.

Why This Role is Essential

Vision without execution remains merely a dream. The CEO role ensures that your philosophical ideals and creative aspirations materialize through deliberate action and strategic decision-making. Without this executive function, even the most profound insights and inspiring visions may never become reality. The CEO transforms abstract concepts into tangible outcomes.

From a management perspective, your role as CEO involves developing and implementing systems, routines, and processes that support the realization of your creative vision. You establish clear goals and milestones, create action plans, and allocate resources in ways that maximize your creative output and progress. By creating a structured approach to managing your creative pursuits, you ensure your efforts remain focused, efficient, and aligned with your overarching philosophy and purpose.

One of your key responsibilities as CEO is making strategic decisions that steer your creative life in the right direction. This requires regularly assessing your progress, evaluating opportunities and challenges, and making informed choices that align with your values and long-term objectives. By applying your philosophical framework to your decision-making process, you ensure that your creative management remains grounded in your core beliefs while adapting to changing circumstances.

Your CEO role also encompasses fostering collaboration and communication within your creative ecosystem, which includes family, friends, colleagues, and mentors. By building strong relationships and maintaining open communication, you create a supportive network that enhances your success and well-being. The CEO recognizes that creative achievement rarely happens in isolation and strategically cultivates beneficial connections.

Being an effective CEO of your creative life means cultivating an adaptive mindset to navigate an ever-changing landscape. You embrace lifelong learning and practices that ensure you remain resilient and energized. Through a balanced approach to goal-setting, decision-making, and resource management, you align your daily actions with your larger vision, creating a fulfilling and sustainable creative life.

The CEO role doesn't operate in isolation but draws upon and coordinates with your other roles. It receives philosophical guidance from your philosopher, creative inspiration from your artist, skill development plans from your architect/builder, and resource assessments from your resource manager. By integrating these perspectives, your CEO role creates a cohesive and effective approach to realizing your creative potential.

When to Activate This Role

Step into your CEO perspective when planning your week or day, making important decisions about resource allocation, evaluating new opportunities, establishing systems and routines, or whenever you need to translate inspiration into practical action steps. Return to this role regularly to ensure your creative life maintains momentum and direction.

Through the effective embodiment of the CEO role, you bridge the gap between aspiration and achievement, ensuring your creative management is not just inspired but also implemented with consistency and strategic focus.

Creative Life Project Vision

You are the artist, imagining a vision for your life and how to navigate through the problems, challenges, and opportunities you will face as you work to make it real.

As the artist, your role extends beyond creating a vision to actively managing the process of bringing that vision to life. While the philosopher establishes your beliefs and the CEO implements systems, the artist's role in Creative Self Management emphasizes the imaginative envisioning and adaptive navigation needed to transform possibilities into reality.

Why This Role is Essential

Without vision, there is no destination. The artist role ensures you have a compelling and meaningful creative direction that resonates with your authentic self. This role provides the inspirational blueprint that guides all other aspects of your creative management. Without the artist's perspective, your efforts may be efficient but lack purpose, meaning, and the spark of originality that makes your creative journey uniquely yours.

From a management perspective, your artistic vision serves as a guiding blueprint for your creative journey. It provides clear direction and purpose, helping you prioritize your efforts and allocate your resources effectively. As the artist in Creative Self Management, you take responsibility for translating your vision into actionable goals, milestones, and projects that progressively move you closer to your desired outcomes.

To effectively manage the realization of your vision, you develop a systematic yet flexible approach to planning and execution. This involves breaking down your overarching vision into smaller, manageable steps and creating a roadmap that outlines specific actions, timelines, and resources. By creating a structured yet adaptable plan, you provide yourself with a clear path forward that can accommodate the unpredictable nature of the creative process.

As you navigate the challenges and opportunities of your creative journey, you apply your artistic sensibilities to your management approach. You remain open to new ideas, perspectives, and possibilities, continuously seeking ways to refine and enhance your vision. You embrace an iterative process of experimentation, feedback, and adaptation, using each experience as an opportunity to learn, grow, and improve your creative strategies.

The artist in you actively cultivates the balance between creativity and practicality. While your artistic vision provides inspiration and direction, you also recognize the importance of grounding your efforts in the realities of your circumstances. You make strategic decisions that align with your available resources, time constraints, and other practical considerations, ensuring your creative pursuits remain sustainable and achievable while still honoring your vision.

Throughout the process of managing your CLP Vision, you draw upon your philosophical foundation for values that guide your decision-making, while your CEO mindset equips you with the organizational structure to execute your vision. The artist role adds the elements of imagination, intuition, and adaptability that allow your creative management to remain vibrant, meaningful, and responsive to emerging opportunities.

When to Activate This Role

Step into your artist perspective when you need to envision new possibilities, when facing seemingly insurmountable obstacles that require creative solutions, when your path forward feels unclear or uninspiring, or whenever you need to reconnect with the deeper meaning and purpose of your creative journey. Regular visits to this perspective keep your creative management infused with passion and possibility.

By embracing the artist role in your Creative Self Management, you ensure that your creative journey remains not only structured and effective but also deeply meaningful, personally fulfilling, and responsive to the ever-changing landscape of creative possibilities.

Life Skill of Being Creative

You are the architect and builder, developing and using your skills to transform your vision into reality.

As the architect and builder within the Creative Self Management framework, your role focuses on strategically developing and effectively deploying your skills to transform your CLP Vision into reality. While the philosopher establishes your beliefs, the CEO implements systems, and the artist envisions possibilities, the architect and builder role emphasizes the practical mastery and application of skills needed to create tangible results.

Why This Role is Essential

Vision without skill remains unfulfilled potential. The architect and builder role ensures you develop the necessary capabilities to bring your creative ideas into the world. Without this perspective, you might have inspiring visions and well-organized plans but lack the practical abilities to execute them effectively. This role bridges the gap between what you can imagine and what you can create.

From a management perspective, your role as the architect and builder involves creating a comprehensive approach to skill acquisition and utilization. You conduct a thoughtful assessment of your current skills and identify the gaps between your existing capabilities and the skills required to realize your vision. Based on this assessment, you develop a strategic roadmap that outlines the specific skills you need to acquire, the resources and support you'll need, and the timeline for achieving your skill development goals.

As you execute your skill development plan, you take a proactive and disciplined approach to manage your learning and growth. You prioritize efforts, allocating time and resources to the skills that are most critical to your vision. You create a structured learning path while establishing clear milestones to track your progress and hold yourself accountable for your development.

Beyond acquiring new skills, you focus on managing the application and integration of your skills in real-world contexts. You actively seek opportunities to put your skills into practice through personal projects, professional assignments, or community involvement. By consistently applying your skills, you not only deepen your mastery but also generate tangible results that demonstrate the value and impact of your capabilities.

The architect and builder in you recognizes that skill management is an ongoing process that requires regular evaluation and adaptation. As you gain new experiences and insights, you revisit your skill development plan and make necessary adjustments to ensure it remains aligned with your evolving vision and circumstances. You stay attuned to emerging trends and best practices in your field, continuously updating your skill set to maintain relevance and effectiveness.

Your architect and builder perspective works in concert with your other roles. It takes direction from your philosophical values, follows the systems established by your CEO role, and brings to life the possibilities imagined by your artist role. By integrating these elements, you create a cohesive approach to skill development that is principled, organized, creative, and effective.

When to Activate This Role

Step into your architect and builder perspective when identifying skills you need to develop, creating learning plans, facing technical challenges that require expertise, evaluating your skill progress, or whenever you need to focus on the craftsmanship aspects of your creative work. This perspective is particularly valuable when you encounter obstacles that can only be overcome through increased capability or technical mastery.

Through effective embodiment of the architect and builder role, you ensure that your creative management is grounded in practical competence, enabling you to transform your vision into reality through skilled execution and continuous growth.

Creative Self Management

You are the resource manager, monitoring, nurturing, and allocating the appropriate resources to realize your vision.

As the resource manager within the Creative Self Management category, your role extends beyond simply monitoring and allocating resources to actively optimizing their utilization for the realization of your CLP Vision. While the previous roles establish what you believe, organize your approach, envision possibilities, and develop necessary skills, the resource manager role ensures you have the fuel and materials needed for your creative journey.

Why This Role is Essential

Even the most inspired vision, best-organized plan, and most refined skills cannot manifest without proper resources. The resource manager ensures you identify, cultivate, and strategically deploy both internal resources (energy, focus, creativity, resilience) and external resources (time, space, relationships, materials, finances) needed to sustain your creative journey. Without this perspective, your creative efforts may stall due to resource depletion or inefficient allocation.

From a management perspective, your role as the resource manager involves developing a comprehensive system for identifying, acquiring, and deploying the resources necessary to support your creative endeavors. This includes conducting regular assessments of your current resources, both internal and external, and identifying any gaps or areas for improvement. Based on these assessments, you create a strategic plan that outlines the specific resources you need to acquire or optimize, the steps required to do so, and the metrics for measuring your progress.

As you execute your resource management plan, you take a proactive and disciplined approach to ensure the optimal utilization of your resources. This involves setting clear priorities and boundaries and ensuring that your time, energy, and focus are allocated to the activities and projects that are most critical to your vision. You establish routines and rituals that support your creative productivity, such as dedicated work blocks, regular breaks, and self-care practices that replenish your internal resources.

In addition to managing your internal resources, you also take a strategic approach to cultivating and leveraging your external resources. This involves actively seeking out and nurturing relationships with individuals and organizations that can support your creative journey, such as mentors, collaborators, and industry partners. You develop a network of trusted advisors and advocates who can provide guidance, feedback, and opportunities for growth and exposure.

As the resource manager, you also prioritize the creation of an enabling environment that supports your creative productivity and well-being. This involves designing your physical workspace to optimize focus, inspiration, and comfort, as well as establishing clear boundaries between your work and personal life. You also curate your digital environment, using technology and tools that enhance your creativity and productivity while minimizing distractions and information overload.

You recognize that effective resource management requires ongoing evaluation and adaptation. As you gain new insights and experiences, you regularly reassess your resource allocation and make necessary adjustments to ensure it remains aligned with your evolving vision and circumstances. You stay attuned to emerging trends and best practices in your field, continuously seeking out new resources and strategies to support your creative growth and impact.

When to Activate This Role

Step into your resource manager's perspective when planning resource needs for projects, experiencing energy depletion, facing time constraints, making decisions about investments in tools or materials, building your support network, or whenever you need to ensure the sustainability of your creative efforts. This perspective is especially valuable during periods of high demand or when multiple projects compete for limited resources.

Through the effective embodiment of the resource manager role, you ensure that your creative journey is sustainable, well-supported, and optimally resourced, allowing your creative vision to flourish without being compromised by resource limitations or inefficient allocation.

You are the project manager, curating, funding, and managing the portfolio of projects, serving as the building blocks for your CLP Vision and Story.

As the project manager within the Creative Self Management framework, your role extends beyond curating and overseeing your project portfolio to actively managing the execution and integration of these projects to bring your CLP Vision and Story to fruition. While previous roles establish your beliefs, organize your approach, envision possibilities, develop skills, and manage resources, the project manager role ensures your creative efforts are structured into well-defined projects that collectively advance your vision.

Why This Role is Essential

Visions are realized through concrete projects. The project manager ensures your creative energy is channeled into specific, bounded initiatives that collectively build toward your larger vision. Without this perspective, your creative efforts might remain scattered, unfinished, or disconnected from one another. This role transforms abstract aspirations into tangible accomplishments through the art of effective project design and execution.

From a management perspective, your role as the project manager involves developing a comprehensive system for selecting, planning, and executing projects that align with your CLP Vision. This system includes establishing clear criteria for project selection, such as alignment with your values, potential impact, and feasibility. You create a structured process for evaluating and prioritizing potential projects, ensuring that your project portfolio remains focused, balanced, and manageable.

As you plan your projects, you take a strategic approach to ensure their successful execution. This involves breaking down each project into smaller, actionable tasks and creating detailed project plans that outline the objectives, timelines, resources, and dependencies involved. You also identify potential risks and challenges associated with each project and develop contingency plans to mitigate them. By creating comprehensive project plans, you provide a clear roadmap for execution and increase the likelihood of successful outcomes.

During the execution phase, you take an active role in managing the day-to-day progress of your projects. This involves monitoring project milestones, tracking key metrics, and ensuring that tasks are completed on time and within budget. You regularly communicate with project stakeholders, providing updates on progress and addressing any issues or concerns that arise. You also remain flexible and adaptable, making necessary adjustments to project plans as circumstances change or new information becomes available.

In addition to managing individual projects, you also focus on integrating your projects to create a cohesive and meaningful narrative. This involves identifying connections and synergies between projects and leveraging them to amplify their impact. You look for opportunities to cross-pollinate ideas and insights across projects, using the learnings from one project to inform and enhance others. By actively managing the integration of your projects, you ensure that they collectively contribute to the realization of your CLP Vision and Story.

As the project manager, you also prioritize the continuous improvement of your project management skills and processes. You regularly evaluate the effectiveness of your project management system, seeking feedback from stakeholders and identifying areas for improvement. You stay up-to-date with project management best practices, incorporating new tools and techniques that can enhance your capabilities.

When to Activate This Role

Step into your project manager's perspective when selecting which creative initiatives to pursue, planning project timelines and milestones, facing complex project coordination challenges, evaluating project outcomes, or whenever you need to organize your creative work into structured, manageable units. This perspective is particularly valuable when managing multiple concurrent projects or when transitioning between project phases.

Through the effective embodiment of the project manager role, you ensure that your creative journey progresses through the completion of meaningful projects that collectively build your Creative Life Project & Story™ while advancing you toward your larger vision, transforming abstract aspirations into concrete achievements.

Creative Life Project & Story

You are the author, practicing the art of writing a page in your life story every day...or not.

As the author within the Creative Self Management framework, your role extends beyond simply writing your Creative Life Project & Story to actively managing the narrative arc and ensuring that your story aligns with your CLP Vision. While previous roles establish your beliefs, organize your approach, envision possibilities, develop skills, manage resources, and structure projects, the author's role focuses on crafting a meaningful narrative from your experiences and choices.

Why This Role is Essential

Life becomes meaningful through the stories we tell about it. The author ensures you are consciously crafting a coherent and purposeful narrative rather than merely experiencing disconnected events. Without this perspective, your creative journey might lack meaning, direction, and the sense of progression that comes from a well-crafted story. This role transforms random occurrences into a purposeful life narrative that reflects your values and aspirations.

From a management perspective, your role as the author involves developing a comprehensive approach to planning, executing, and refining the story of your life. This includes establishing a clear vision for your desired narrative arc, identifying the key themes and values that will guide your storytelling, and creating a roadmap for how your story will unfold over time. By taking a strategic approach to authorship, you ensure that your life story remains coherent, purposeful, and aligned with your long-term goals.

As you manage your narrative, you focus on creating an interesting and meaningful story structure. This involves identifying the key chapters or phases of your life story, each with its own specific goals, challenges, and growth opportunities. You consider how these chapters build upon one another, creating a sense of progression and development throughout your narrative. You also pay attention to the pacing of your story, ensuring there is a balance between moments of tension and resolution, action and reflection, stability and change.

Beyond managing the overall structure of your story, you also focus on crafting impactful scenes and moments within each chapter. This involves being intentional about the choices you make, the actions you take, and the way you interpret and respond to the events of your life. You look for opportunities to create meaningful turning points, overcome obstacles, and demonstrate growth and transformation. By actively managing the key scenes and moments of your story, you create a narrative that is engaging, inspiring, and reflective of your authentic self.

As the author of Creative Self Management, you also prioritize the integration of your life story with your broader creative goals and aspirations. You ensure your narrative aligns with your CLP Vision; you create chapters and scenes that advance you toward your desired outcomes. You regularly assess your story's progression, making necessary adjustments and revisions to keep it on track. You also look for opportunities to leverage your life experiences and insights to inform and enhance your creative projects and pursuits.

Throughout your authorship journey, you draw upon all your other roles. Your philosophical foundation provides the values that guide your storytelling choices, your CEO mindset offers structure, your artist vision supplies creativity, your architect skills provide the tools for crafting a narrative, your resource management ensures sustainability, and your project management transforms episodes into coherent chapters. The author's role integrates all these perspectives into a unified narrative.

When to Activate This Role

Step into your author's perspective when reflecting on your life journey, making significant life decisions, facing major transitions, processing challenging experiences, celebrating achievements, or whenever you need to find meaning in your experiences. This perspective is particularly valuable when you feel disconnected from your life's purpose or when you need to reframe your understanding of past events.

Through the effective embodiment of the author role, you ensure that your life unfolds as a meaningful story rather than a series of random events, creating a narrative that is not only well-crafted but also aligned with your deepest values and aspirations, empowering you to live a life that is authentic, purposeful, and worthy of telling.

Creative Self Expression Practice

You are the coach, reinforcing the value of your Creative Self Development Process and practice to establish your creative independence.

As the coach within the Creative Self Management framework, your role extends beyond simply reinforcing the importance of your daily practice to actively managing and optimizing your creative life practice for maximum growth and impact. While previous roles establish your beliefs, organize your approach, envision possibilities, develop skills, manage resources, structure projects, and craft your narrative, the coach role ensures consistent action and ongoing development through deliberate practice.

Why This Role is Essential

Vision without consistent practice remains unrealized. The coach ensures that your creative development becomes an ongoing process rather than an occasional event. Without this perspective, your creative journey might be characterized by sporadic effort, inconsistent progress, and unfulfilled potential. This role transforms creative aspirations into habitual actions that steadily build toward mastery and meaningful achievement.

From a management perspective, your role as the coach involves developing a comprehensive system for designing, implementing, and continuously improving your creative life practice. This includes establishing clear goals and objectives for your practice, identifying the specific habits, routines, and rituals that will support your creative development, and creating a structured plan for consistently engaging in these activities. By taking a strategic approach to coaching, you ensure that your practice remains focused, purposeful, and aligned with your larger creative vision.

As you manage your practice, you focus on creating an optimal environment and set of conditions for your creative growth. This involves identifying and managing the various factors that can impact your practice, such as your physical space, time management, energy levels, and social support. You actively seek resources, tools, and techniques that can enhance the effectiveness and efficiency of your practice, and you make necessary adjustments to your environment and routines to ensure they are conducive to your creative development.

Beyond managing the external factors of your practice, you also focus on developing the internal skills and capacities essential for sustained creative growth. This includes cultivating self-awareness, emotional intelligence, and mental resilience. You actively seek opportunities to challenge yourself, push past your comfort zone, and develop new skills and perspectives. You also prioritize self-care and stress management, recognizing that a balanced approach to your practice is essential for long-term sustainability and success, all supported by enriching and positive self-talk.

As the coach in Creative Self Management, you prioritize the integration of your practice with your broader creative goals and aspirations. This involves regularly assessing the alignment between your daily activities and your larger vision, making necessary adjustments to ensure your practice moves you closer to your desired outcomes. You also leverage your practice as a source of inspiration and insight for your other creative projects, using the skills, ideas, and experiences gained through your practice to inform and enhance your overall creative development.

Your coach role works in harmony with your other roles: implementing the values established by your philosopher, following the systems created by your CEO, exploring the possibilities envisioned by your artist, developing the skills identified by your architect/builder, utilizing the resources managed by your resource manager, advancing the projects overseen by your project manager, and living the story crafted by your author.

When to Activate This Role

Step into your coach's perspective when establishing daily practices, facing motivation challenges, experiencing plateaus in your development, designing learning experiences, evaluating your progress, or whenever you need to focus on the disciplined, day-to-day actions that build toward mastery. This perspective is particularly valuable during periods of distraction or when you need to recommit to consistent creative practice.

Through the effective embodiment of the coach role, you ensure that your creative development becomes an ongoing journey of growth and mastery rather than an unfulfilled aspiration, transforming creative potential into lived reality through consistent, deliberate practice.

Share Component of Practice

You are an ambassador, representing your fresh perspective on creativity through your own Creative Life Project & Story to ignite the spark in others wanting to do the same.

As an ambassador within the Creative Self Management framework, your role extends beyond simply sharing your Creative Life Project & Story to actively managing the impact and influence of your creative journey on others and the world around you. While previous roles focus on personal development and execution, the ambassador role emphasizes how your creative journey can inspire and contribute to broader communities and cultures.

Why This Role is Essential

Creativity flourishes in the community. The ambassador ensures that your creative journey extends beyond personal achievement to create a meaningful impact in the world. Without this perspective, your creative development might remain self-contained, and you might miss opportunities for both greater influence and collaborative growth. This role transforms individual creative practice into a force for positive cultural change.

From a management perspective, your role as an ambassador involves developing a comprehensive approach to planning, executing, and optimizing your creative outreach and engagement. This includes establishing clear goals for your sharing activities, identifying the specific audiences and communities you wish to reach, and creating a structured approach to how you will communicate and engage with these groups. By taking a strategic approach to ambassadorship, you ensure that your sharing efforts remain focused, purposeful, and aligned with your values.

As you manage your outreach, you focus on creating compelling and authentic content and experiences that showcase your creative journey and inspire others to embark on their own. This involves developing a deep understanding of your unique creative voice, perspective, and story, then finding ways to articulate and express these elements in a way that resonates with your intended audiences. You look for opportunities to collaborate and engage with others in your creative community, building relationships and networks that amplify the impact and reach of your sharing efforts.

Beyond content and relationship management, you cultivate crucial skills for impactful creative communication and engagement. This involves developing your ability to listen deeply, communicate clearly, and facilitate meaningful dialogue. You also work on developing your leadership and advocacy skills, learning how to inspire and mobilize others around shared creative goals and visions that contribute to more vibrant, innovative, and supportive creative cultures.

As an ambassador in Creative Self Management, you prioritize the alignment of your sharing efforts with your broader creative goals and aspirations. This involves regularly assessing the impact and effectiveness of your outreach activities and making necessary adjustments to ensure they contribute to your desired outcomes and values. You also leverage your sharing efforts as a source of learning and growth for your own creative development, using the feedback, insights, and connections gained through your outreach to inform and enhance your practice.

The ambassador role integrates all your previous roles: sharing the wisdom developed as a philosopher, the systems created as a CEO, the vision crafted as an artist, the skills honed as an architect/builder, the resources cultivated as a resource manager, the projects completed as a project manager, the story written as an author, and the practices developed as a coach. By sharing all these aspects of your creative journey, you provide a comprehensive model that others can learn from and adapt to their own circumstances.

When to Activate This Role

Step into your ambassador perspective when sharing your creative work publicly, mentoring others, building creative communities, advocating for creative approaches in organizations, collaborating on cultural projects, or whenever you seek to extend the impact of your creative work beyond personal achievement. This perspective is particularly valuable when you feel ready to transform your individual creative practice into a contribution to broader cultural conversations.

Through the effective embodiment of the ambassador role, you ensure that your creative journey creates ripples of positive influence that extend far beyond your individual experience, contributing to the development of more creative, innovative, and supportive cultures for everyone.

Together, these nine roles form a complete management system for your creative life. Each addresses a specific domain of creative living while contributing to the whole. The philosopher and CEO establish your foundation and direction; the artist and architect/builder generate and manifest your visions; the resource manager and project manager organize and optimize your efforts; the author, coach, and ambassador connect your creative work to meaning, growth, and impact.

This system's power lies in its comprehensiveness. Traditional approaches to creativity often focus narrowly on ideation or execution while neglecting the philosophical grounding, resource sustainability, or social dimensions of creative living. The CLP approach recognizes that truly transforming your blueprint into your fingerprint requires engagement across all these domains. By developing fluency in each role and understanding their interconnections, you create a management approach capable of navigating the complete spectrum of creative challenges and opportunities.

The Integrative Power of Perspective Fluidity

Through the exploration of each role within the Creative Self Management category, you have gained insight into the diverse perspectives needed to realize your creative potential fully. The power of this approach lies not in permanently adopting any single role perspective but in developing the ability to shift fluidly between perspectives as circumstances require. This fluidity is directly connected to the CLP Philosophy's emphasis on adaptability and the Creative Self Mindset's principle of openness. Just as the Life Force of Creation manifests in countless forms throughout the universe, your creative management capacity expresses itself through these different roles, each channeling this fundamental force in unique ways while maintaining a connection to its source.

Developing Perspective Fluidity

Perspective fluidity—the ability to recognize which perspective is needed in a given moment and shift into it intentionally—is a significant component of the Life Skill of Being Creative.

- *Respond with precision* to the specific demands of each situation.
- *Access the full range* of your internal resources rather than being limited to familiar patterns.
- *Maintain a balance* between seemingly opposing needs (structure and flexibility, vision and practicality).

- *Navigate complexity* by bringing the optimal empowering mindset to each challenge.
- *Integrate insights* across perspectives for more comprehensive solutions.

As you practice perspective shifting, you'll develop greater self-awareness about which roles come naturally to you and which require more conscious cultivation. Most people have preferred perspectives they default to, often missing the benefits of less familiar viewpoints. Creative Self Management involves strengthening your capacity across all perspectives while becoming increasingly fluid in your transitions between them.

Over time, this becomes more intuitive; you'll learn to recognize the signals that indicate which perspective is needed. Feelings of confusion about priorities might call for the CEO; creative blocks might require the artist; skill plateaus might need the architect/builder; burnout could signal that the resource manager is needed.

The most masterful creative practitioners can shift perspectives rapidly, sometimes cycling through multiple viewpoints in a single session—stepping back for philosophical grounding, generating artistic possibilities, evaluating resource constraints, and then structuring project steps—all while maintaining a coherent through-line.

Perspective Shifting Beyond Creative Self Management

The power of perspective shifting extends far beyond Creative Self Development. It represents a fundamental approach to creative problem-solving in virtually any domain.

Breaking Through Cognitive Barriers

When we encounter seemingly insurmountable problems, it's often because we're viewing them through a limited perspective. The deliberate practice of shifting viewpoints allows us to see previously invisible solutions. What appears impossible from one angle may be straightforward from another. This explains why creative breakthroughs often come when we step away from a problem and return with fresh eyes—we've unconsciously shifted our perspective.

Enhancing Collaborative Innovation

In collaborative settings, perspective shifting becomes even more powerful. Different team members naturally embody different role perspectives—some are visionaries; others are pragmatic builders; still others are resource-conscious managers. By recognizing these diverse perspectives as complementary rather than competing, teams can leverage their cognitive diversity for enhanced problem-solving. The most innovative organizations deliberately cultivate this perspective diversity and teach members to appreciate viewpoints different from their own.

Resolving Complex Challenges

Our most pressing global and personal challenges rarely yield to single-perspective solutions. Complex environmental issues require both visionary imagination and practical implementation; personal health demands both scientific understanding and behavioral coaching; educational transformation needs philosophical grounding and systematic execution. By deliberately cycling through multiple perspectives, we can develop more comprehensive, nuanced approaches to complex problems.

Transcending Either/Or Thinking

Perspective shifting helps us move beyond binary thinking to recognize that seemingly contradictory approaches can be integrated. Should we focus on structure or freedom? Analysis or intuition? Individual excellence or collaborative harmony? The answer, through a perspective-shifting lens, is not either/or but both/and at the appropriate times and in the appropriate contexts.

Fostering Adaptability in Changing Environments

In rapidly changing environments, those who can shift perspectives quickly have a distinct advantage. They can assess situations through multiple lenses, rapidly determining which approach best fits current conditions. As circumstances change, they adapt not by abandoning their principles but by accessing different aspects of their perspective repertoire.

As you practice integrating these diverse perspectives in your creative journey, you're simultaneously developing one of the most valuable capabilities for navigating our complex, rapidly changing world—the ability to see through many eyes, think with many minds, and bring the right perspective to each moment of opportunity or challenge.

Creative Self Management as Integration

Creative Self Management, like the biology of being creative, is ultimately about integration—bringing together diverse aspects of your Creative Self into a coherent whole that can respond dynamically to life's challenges and opportunities. By developing a facility with each role perspective and the ability to shift between them fluidly, you create an internal ecosystem where your creative potential can fully flourish.

This perspective-shifting approach recognizes that being fully human means embodying many roles, not identifying exclusively with any single one. The philosopher, CEO, artist, architect/builder, resource manager, project manager, author, coach, and ambassador are all aspects of your integrated Creative Self.

Through the art and practice of Creative Self Management, you develop the meta-skill of knowing when and how to apply each facet of yourself. This is the path to creative wholeness and creative independence—where managing your creative life becomes a profound creative act.

PART 07

CATEGORY–CREATIVE LIFE PROJECT & STORY

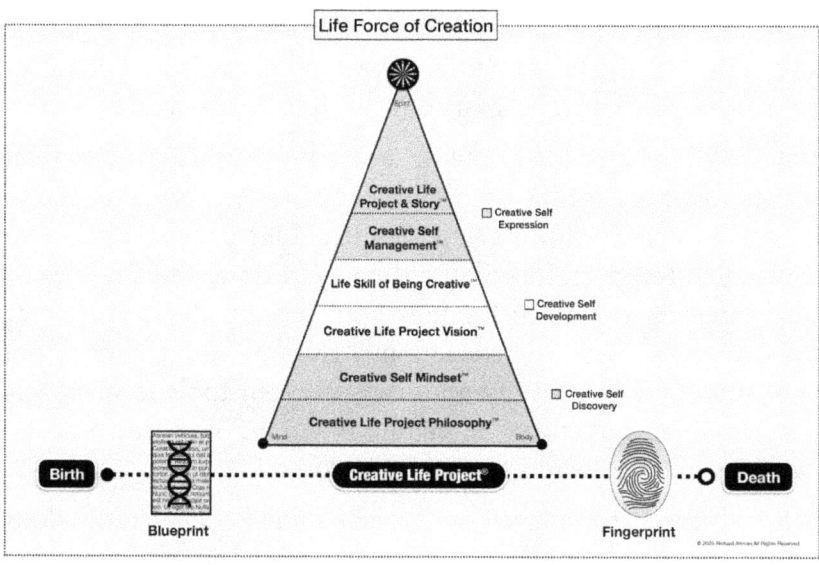

The central theme of the CLP emerges from this transformative idea: viewing your life beyond being a collection of random events and disconnected experiences—but, instead, as an ongoing creative project, a continuous work of art, and an ever-evolving story. This perspective invites you to see your life through the lens of Creative Self Expression and empowers you to shape your journey, transforming what you've inherited actively—your "blueprint"—into something uniquely yours—your "fingerprint."

This view of life as a creative project is deeply rooted in the foundational philosophy established earlier in our journey. When we recognize creativity as "the trait empowering humans to imagine and craft clever and strategic solutions to survive, thrive, and flourish in a constantly changing world," we understand that our entire life story becomes a canvas for this creative expression. The functional definition of creativity we explored in the CLP Philosophy directly informs how we approach our life as a project—with intentionality, adaptability, and a commitment to both personal fulfillment and contribution to others.

The Cloud of Confusion that once obscured our understanding of creativity now gives way to a clear perspective on how creativity manifests in the narrative arc of our lives. By viewing life as a creative project, we transcend the limiting notion that creativity belongs only in specialized domains. Instead, we embrace the understanding that creativity is the fundamental force through which we shape our experiences, relationships, and contributions to the world.

Think of life as a project, like an artist moving from preliminary sketches to a fully realized sculpture. Your vision served as the initial concept; your empowering Creative Life Project Philosophy, Creative Self Mindset, Life Skill of Being Creative, and Creative Self Management were the techniques you developed along the way. Now comes the time for execution, curation, and composition—turning potential into reality and using all your tools to make your vision tangible, your story compelling, and your life a true reflection of who you are and who you wish to become.

The term "project management" might initially seem intimidating or overly technical. But the CLP is not a rigid methodology; rather, it is something deeply personal and profound. It provides a structured approach to apply what you've learned meaningfully to your life. It's about curating your experiences, expressing your creativity, and managing your resources—mental, emotional, and material—in alignment with your vision of living your best life.

Your CLP is ultimately your story—the one you write, direct, curate, and live. It's an ongoing work where you make intentional choices about what belongs in your narrative and how each element fits into a larger, meaningful whole. Each day, you craft a new chapter, whether consciously or not, and this part empowers you to do so with awareness, intention, and creativity. By viewing your life as a creative project, you actively decide what goes into your story and what kind of narrative you wish to create.

Projects on a Continuum

Not all projects require grand ambitions, just as not every moment in life needs to be pivotal. Projects, like creativity itself, exist on a continuum—from small everyday tasks and brief experiments to major endeavors spanning years. Whether you're tackling a short-term goal, developing a new habit, or pursuing a lifelong dream, each project contributes to the broader story of your life.

Understanding this continuum relieves the pressure to constantly be doing something extraordinary. Instead, it emphasizes that every creative act, no matter how small, adds meaning to your life's narrative. From simple to-do lists to ambitious long-term goals, the CLP embraces everything you undertake in service of your vision.

Each small project, task, moment of reflection, and creative effort is part of something larger. These small steps aren't insignificant—they build momentum, cultivate growth, and ultimately bring your vision to life. They are the building blocks of meaningful progress.

A Unified Creative Life Project & Story

The CLP and your life story are essentially the same reality viewed from two different perspectives. The project represents the plan—your conscious choices, strategies, and actions you take to build your creative life. The story is the experience—the lived narrative, the emotional journey, and the legacy you leave behind.

Together, they form the essence of creative living: a life where every action carries intention, where each project contributes to a larger story, and where every day offers an opportunity to bring your vision closer to reality.

CHAPTER 18:
VIEWING LIFE AS A CREATIVE PROJECT

Framing your life as your ultimate creative project provides a fresh perspective that brings intention and clarity to both everyday decisions and long-term goals. This mindset shifts you from merely responding to circumstances to actively designing the path you wish to follow. When viewed as a creative project, life becomes more than random experiences—it evolves into an organized, cohesive journey purposefully aimed at creating your most fulfilling and creative life.

This perspective doesn't reduce your life to mechanical tasks and deadlines. Instead, it invites creativity into every aspect of your existence, providing gifts:

- Structure where there is chaos
- Direction where there is uncertainty
- Motivation where there is resistance

Your CLP is inherently dynamic—evolving, changing, and growing over time. Projects adapt to new circumstances, challenges, and opportunities. This framework embraces both adaptability and creativity, encouraging you to navigate life's unpredictability while staying anchored to your deeper values and aspirations.

Every project begins with a vision—your CLP Vision—capturing what you want to build, experience, and leave as your legacy. The CLP gives form to that vision by breaking it into tangible, actionable elements. Whether you're exploring new passions, developing creative skills, overcoming challenges, or nurturing relationships, each project contributes to the bigger picture of your creative life story. This approach helps you recognize that every effort, regardless of size, forms part of an interconnected whole, allowing you to find meaning in each endeavor.

Projects vary in scale—some are ambitious visions requiring years to realize, while others may be smaller daily endeavors, each valuable in its own right. By approaching each aspect of life as a project, you can more effectively allocate your energy and resources toward what matters most, aligning each effort with your overarching vision. With a clear purpose guiding your actions, even the smallest project becomes meaningful and rewarding.

This approach encourages ongoing growth and reflection. Projects have a natural rhythm: they begin, evolve, and reach completion, providing moments to reflect, celebrate, and learn. Each project—whether successful or filled with unexpected detours—offers valuable insights that inform future actions, strengthen resilience, and refine your creative vision. Reflection is essential, helping you understand not just what you did but why it mattered and how it fits into your broader journey.

Framing your life as a project unifies all aspects of the Creative Self Development Framework into a cohesive approach. It's about engaging with your life with the mindset of a creator: imagining, building, managing, and ultimately expressing your unique story. This perspective helps you see potential in every challenge, purpose in every task, and connections between all aspects of your life.

By framing your life as a creative project, you shift from being a passive recipient of circumstances to an active creator of your experience. This shift represents the philosophical core of the CLP—that creativity is not something you occasionally do but something you fundamentally are. Your life becomes the primary expression of your Creative Self, the ultimate manifestation of your journey from Blueprint to Fingerprint.

Intentional Living: The Foundation of a Meaningful Creative Life Project

Viewing your life as a creative project provides an overarching purpose that transforms how you make decisions. This intentional approach ensures your actions align with your values and aspirations, making each choice meaningful and purposeful.

In today's fast-paced world, we often find ourselves swept along by routines and external pressures, reacting to circumstances without considering how they connect to our deeper desires. Intentional living represents a deliberate shift from this passive stance toward purposeful action. It recognizes that every day presents opportunities to make choices that shape your life story.

When you frame your life as a project, applying this principle becomes more intuitive. Projects naturally require clarity of purpose and planned outcomes, encouraging ongoing reflection about whether your actions align with your long-term vision.

Intentionality doesn't mean micromanaging every moment. Rather, it ensures that the broader trajectory of your life remains consistent with your values and goals. This perspective allows you to focus your energy, time, and resources on activities that meaningfully contribute to your CLP Vision instead of being diverted by distractions that don't serve your purpose.

At its core, intentional living means recognizing that your life is yours to shape. Every project, whether significant or modest, contributes to your CLP—each one reflecting aspects of who you are and who you aspire to become. By committing to an intentional approach, you empower yourself to make choices that resonate with your true aspirations, leading to a life that isn't just productive but profoundly fulfilling.

This practice creates a life that doesn't simply happen to you but one you consciously craft, infusing each day with purpose, clarity, and a sense of personal agency. The difference is transformative—moving from being a passive participant in your life to becoming its active designer.

Clarity and Vision: Projects Start with a Vision

The Creative Self Development Framework provides a structured approach to transforming your vision into reality by framing your life as an ongoing creative project. This framework offers tools and principles that help you translate your aspirations into actionable steps, bringing clarity and focus to your daily decisions and actions.

Imagine embarking on a journey equipped with both intention and adaptable tools—the framework functions as a navigational system for your creative life. It enables you to visualize your best possible life while supporting you in taking deliberate actions toward that vision. Your CLP becomes an ongoing process of imagining, articulating, and actualizing what success, fulfillment, and creativity mean specifically to you.

The framework ensures your vision remains a central reference point, guiding you through challenges and decisions with a sense of purpose. It anchors your CLP while allowing for flexibility and adaptability. As you develop, your vision evolves with you, shaped by new experiences, challenges, and opportunities. This iterative process keeps your CLP relevant and aligned with your current state of being.

Your vision serves as a powerful source of motivation, fueling your passion and inspiring you to recognize the value of each small step and effort. The framework structures these steps, connecting them to the larger story you're creating. It transforms your vision from an abstract concept into a living, breathing guide that keeps you focused, energized, and resilient when facing obstacles.

By aligning your actions with a dynamic, well-supported vision, you actively shape a fulfilling and authentic existence. Your CLP becomes the manifestation of this vision—a tangible expression of your ability to imagine, adapt, and take intentional steps toward the life you desire.

Structured Growth: Breaking Down Your Life into Manageable Projects

Framing your life as a series of projects allows you to break down the complexity of personal growth into manageable, actionable steps. Growth often feels intimidating when viewed as a distant, abstract concept—something vague you strive toward without knowing how to reach it. By dividing your life into smaller projects, you transform this abstract idea into concrete, achievable actions, making the process less overwhelming and more approachable.

Consider your CLP as a construction plan and strategy. You don't build an entire house in a day, and you certainly don't build without a blueprint or phased approach. Each room is built one at a time, each layer of foundation carefully laid, each nail driven with intention toward the greater goal. This same principle applies to structuring your growth through projects. By focusing on one "room" at a time, you make progress strategically and systematically, ensuring each phase is completed effectively before moving to the next.

Each smaller project represents a stepping stone in your personal growth journey. These projects vary widely—a skill to acquire, a relationship to nurture, or an experience to have. What matters is that each has a clear purpose, timeline, and outcome, creating essential structure. This approach prevents feeling overwhelmed by the enormity of your aspirations. Instead of being burdened by your entire vision, you focus on what's within reach now, making steady progress toward your bigger picture.

Breaking down your life into projects also makes growth measurable. It allows you to set smaller, realistic goals that lead to larger milestones. This measurability creates a sense of progress and accomplishment, reinforcing your motivation to continue. Each successfully completed project builds confidence, showing that even the most daunting vision can be achieved through deliberate, sequential actions.

Structured growth through projects encourages meaningful reflection. When you complete a project, you can assess what worked well, what could be improved, and what you learned. This reflection informs your next project, creating a continuous cycle of learning and application. Rather than moving forward blindly, you adapt and refine your approach as you grow, making each subsequent project more effective and aligned with your vision.

By breaking growth into manageable projects, you make creative living less intimidating and more actionable. Structured growth transforms aspirations into achievable steps, each contributing to the life you want to create. Your CLP becomes not an overwhelming challenge but a series of meaningful endeavors that together form a transformative journey of personal fulfillment.

Adaptability: Embracing Change and Iteration Through Projects

Life is inherently unpredictable, filled with unexpected turns and challenges. By framing your life as a series of creative projects, you cultivate adaptability—recognizing that, like any well-planned endeavor, things rarely unfold exactly as envisioned. Projects naturally evolve, change, and sometimes require complete redirection. Similarly, viewing your life as a project enables you to become comfortable with this dynamic nature of change, growth, and redefinition.

When you approach life as an ongoing creative project, adaptability becomes essential rather than optional. Every project, despite careful planning, requires adjustment. Creative Self Management involves continuously evaluating the environment, circumstances, and context of each project and making strategic adjustments as needed. This ability to adapt helps you navigate unexpected changes with resilience, transforming obstacles into opportunities for learning and growth.

Adaptability means a willingness to pivot when circumstances demand it. When you initiate your CLP, you begin with a vision, but the path to realizing that vision is rarely straight. You may need to alter strategies, adjust goals, or shift expectations in response to new information or changing circumstances. Adaptability allows you to make these shifts gracefully rather than viewing them as setbacks. It encourages you to embrace iteration, using each phase of your journey as an opportunity to refine and evolve.

Consider the metaphor of a river flowing toward the sea. Along its path, the river encounters rocks, branches, and other obstacles. Rather than stopping, it finds a way around these barriers, sometimes changing course slightly, sometimes carving an entirely new channel. This fluid, adaptive approach embodies the CLP mentality. You are the river, flowing toward your vision of your best life, and the challenges you encounter become opportunities to shape a new, often better path forward.

Creative Problem-Solving: Embracing Challenges as Opportunities

Projects rarely proceed without obstacles. They inherently present challenges that require creative solutions, and when you frame your life as a series of projects, you naturally activate your Creative Self Mindset. Rather than being discouraged by difficulties, you learn to view them as opportunities to tap into your creative potential, draw upon your knowledge, and employ innovative strategies to overcome whatever hurdles arise.

Viewing life as a creative project transforms each challenge from a potential endpoint into a puzzle to solve. You become both architect and builder, continuously developing and refining approaches to move forward. This perspective reframes setbacks as platforms for growth, encouraging you to leverage your creativity to develop resourceful, innovative solutions. Whether addressing a professional challenge, navigating relationship dynamics, or pursuing personal development, the ability to solve problems creatively becomes an invaluable skill guiding your journey.

Creative problem-solving empowers you to experiment with different approaches without letting fear halt your progress. Just as any project might require multiple iterations before achieving the desired result, life's challenges can be approached from various angles. Your CLP becomes a living tapestry of experimentation, innovation, and resilience.

This approach encourages both divergent and convergent thinking—generating numerous potential solutions and then selecting the most viable option. By recognizing that creative problem-solving isn't about finding a "perfect" answer but rather about finding a way forward, you reduce perfectionism's pressure and open yourself to unexpected outcomes that may prove even more rewarding than initially imagined.

Framing life as a project means acknowledging that obstacles are integral to any creative endeavor. With the mindset that challenges exist to be solved rather than avoided, you enrich your creative journey and become more adept at handling complexity and uncertainty in all areas of life. Through creative problem-solving, you transform obstacles into opportunities, steadily progressing toward your vision with ingenuity and purpose.

Meaningful Reflection: Learning Through Evaluation

In project management, one of the most critical phases is reflection—evaluating what succeeded, what could improve, and what lessons emerged. When you apply this project-based perspective to your life, you create space for regular, meaningful reflection that transforms experience into wisdom. Through reflection, you understand the true value of your actions and their impact, gaining insights needed to adjust your approach and enhance future efforts.

Viewing your life as a series of projects encourages consistent evaluation, the foundation for ongoing growth and development. Each project, whether it unfolded as planned or took unexpected directions, contains valuable information to inform your next steps. Reflection extracts these lessons and integrates them into your path forward. It transforms every challenge, victory, and mistake into a stepping stone for further progress. Reflection also fosters deeper self-understanding—illuminating your motivations, strengths, and areas where growth is still needed.

By taking time to honestly assess the projects you've undertaken, you become more attuned to the nuances of your creative process and better equipped to make choices aligned with your vision. This level of introspection helps you recognize behavioral patterns, refine your methods, and reinforce positive habits while identifying those that need modification.

Reflection in your CLP goes beyond self-assessment; it also celebrates the progress you've made. Too often, in our rush to achieve the next goal, we forget to acknowledge what we've already accomplished. By viewing your life as a project and committing to regular reflection, you ensure that you honor your achievements, learn from your experiences, and maintain a sense of gratitude and fulfillment.

Meaningful reflection serves as a tool for transformation. It allows you to see your life not as disconnected events but as an interconnected, evolving project continuously shaped by your actions, choices, and experiences. Through thoughtful reflection, you deepen your understanding of your journey, gain clarity for the path ahead, and cultivate the wisdom necessary to craft a fulfilling and purpose-driven life story.

Momentum and Motivation: Creating Positive Feedback Loops

In any project, momentum is key to maintaining motivation. The sense of accomplishment that comes from achieving project milestones—whether small or significant—creates powerful forward motion. Framing your life as a series of projects allows you to harness this power, using each milestone as a source of motivation to propel you toward the next. The concept of momentum becomes a positive feedback loop that drives your creativity and enthusiasm forward.

As you work through your CLP, each completed step creates a tangible sense of progress. This feeling is crucial for staying motivated, especially when overarching goals seem distant or challenging. Breaking your life down into smaller, manageable projects enables you to see results more frequently, providing the encouragement needed to persist even when faced with difficulties.

Momentum also fosters resilience. Inevitably, you will face setbacks or discouragement, but the momentum generated by earlier successes helps you push through these challenges. The experience of having moved forward—even in small increments—reminds you that progress is possible despite obstacles. This perspective is particularly valuable in creative endeavors, where uncertainty is common and maintaining forward movement is essential.

Momentum in life projects isn't about speed but consistency. A CLP builds not through occasional bursts of inspiration but through sustained effort and commitment. By celebrating each milestone, you generate the energy needed to continue, ensuring your vision remains vibrant and actionable. This momentum-driven approach ensures every action meaningfully contributes to your creative life story, adding depth, purpose, and impact.

When you frame your life as a series of projects, you create an environment where momentum and motivation reinforce each other, driving you toward your vision. This dynamic approach encourages persistence, even during challenges, helping you build a fulfilling, resilient, and progressively developing CLP.

Purposeful Resource Allocation: Focusing on What Truly Matters

Every project operates within constraints—whether time, energy, finances, or other resources. Framing your life as a project compels you to think critically about how to allocate these resources to support your vision. It encourages purposeful investment in what truly matters, aligning your time and energy with the goals most meaningful to you.

Resource allocation requires recognizing that while demands on your time are many, your resources are finite, making effective prioritization crucial. By viewing your life as a creative project, you learn to focus on what brings you closer to your creative vision. This means consciously deciding where your attention goes, choosing activities and commitments aligned with your values and aspirations, and releasing those that don't serve your higher purpose.

Purposeful resource allocation extends beyond managing time. It also encompasses emotional, mental, and physical resources. You might allocate mental space to learning new skills or dedicate emotional energy to nurturing supportive relationships. This approach ensures you aren't living reactively, overwhelmed by endless tasks, but rather strategically directing your resources to align with your CLP.

Viewing your life as a series of creative projects helps identify opportunities to build and conserve resources. You begin to recognize where you can leverage existing strengths, develop new capacities, and optimize your efforts. Every decision becomes an investment in your creative journey, and the purposeful allocation of resources allows you to maximize these investments for optimal growth and fulfillment. By focusing on what matters most, you build a life truly aligned with your goals, values, and aspirations—one that authentically reflects your unique blueprint.

Personal Accountability: Taking Ownership of Your Journey

In any project, there must be accountability—someone responsible for driving progress, making decisions, and ensuring advancement. That responsibility belongs to you. You are the project manager of your own life, and with that comes personal accountability—the understanding that you have the power to shape your journey through the choices you make.

Taking ownership of your CLP means becoming responsible for both successes and setbacks. It's about embracing the reality that you are the primary agent of change in your life and that your actions, thoughts, and decisions will ultimately determine the outcome. This perspective empowers you to stop waiting for external factors to shape your life and to start taking active, intentional steps to make your vision a reality.

Personal accountability also means recognizing the impact of your choices. When you steer the course of your project, each decision carries weight. This encourages a more thoughtful, deliberate approach to living—where actions align with values and long-term goals. Instead of drifting aimlessly, you make decisions guided by a clear sense of purpose, ensuring your life's direction results from conscious effort rather than circumstance.

This form of accountability cultivates resilience. By owning your role as project manager, you recognize that setbacks offer opportunities to learn and adapt. You develop the mental fortitude to reassess strategies and pivot when necessary, always keeping your CLP Vision in focus. This accountability empowers you to maintain forward momentum, even when facing challenges, knowing that each step—successful or not—is an integral part of your journey.

Personal accountability transforms how you view your life. It reinforces that you are the author of your own story and that, through intentional choices and actions, you have the power to bring your creative vision to life. This sense of responsibility drives genuine progress and ensures your life reflects the values, dreams, and aspirations that are uniquely yours.

Sustained Focus on What Matters: Eliminating Distractions

Projects inherently have clear purposes and defined outcomes, and this structure is crucial for maintaining focus. Framing your life as a series of creative projects helps eliminate distractions by consistently bringing you back to what matters most. It encourages aligning your actions with your long-term vision and minimizing activities that don't serve your larger purpose.

In a world saturated with distractions—from social media to endless to-do lists—maintaining focus on your creative vision can be challenging. Viewing life through the lens of project management gives you a clear framework to determine where to invest your energy. This approach helps filter out unnecessary noise, ensuring your efforts are directed toward meaningful and impactful pursuits.

From this perspective, you regularly evaluate whether your actions move you closer to your vision. This focused attention helps prevent burnout by teaching you to release unimportant tasks that don't contribute to your creative journey. Rather than getting lost in daily minutiae, you become skilled at identifying and prioritizing activities aligned with your goals, ensuring every effort contributes to the bigger picture.

Sustained focus centers on clarity of purpose. It enables you to build a life where every decision, action, and effort serves the vision you've set for yourself. By maintaining concentration on what truly matters, you ensure your CLP authentically reflects your values, aspirations, and unique potential.

Integration of Multiple Roles: Understanding the Bigger Picture

Your projects bring clarity to the various roles you play throughout your journey. As you navigate the Creative Self Development Framework, you'll embody different perspectives: philosopher, artist, CEO, builder, manager, and more. Understanding how each role contributes to your project helps you integrate them effectively, ensuring all aspects align in service of your vision.

The philosopher helps define your guiding principles and values, while the CEO translates these into actionable daily strategies. The artist imagines your vision, the builder brings it to life through skill development and action, and the resource manager ensures you have what you need to achieve it. Each role is vital, and knowing when and how to shift between them is key to managing your project effectively.

Integration means recognizing that you don't function in just one capacity at any time. Life often requires fluid transitions between different mindsets and approaches. For example, you might need the creative artist's mindset when envisioning goals while simultaneously adopting the CEO's pragmatism to implement them. Viewing life as a creative project helps you understand how these perspectives aren't separate, but are interconnected parts of a larger whole, each playing a unique role in helping you navigate, build, and live your creative life.

This integration fosters balance. By understanding and embracing each role, you ensure no aspect of your life is neglected. You're not solely focused on strategic elements of your creative journey; you're also nurturing your Creative Self, developing skills, managing resources, and continuously growing. This holistic approach ensures all facets of your life contribute to your overall creative vision, making your journey more fulfilling and well-rounded.

Alignment with Your Creative Life Project Vision: Turning Your Blueprint into Your Fingerprint

The life-as-creative-project perspective fundamentally centers on alignment—helping you bridge the gap between dreams and daily realities to transform an abstract blueprint into a tangible fingerprint that leaves your unique mark on the world.

The blueprint represents your CLP Vision—a comprehensive yet evolving plan defining who you want to be and what you want to accomplish. It embodies the dreams, values, and aspirations that make you uniquely you. However, the blueprint remains theoretical, showing direction without yet existing in the physical world. By viewing your life as a creative project, you gain the power to bring this blueprint into reality, transforming ideas into experiences and dreams into actions. Each project becomes a building block, gradually constructing your creative life.

The fingerprint concept signifies the uniqueness of your creative journey. Just as no two fingerprints are identical, your CLP will be unlike anyone else's. Your approach to each project, the values you bring, and the experiences shaping your perspective make your journey inherently personal. By aligning your projects with your vision, you ensure your life story reflects not only what you've accomplished but who you truly are. This approach guarantees that as you navigate different phases of your creative journey, you remain connected to your larger purpose and true to your Creative Self.

Summary

Viewing your life through the lens of a creative project offers a powerful reframe—one that invites you to take ownership, apply creativity, and bring clarity to your journey. This perspective transforms your experiences from disconnected events into a purposeful narrative reflecting your values, aspirations, and creative potential. Life becomes not something that happens to you but a canvas on which you actively create, adjust, and refine your story.

Consider how you might apply this perspective to different areas of your life. What projects currently call to you? How can you align your daily actions with your greater vision? Remember, the value of this framework lies in its ability to bring meaning and purpose to every moment. Whether you're starting a new adventure, solving a challenging problem, or reflecting on what matters most, each project offers an opportunity to create, learn, and grow.

Fundamentally, your CLP is your story to tell—the expression of your Creative Self in action, unfolding through each project, decision, and chapter. With intentionality, adaptability, accountability, and vision guiding your journey, you're equipped to craft a deeply meaningful life—a story reflecting the best of who you are and what you wish to contribute to the world.

CHAPTER 19:
YOUR CREATIVE LIFE PROJECT & STORY—THE HERO RETURNS

Remember when you first opened this guide? You stood at the threshold of your own Hero's Journey, uncertain about your creative potential, perhaps questioning whether creativity had any meaningful role in your life. You answered those initial questions about your relationship with creativity—some responses revealing confidence, others uncertainty, all of them honest snapshots of where you began.

Now, having traveled through the Creative Self Development Framework, you find yourself in a different place entirely. You've navigated the Cloud of Confusion, developed creative literacy, embraced an empowering Creative Self Mindset, contemplated your vision, and learned about the Life Skill of Being Creative and managing your creative resources. You've transformed your understanding of what it means to be creative and discovered your role as the creator in your life and of your life.

This is the classic return phase of the Hero's Journey—the moment when the transformed hero comes back to their ordinary world, carrying new wisdom, skills, and perspectives that can benefit not only themselves but their entire community.

The Hero's Transformation

Your story—your journey through this guide and beyond—holds profound value and purpose that extends far beyond what you might initially recognize. The significance of your narrative lies not in meeting conventional definitions of success or achievement, but in the unique transformation you've undergone and the distinctive mark you're now prepared to leave on the world.

Every hero's story follows this pattern: they begin as ordinary people, face extraordinary challenges, undergo a fundamental transformation, and return with gifts that can help others. Your Creative Life Project & Story follows this same archetypal pattern, but with a crucial difference—your transformation is ongoing, your story is still being written, and your greatest adventures may yet lie ahead.

Your Unique Significance

Your creative journey is uniquely yours, shaped by your specific experiences, choices, and creative expressions. This uniqueness holds inherent value and deserves recognition. No one else has lived your life, faced your particular challenges, or developed the specific creative solutions you've discovered. Your story matters precisely because it represents a one-of-a-kind narrative that adds richness and diversity to the tapestry of human creative experience.

Like Luke Skywalker discovering his connection to the Force or Frodo finding courage he never knew he possessed, you've uncovered aspects of your creative potential that were always there but perhaps hidden or dormant. But perhaps no story better illustrates the profound significance of an ordinary person's creative journey than that of George Bailey in *It's a Wonderful Life*.

George has dreams of grand adventures—traveling the world, building magnificent structures, experiencing life on a grand scale. Yet circumstances keep calling him back to his small town of Bedford Falls, where he faces what seems like mundane challenges: running a modest savings and loan, helping neighbors with their financial struggles, and raising a family in a house that needed constant repair. To George, this feels like failure, like a life unlived.

When despair finally overwhelms him and he wishes he had never been born, George is given an extraordinary gift: the chance to see what Bedford Falls—and the lives of everyone he knew—would have looked like if he had never existed. Through this supernatural glimpse into an alternative reality, he witnesses the quiet but profound ways his creative responses to ordinary challenges have shaped everything around him.

George's story reveals a profound truth about being creative and creative living: sometimes our most meaningful adventures unfold not through the dramatic journeys we envision but through the creative ways we respond to the circumstances we're given. George's willingness to approach each challenge with resourcefulness, compassion, and cleverness—his creative responses to ordinary problems—transformed not only his own life but the entire community around him.

When George finally sees his true impact, he discovers that his creative solutions to everyday challenges created ripples of positive change that extended far beyond what he could have imagined. His small acts of creative problem-solving, his innovative approaches to helping others, his resourceful responses to financial crises—all of these seemingly ordinary applications of creativity had extraordinary consequences.

If you haven't seen this movie, you owe it to yourself to find it and watch it.

The experiences that have shaped your creative development—both the victories and the setbacks, both the grand aspirations and the everyday responses to circumstances—are not random events but the raw material from which your unique creative wisdom has emerged.

Your Creative Life Project & Story becomes a representation of the universal truth that creativity is not reserved for a chosen few but is available to anyone willing to undertake the journey of discovery and development. By embracing your Creative Self Potential, you've demonstrated that transformation is possible, that ordinary people can become extraordinary through commitment to their Creative Self Development.

The Power of Personal Fulfillment

Crafting and living your story with intention brings profound personal fulfillment that goes far beyond external achievements. By acknowledging your creative journey's significance, you find meaning and purpose in everyday actions, leading to a more satisfying and enriched life.

This fulfillment does not come from comparing your story to others but from recognizing the authentic progress you've made. Like Daniel in *The Karate Kid*, discovering that his seemingly simple training exercises were actually building real strength, you may find that the small, daily practices of creative development have accumulated into significant transformation.

Your Creative Life Project & Story provides a framework for intentional living—making conscious choices aligned with your creative values and vision. This purposeful approach helps you focus on what truly matters, fostering a sense of direction and clarity that enhances satisfaction and achievement in all areas of life.

Your Impact on Others

Perhaps most importantly, your Creative Life Project & Story has the power to inspire and influence those around you. By living your creative journey authentically, you provide insights, motivation, and encouragement to others who may be struggling to recognize their own creative potential.

Your story offers inspiration to others facing similar challenges or pursuing similar goals. Your journey provides hope and encouragement, showing others that they, too, can overcome obstacles and develop their creative abilities.

Like George Bailey discovering the profound impact of his seemingly ordinary life, you may never fully realize how your creative journey influences others. Your willingness to approach everyday challenges creatively, to solve problems with resourcefulness, to express yourself authentically in small daily choices—these acts of being creative, living a creative life, trigger ripples that extend far beyond your immediate awareness.

The insights and lessons you've gained through your creative journey offer valuable wisdom to guide others. These insights help others navigate their own paths with greater understanding and awareness. Every challenge you've overcome, every skill you've developed, every mindset shift you've experienced becomes potential guidance for someone else's journey.

The Return: Sharing Your Gifts

In the classic Hero's Journey, the return phase is not just about coming home—it's about sharing the gifts, wisdom, and capabilities gained during the adventure. As someone who has developed creative literacy and embraced your Creative Self, you now carry something valuable that extends beyond personal transformation.

George Bailey's story reminds us that this sharing often happens in the most ordinary ways. He never traveled the world as he dreamed, never built the magnificent structures he envisioned, yet his creative responses to everyday challenges created an extraordinary impact. His gifts were shared not through grand gestures but through creative living itself.

This doesn't mean you need to become a teacher or mentor in any formal sense. Like George, you may find that your most meaningful contributions happen through how you creatively navigate your actual circumstances rather than through the dramatic adventures you might have originally envisioned. When you approach problems creatively, when you express yourself authentically, when you manage your life with intention and vision, you model a way of being that others can recognize and aspire to.

Your willingness to embrace your creative journey—with all its imperfections and uncertainties—gives others permission to begin their own explorations. Your story becomes living proof that creativity is not about perfection but about engagement, not about extraordinary talent but about ordinary commitment to growth and authentic expression.

The fresh perspective on creativity you've gained through this guide becomes a gift you naturally share simply by embodying it in your daily life. You become part of the solution to the Cloud of Confusion that surrounds creativity, helping to clear the way for others to discover their own creative potential.

The Ongoing Adventure

Unlike many traditional stories that end with the hero's return, your Creative Life Project & Story represents a new beginning rather than a conclusion. The framework you've learned, the mindset you've developed, the vision you've crafted, and the understanding you've gained are not endpoints but tools for the lifelong adventure of creative living.

As you continue to engage with life through this fresh perspective on creativity, your story will evolve and deepen. New challenges will arise that call for creative solutions. New opportunities will present themselves that invite innovative thinking. New relationships and communities will offer possibilities for creative collaboration and mutual growth.

Your story will continue to transform because you have become someone who approaches life creatively. You've developed the capacity to navigate change with resilience, to solve problems with innovation, and to express yourself with authenticity. Most importantly, you've learned to see yourself as the author of your own story rather than a passive character in someone else's narrative.

Recognizing Your Heroic Journey

Looking back on your journey through this guide, you can now recognize the classic elements of heroic transformation:

- **The Call**: Your initial sensing that there was more to creativity and to your life than you were experiencing
- **The Mentor**: This guide and the framework it provided for your development
- **Crossing the Threshold**: Your decision to take your creative potential seriously and begin intentional exploration
- **Trials and Revelations**: The challenges to old thinking and the insights you've gained along the way
- **Transformation**: The shifts in understanding, capability, and confidence you've experienced

- **The Return**: Your emergence as someone equipped to live creatively and inspire others

This pattern isn't just a literary device—it reflects how real transformation occurs in human lives. By recognizing your journey as heroic, you honor the courage it took to begin, the persistence required to continue, and the growth you've achieved.

Your Story Continues

Your Creative Life Project & Story is both deeply personal and universally significant. It represents your unique way of engaging with the fundamental human capacity for creativity while contributing to the larger conversation about what it means to live a creative life.

The person who began this guide still exists within you, but they've been joined by someone new—someone with creative literacy, someone with tools for ongoing development, someone who understands their role as the creator in their life and of their life. This integration of who you were with who you're becoming is the essence of the Blueprint to Fingerprint transformation.

As you move forward, your story will continue to evolve with each choice you make, each challenge you approach creatively, and each moment you choose to engage fully with your creative potential. The framework you've learned becomes part of your toolkit for navigating whatever adventures lie ahead.

Remember that your story matters—not because it's perfect or because it matches someone else's definition of success, but because it's authentically yours. It represents your unique way of transforming your inherited blueprint into your distinctive fingerprint, leaving a mark that only you can make.

Your adventure in creative living continues to unfold. The hero has returned, transformed, and ready for whatever comes next. Your Creative Life Project & Story advances with each creative choice you make, each problem you solve innovatively, and each moment you choose to embrace your role as the creator of your own life.

The world needs your story. It needs your unique perspective, your creative solutions, your authentic expression. As you continue writing this story through your daily choices and creative expressions, you join the long tradition of those who have discovered that creativity is not a special gift for the few but a fundamental capacity that empowers all of us to navigate, build, and live our best lives.

Your story is far from over. In many ways, it's just beginning.

PART 08

CATEGORY–CREATIVE SELF EXPRESSION PRACTICE

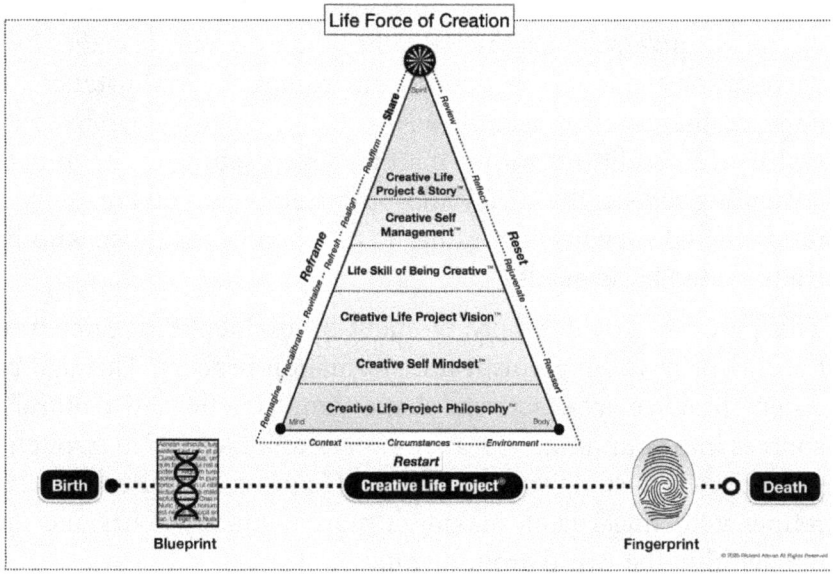

The Creative Self Expression Practice represents the final category of the Creative Self Development Framework—a fresh perspective on being creative. This practice is an ongoing commitment to integrating creativity into every aspect of your life. It transforms your creative expression into an evolving story where each action becomes an opportunity to apply your learning, respond to your environment, navigate circumstances, and adapt your approach. Here, the framework transitions from concept to practice, becoming a living, breathing force that helps you actively cultivate and express your Creative Self in all life domains.

This practice embodies the philosophical foundations established throughout the CLP. The practice cycle—Restart, Discover/Develop/Express, and Reset—operationalizes the understanding that creativity is not a one-time event but an ongoing process of engagement with life's ever-changing circumstances. This reflects the CLP's fundamental definition of creativity as the trait empowering us to navigate a constantly changing world. Each component of the practice cycle connects directly to this definition: "Restart" acknowledges changing circumstances; "Discover/Develop/Express" encompasses the imagination and crafting of solutions; "Reset" enables continued thriving and flourishing through reflection and renewal.

The practice also honors the philosophical understanding that creativity is universally accessible rather than domain-specific. By incorporating elements that address environment, circumstances, and context, the practice acknowledges that creativity operates within real-world conditions rather than idealized settings. This practical grounding reflects the CLP Philosophy's emphasis on creativity as a fundamental survival trait rather than a luxury for those who have transcended basic needs.

This practice provides daily, moment-by-moment engagement with the Blueprint to Fingerprint transformation process. Through consistent practice, you actively shape your genetic and cultural resources into your unique creative expression. Each cycle through the practice—Restart, Discover/Develop/Express, and Reset—further refines your fingerprint, making it more distinctly yours and more impactful in the world around you.

Process vs. Practice

Understanding the distinction between process and practice is essential for grasping how the different components of the CLP work together to transform your relationship with creativity.

The CLP is the overarching idea and philosophy that frames life as a creative project. It invites you to view your entire life as a creative endeavor where you are both the artist and the masterpiece in progress.

The Creative Self Development Framework supports the process of Creative Self Development—a structured approach for discovering, developing, and expressing your creative potential. This process emphasizes you as the creator in your life and of your life. It provides strategies for developing your creative capacities through deliberate, intentional growth. Unlike other creative processes (such as design thinking or creative problem-solving) that focus on external problems or specific projects, the Creative Self Development Process centers on developing you as a creative individual.

The Creative Self Expression Practice is the ongoing *practice* of the Life Skill of Being Creative. It's how you act daily to navigate, build, and live your best life through Creative Self Expression. This practice isn't a series of steps to follow but a way of being and engaging with the world that permeates every aspect of your existence. Through this practice, creativity becomes integrated into how you perceive, think, interact, and contribute—it becomes part of your identity rather than just something you occasionally do.

This integrated approach distinguishes the CLP perspective on creativity and being creative from other approaches to developing creative potential:

- The CLP Philosophy establishes creativity as the core of what it means to be human and a trait that can be developed and expressed rather than a special talent for the gifted few.
- The Creative Self Development Framework provides a structured process for developing yourself as the creator in your life and of your life.

- The Creative Self Expression Practice transforms creativity from an occasional activity into a continuous way of navigating, building, and living your best life.

By understanding how philosophy, process, and practice function together within the CLP, you can more effectively develop your creative potential while simultaneously living creatively each day. The CLP Philosophy provides the foundation, the Framework provides the process, and the Practice allows you to embody and express your creativity daily.

This integration transforms creativity from something you occasionally engage in to solve specific problems into a fundamental orientation toward life itself—a way of living that enriches every experience, relationship, and endeavor with the unique development and expression of your Creative Self.

Organization of the Creative Self Expression Practice Components

The Creative Self Expression Practice offers a comprehensive set of components that support the continuous growth and application of your creative potential. While these components appear in a specific arrangement within the framework diagram, this organization doesn't represent a rigid, linear process.

In practice, your engagement with these components will be fluid, dynamic, and responsive to your unique needs and circumstances. You may find yourself moving between different elements in whatever order is best for your current circumstances rather than following a predetermined sequence. You will also notice that, unlike previous versions of the framework diagram, this version blends the specific colors for each category to further reinforce the reality that these components are not isolated from each other and are available for random access as required.

This practice is designed as a flexible, adaptable tool supporting your ongoing creative development. By understanding how these components relate to each other within the framework, you can better navigate the practice and leverage its elements to enhance your creative potential.

In the following chapter, we'll explore each component, providing guidance on effectively incorporating them into your creative journey. Remember that this practice is dynamic and iterative—the key is engaging with the components in ways that best support your current circumstances and Creative Self growth and development.

CHAPTER 20:
CREATIVE SELF EXPRESSION PRACTICE COMPONENTS

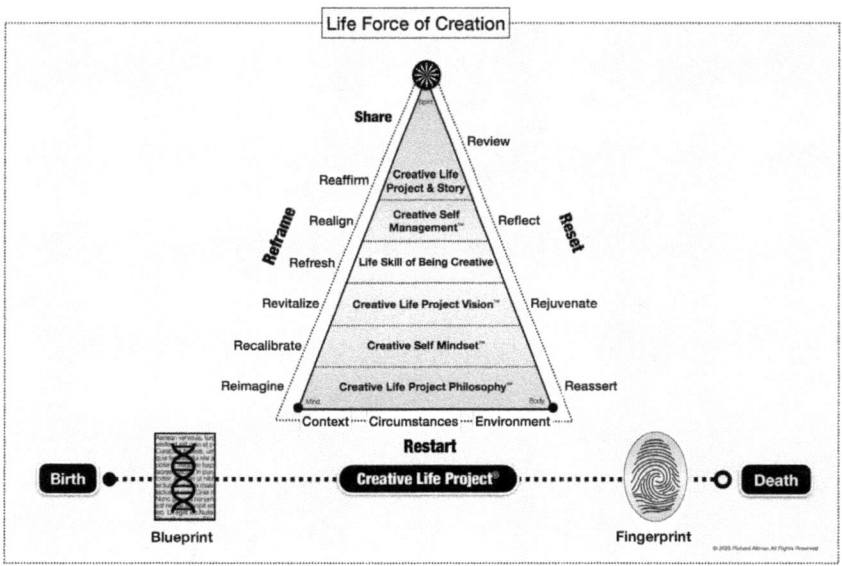

The Creative Self Expression Practice is a dynamic, cyclical approach to nurturing and expressing your creative potential. Review the graphic of the complete framework above and notice that each side of the triangle represents a crucial phase in your creative journey.

At the triangle's base lies the foundation: *Restart*. This phase encompasses environment, circumstances, and context. Restart embodies our ability to begin anew, adapting to life's ever-changing landscape.

It reminds us that creativity isn't linear but requires constant renewal and adaptation.

The left side of the triangle represents the *Reframe* elements of the creative journey. This phase includes the keywords from Reimagine to Share, representing the active process of uncovering our creative potential, honing our skills, and bringing ideas to life. This side encourages us to explore, grow, and manifest our creative visions.

The right side focuses on reflection and renewal: *Reset*. Covering keywords from Review to Reassert, Reset emphasizes the importance of stepping back, evaluating progress, and recommitting to creative goals. It allows us to learn from experiences, refine our approach, and reinvigorate our creative spirit.

Together, these three sides—Restart, Discover/Develop/Express, and Reset—form a continuous cycle of creative growth. As we move through this cycle, we refresh our perspective, expand our capabilities, and deepen our commitment to our creative journey.

By engaging with each phase, we cultivate a holistic, sustainable approach to creativity that permeates all aspects of our lives. This practice empowers us to navigate life's challenges and opportunities with resilience, innovation, and authenticity, empowering us to navigate, build, and live our best lives. Let's explore each practice component represented in the diagram.

Environment

As we engage with the Creative Self Expression Practice, we quickly recognize the profound influence our environment has on our creative process and output. The spaces where we live, work, and interact can either nurture or hinder our creativity. This environment extends beyond physical spaces to include our social and psychological surroundings.

Cultivating a supportive, nurturing environment is essential to this practice. This involves intentionally designing the physical, social, and psychological spaces where we operate to foster creative exploration, experimentation, and growth across all life areas.

Physically, this might mean creating dedicated spaces that are comfortable, functional, and inspiring. These spaces should be free from distractions and clutter while including the tools and resources needed for our creative work—whether in business projects, personal endeavors, or daily problem-solving. It may also involve incorporating elements of nature, beauty, and sensory stimulation to spark imagination and inspire fresh ideas.

Socially, cultivating a supportive, creative environment means surrounding ourselves with people who encourage, challenge, and inspire us. This could include joining communities of like-minded individuals, collaborating on projects, or seeking mentors who provide guidance and support. These social connections offer fresh perspectives, constructive feedback, and emotional support vital for creative growth.

Psychologically, nurturing our creative environment involves developing mental and emotional habits that enable full engagement in the creative process. This might include practicing mindfulness and self-awareness, cultivating a Creative Self Mindset, or learning to manage stress and anxiety productively. It's about creating an internal landscape open to new ideas, resilient in the face of challenges, and receptive to creative possibilities in everyday situations.

Ultimately, cultivating a supportive, creative environment means taking responsibility for the context in which we create. By intentionally designing our living and working spaces, we create conditions for creativity to flourish in all aspects of life. This environment becomes a catalyst for innovative thinking, problem-solving, and personal growth, enabling us to approach life's challenges and opportunities with creativity and resourcefulness.

As we embrace the power of the environment in our creative practice, we recognize that our surroundings are both the backdrop to and an integral component of the creative process itself. By cultivating spaces that inspire, support, and challenge us, we unlock new levels of creativity, productivity, and fulfillment, becoming more capable of bringing our unique gifts to every situation we encounter.

Circumstances

As we navigate the complex, ever-changing landscape of our lives within the Creative Self Expression Practice, we quickly understand the importance of adaptability when facing unpredictable circumstances. These circumstances refer to the specific situations and events currently unfolding in our lives, closely related to our environment and context.

If we consider our environment as answering "Where am I?" and context as providing the broader perspective of how our current situation fits into our life's bigger picture, then circumstances can be understood as "What is happening right now where I am?" Circumstances encompass the immediate challenges, opportunities, and changes we encounter within our environment and context.

Life presents unexpected circumstances that can either derail our creative progress or propel us in exciting new directions. The Creative Self Expression Practice encourages us to cultivate a flexible, open-minded approach to these changing circumstances. Rather than resisting life's inevitable ups and downs, we learn to embrace them as integral parts of the creative journey and find ways to use them advantageously.

This adaptability requires developing keen awareness and responsiveness to our current circumstances. We must learn to notice subtle shifts and signals in our environment and adjust our strategies accordingly. This might involve pivoting projects in response to emerging trends, shifting priorities when facing personal or professional challenges, or finding new ways to collaborate amid social or technological changes.

The practice of resourcefulness and adaptability within the Creative Self Expression Practice requires cultivating deep trust and resilience when facing uncertain circumstances. We must learn to release attachment to specific outcomes or expectations and remain open to possibilities that emerge in the present moment. This might involve taking risks, experimenting with new approaches, or simply surrendering to the creative process's natural ebb and flow.

At the same time, the Creative Self Expression Practice reminds us to stay true to our core values, vision, and purpose even as we adapt to changing circumstances. While the specific manifestations of our creative work may shift and evolve in response to our circumstances, the deeper intentions and aspirations driving us remain constant.

Ultimately, the practice of adaptability within the Creative Self Expression Practice is about developing the mental and emotional flexibility needed to thrive amid ever-changing circumstances. By cultivating a responsive, resilient approach to situations we encounter, we become more capable of navigating life's journey with grace, courage, and authenticity.

Context

As we engage in this practice, we quickly understand the critical role context plays in shaping our creative experiences and outcomes. Context refers to the complex web of factors and influences surrounding and informing our creative work, including our personal history, cultural background, social relationships, and broader environmental and societal conditions.

The Creative Self Expression Practice encourages us to develop a deep, nuanced understanding of the contexts in which we create and to consider how these contexts impact our creative process and output. This involves looking beyond the immediate circumstances of our creative work and considering how our current situation fits into the larger tapestry of our lives and the world around us.

On a personal level, this may involve reflecting on how our unique experiences, values, and beliefs shape our creative perspective and voice. By gaining insight into our own cultural and historical context, we better understand the sources of our creative inspiration and the deeper meanings behind our work. This self-awareness allows us to tap into authentic expressions of creativity that resonate with our true selves.

On a social level, considering the context within the Creative Self Expression Practice involves examining how our relationships and interactions influence our creative process and outcomes. This might include exploring how our collaborations, partnerships, and community involvement shape our creative vision and impact or considering how different audiences and stakeholders receive and interpret our work. Understanding these social dynamics helps us communicate more effectively and create work that resonates with others.

On a broader level, considering context involves situating our creative work within larger environmental, economic, and political systems. This might include examining how technological disruption, social movements, or environmental challenges impact our creative industries and communities or considering how our work can contribute to positive change on a global scale.

By developing a holistic understanding of context, we become more adept at recognizing opportunities for creative expression and problem-solving in daily life. We can see how seemingly unrelated elements might connect in innovative ways, leading to fresh insights and novel solutions.

Ultimately, considering the context within the Creative Self Expression Practice is about developing a holistic, integrated understanding of our creative lives. By situating our current circumstances within the bigger picture of our personal, social, and global contexts, we gain a deeper appreciation for the complex factors shaping our creative experiences and outcomes.

As we embrace the power of context in our practice, we recognize that our work doesn't exist in isolation but is intimately connected to the world. By considering the broader contexts in which we create, we become more aware, empathetic, and engaged in our creative pursuits and more capable of creating meaningful, relevant, and transformative work in all aspects of our lives.

Reimagine

At the foundation of our practice lies the transformative act of reimagining. This crucial step involves challenging conventional beliefs and assumptions that often limit creativity's potential and scope. By actively reimagining our approach to creativity and our creative potential, we open ourselves to a world of possibilities, recognizing that creative expression isn't a rare gift bestowed upon a select few but an intrinsic part of our human experience.

The Creative CLP Philosophy encourages us to embrace creativity as a fundamental way of being—a lens through which we perceive and engage with the world. This perspective shift empowers us to infuse our daily experiences with wonder, curiosity, and possibility, recognizing that every creative expression testifies to our unique voice and perspective.

Reimagining creativity means breaking free from narrow definitions that confine it to artistic pursuits alone. Instead, we begin to see creativity as a vital force permeating all aspects of life—from workplace problem-solving to navigating personal relationships, from managing finances to pursuing personal growth. This expanded view helps us recognize and cultivate creative potential in areas we might have previously overlooked.

As we reimagine our relationship with creativity, we give ourselves permission to dream big, explore uncharted territories, and push the boundaries of what we believe possible. We begin questioning limiting beliefs about our abilities and start viewing challenges as opportunities for creative solutions rather than insurmountable obstacles.

This reimagining process also involves reconsidering our understanding of the creative process itself. Rather than viewing creativity as a linear path from inspiration to finished product, we begin to appreciate it as a cyclical, iterative journey of exploration, experimentation, and refinement. We learn to value the messy middle stages of creation and find joy in the process itself, not just the end result.

Moreover, reimagining creativity means redefining what success looks like in our creative endeavors. Instead of measuring our worth by external standards or comparisons to others, we learn to value our unique creative voice and the personal growth that comes from engaging in the creative process.

By embracing reimagining as a foundational element of the Creative Self Expression Practice, we reclaim our inherent creative birthright and recognize our capacity to shape our lives and world through creative expression. This sets the stage for the Learning Spiral's continuous process, encouraging us to consistently build upon our evolving knowledge, experiences, and creative intuition.

Ultimately, reimagining creativity is about cultivating openness, adaptability, and resilience. It's about recognizing that creativity isn't just a skill to hone but a way of life to embrace. As we reimagine creativity, we open ourselves to endless possibilities, ready to approach each day with fresh eyes and an innovative spirit.

Recalibrate

The next component we encounter is the essential process of recalibrating our mindset. This transformative step involves aligning our thoughts, beliefs, and attitudes with the principles of the Creative Self Mindset—a powerful framework for cultivating authentic creative expression and personal growth.

Recalibration emerges from the CLP Philosophy as we transform our reimagined beliefs about creativity into empowering self-talk and practice. By actively recalibrating our mindset through this self-directed narrative, we learn to identify and reframe limiting thought patterns, replacing them with beliefs that support creative growth and self-expression in all life areas.

The recalibration process involves a conscious effort to shift our perspective on creativity and our creative potential. It requires challenging deeply ingrained beliefs about what it means to be creative, who can be creative, and how creativity manifests in daily life. This might involve questioning societal norms, cultural conditioning, or personal experiences that have shaped our understanding of creativity.

As we recalibrate, we begin seeing creativity not as a rare talent reserved for artists or innovators but as a fundamental human capacity we all possess and can develop. We start recognizing creative opportunities in everyday situations—from problem-solving at work to navigating personal relationships, from managing our homes to pursuing our passions.

The Creative Self Mindset Principles serve as guidelines in this recalibration process, moving us toward a more expansive, authentic, and purposeful approach to creativity. These principles help us cultivate a growth mindset, embrace curiosity and experimentation, and develop resilience when facing challenges. By aligning our mindset with these principles, we cultivate deep trust in our creative instincts and develop the resourcefulness necessary to navigate the ups and downs of our creative journey.

Recalibration also involves developing new habits and practices that support creative growth. This might include setting aside regular time for creative exploration, seeking new experiences to stimulate imagination, or developing rituals that help us access creative flow. It's about creating a lifestyle that nurtures and sustains our creative spirit.

Recalibrating our mindset also involves learning to quiet our inner critic and cultivate self-compassion. We learn to view "mistakes" or "failures" not as evidence of lacking creativity but as valuable learning experiences contributing to our growth and development.

Ultimately, recalibrating our mindset through the Creative Self Mindset is about developing deep creative integrity and authenticity. By aligning our thoughts and beliefs with genuine creative expression principles, we become better equipped to stay true to ourselves and our vision, even when facing adversity or self-doubt.

We learn to trust our creative process and value our unique perspectives and contributions. As we embrace this recalibration, we open ourselves to a world of creative possibilities, ready to approach each day with renewed enthusiasm, curiosity, and confidence in our creative abilities.

Revitalize

As we continue engaging with our practice, we encounter the energizing power of revitalizing our CLP Vision. Based on our reimagination of creative potential and recalibration of our mindset, we can now revitalize or revise our vision to align with our evolved understanding of creativity, creative potential, and authentic Creative Self.

Revitalizing our CLP Vision involves bringing clarity, focus, and inspiration to our creative aspirations and developing a roadmap for turning dreams into reality. This process requires a deep dive into our being as we uncover the true nature of our creative desires and passions, giving ourselves permission to dream big and imagine a life rich with purpose, meaning, and creative expression.

This revitalization process encompasses all aspects of our lives. We begin to see how creativity can infuse our work, relationships, personal growth, and everyday problem-solving. We start envisioning how our unique creative gifts can positively impact our communities and the world.

With a clear, compelling vision in place, we can develop specific, measurable, achievable goals and corresponding projects that align with our overall creative aspirations. By revitalizing our vision this way, we create direction and momentum—a framework for making consistent progress toward our creative dreams.

This revitalization process also involves reassessing our priorities and values. As our understanding of creativity evolves, so too may our goals and desires. We might discover new interest areas or realize certain pursuits no longer align with our authentic selves. This ongoing refinement ensures our creative journey remains true to our evolving selves.

Revitalizing our vision also means considering how to integrate creative aspirations into daily life. We look for ways to bring creativity into our routines, work, and interactions with others. This might involve reimagining our career path, finding new ways to express ourselves in relationships, or developing creative solutions to everyday challenges.

Additionally, the revitalization process encourages us to think beyond personal gain and consider how our creative vision can contribute to making the world better for everyone. We begin seeing our creative journey not just as a path to self-fulfillment but as a means of making a positive global impact.

Each creative project we undertake becomes a stepping stone toward realizing our larger vision. By approaching these projects with purpose and intention and staying connected to the deeper meaning and significance of our creative work, we revitalize our commitment to the journey ahead, celebrating small victories and milestones along the way.

Revitalizing is a process of continuous renewal and refinement, ensuring our creative journey remains vibrant, meaningful, and true to our authentic selves.

Refresh

Refreshing our Life Skill of Being Creative is our next practice component. Building upon the Learning Spiral concept, which emphasizes continuous learning and growth, we acknowledge the need to refresh our skills in response to our revitalized or revised vision's requirements.

Refreshing our Life Skill of Being Creative involves committing to lifelong learning, recognizing that our creative potential is a dynamic, ever-evolving aspect of our being. This process includes both pursuing domain-specific skills related to our creative projects and the ongoing development of fundamental creative capacities that apply to all areas of life.

By actively seeking new knowledge, experiences, and perspectives, we keep our creative skills fresh, relevant, and adaptable to the changing needs of our creative aspirations. This might involve learning new techniques in our chosen field, exploring entirely new disciplines, or developing soft skills that enhance our creative problem-solving abilities.

The refresh process isn't limited to formal education or training. It encompasses a wide range of activities that stimulate creativity and broaden horizons. This could include reading widely across various subjects, engaging in cross-disciplinary collaborations, attending workshops or conferences, or simply setting aside time for experimentation and play.

Refreshing our skills also involves staying attuned to emerging trends and technologies that may impact our creative work. In our rapidly changing world, new tools and platforms continually emerge that can enhance our creative capabilities. By staying open to these innovations, we can integrate them into our practice in ways that amplify creative expression.

Refreshing our Life Skill of Being Creative involves cultivating self-awareness and engaging in regular reflection to assess our strengths, weaknesses, and improvement areas. This might involve seeking feedback from peers or mentors, analyzing our creative processes, or keeping a creative journey journal. By honestly evaluating our creative process and output, we gain valuable insights that help refine our skills and maintain the freshness and relevance of our creative abilities over time.

It's important to note that the refresh process isn't about constantly chasing the newest trend or technique. Instead, it's about thoughtfully considering which skills and knowledge will truly enhance our creative vision and contribute to our growth as creative individuals. It's about finding a balance between honing existing strengths and exploring new territories.

As we refresh our skills through the Creative Self Expression Practice, guided by the Learning Spiral principles, learning to learn, and lifelong learning, we become more versatile, adaptable, and confident creators. We develop the ability to approach challenges from multiple angles, drawing on a diverse toolkit of skills and perspectives.

This ongoing process of refreshing our skills keeps our creative practice vibrant and exciting. It prevents stagnation and burnout by continually presenting new challenges and growth opportunities. It allows us to stay responsive to the changing needs of our creative vision and the world around us.

Realign

As we move into Creative Self Management within our practice, we embrace the role of resource managers for our individual human resources. This crucial step involves realigning our habits, practices, and strategies to optimize performance and effectively navigate life's complexities.

Creative Self Management requires developing a keen awareness of our internal and external resources and recognizing that our time, energy, focus, and overall well-being are precious assets requiring intentional care. By realigning our habits and practices, we create a solid foundation for sustainable creative expression and personal growth across all life areas.

This realignment process involves assessing our current routines and identifying areas where we can streamline, simplify, or optimize our approach. We may need to release habits or practices that no longer serve our creative goals and implement new strategies supporting productivity, resilience, and overall well-being. This might involve restructuring our daily schedule to align with natural energy rhythms, creating boundaries to protect creative time, or developing rituals to help us transition into a creative mindset.

Effective Creative Self Management also requires cultivating essential skills like organization, time management, and self-awareness. By developing systems and structures that help prioritize tasks, manage schedules, and maintain a clear focus on creative aspirations, we create order and control amid daily life's chaos. This might involve using productivity tools, implementing time-blocking techniques, or developing a personal system for tracking progress on creative projects.

Realigning our Creative Self Management practices involves developing deep self-awareness and emotional intelligence. By tuning into our needs, limitations, and motivation sources, we can make informed choices about resource allocation and navigate challenges with greater ease and resilience. This might involve practices such as mindfulness meditation, journaling, or regular self-reflection to stay connected with our inner creative voice.

Realignment also means creating a harmonious balance between creative pursuits and other life aspects. It's about finding ways to integrate creativity into daily routines, relationships, and professional lives rather than treating it as a separate or isolated activity. This holistic approach ensures our creative practice enhances and enriches our entire life experience.

The process of realigning our Creative Self Management practices is about creating a supportive relationship between our mind space and physical space. By optimizing our habits, practices, and strategies, we cultivate balance, clarity, and purpose that enable us to show up fully and authentically in our creative pursuits and in life as a whole.

Through this realignment, we become more effective stewards of our creative potential, capable of sustaining our creative practice over the long term and adapting to the ever-changing demands of our creative journey and life in general.

Reaffirm

The next practice component we encounter is the power of reaffirming our commitment to our CLP. This vital step involves regularly revisiting our portfolio of creative endeavors, tracking progress, and celebrating achievements along the way.

Our CLP represents the culmination of our creative aspirations, the tangible manifestation of our unique vision and purpose. By consistently reaffirming our dedication to this project, we maintain strong motivation, focus, and momentum, even when facing challenges or setbacks.

The reaffirmation process involves setting clear milestones and success metrics and regularly assessing our progress against these benchmarks. By breaking down larger creative goals into smaller, achievable steps, we create a roadmap for growth and transformation that feels manageable and rewarding. This could involve setting daily, weekly, or monthly goals or defining key milestones for various creative projects.

As we track progress and celebrate achievements, no matter how small, we reinforce the value and significance of our creative pursuits. We cultivate pride and accomplishment in our work, recognizing that each step forward testifies to our commitment and resilience. This positive reinforcement helps build confidence and motivation, fueling continued creative growth.

Reaffirmation also involves reflecting on lessons learned from experiences, both positive and negative. By acknowledging our successes and analyzing setbacks, we gain valuable insights that inform future creative endeavors. This reflective practice helps refine our approach, identify improvement areas, and deepen our understanding of our creative process.

The act of reaffirmation helps us stay connected to the deeper purpose and meaning behind our CLP. By regularly reflecting on the impact and potential of our creative work, we maintain strong alignment between our actions and values, ensuring our efforts are guided by a clear, compelling vision. This might involve revisiting original intentions, reassessing goals in light of new experiences, or exploring how our creative work contributes to personal growth and the world around us.

Reaffirmation also involves nurturing creative relationships and communities. By sharing our progress and challenges with supportive peers, mentors, or collaborators, we create a network of accountability and encouragement that sustains us through the ups and downs of our creative journey.

The process of reaffirming commitment to our CLP is about staying true to ourselves and our creative path. By consistently showing up with dedication, enthusiasm, and a growth mindset, we cultivate profound purpose and fulfillment in our creative endeavors, knowing each step we take is an opportunity to bring our unique gifts and talents to the world.

This ongoing practice of reaffirmation ensures our creative journey remains vibrant, meaningful, and aligned with our deepest values and aspirations, allowing us to navigate life's challenges and opportunities with creativity, resilience, and authenticity.

Share

As we complete a project or reach a milestone in our CLP, we recognize the profound importance of sharing our creations and newly acquired skills with others. This act of sharing goes beyond mere self-promotion or ego gratification; it's a powerful way to enrich our own lives while positively impacting the world around us.

Sharing our creative work and insights allows us to connect with others on a deep, meaningful level, fostering community and belonging. By vulnerably putting ourselves out there, we invite others to witness our growth, struggles, and triumphs, creating opportunities for empathy, understanding, and mutual support. This might involve presenting our work at community events, sharing our creative process on social media, or simply opening up to friends and family about our creative journey.

Additionally, sharing our creations and skills has the potential to inspire and empower others on their own creative journeys. By modeling the courage, resilience, and dedication required to bring creative visions to life, we become beacons of possibility and encouragement for those struggling to find their own voice or path. Our willingness to share can spark creativity in others, creating a ripple effect of inspiration and innovation.

Sharing our work also provides valuable opportunities for feedback, collaboration, and growth. By engaging with others and soliciting their insights and perspectives, we can refine our skills, expand our horizons, and push the boundaries of what we thought possible. This feedback loop can lead to new ideas, unexpected collaborations, and a deeper understanding of our own creative process.

By sharing our creative work, we can contribute to solving real-world problems and addressing societal challenges. Whether through innovative business ideas, community art projects, or creative solutions to everyday family problems, our shared creativity has the power to make tangible differences in the world around us.

It's important to note that sharing doesn't always mean grand gestures or public displays. It can be as simple as offering creative solutions in a work meeting, helping a friend see a problem from a new perspective, or volunteering our skills for a community project. The key is recognizing that our creativity has value beyond personal satisfaction and that by sharing it, we multiply its impact.

As we share, we recognize that our creative work isn't just a personal pursuit but a way to make meaningful differences in others' lives. By generously offering our creations and insights, we become agents of positive change, spreading ripples of inspiration and possibility far beyond our immediate sphere of influence.

Through this sharing practice, we validate our own creative journey while contributing to the collective energy of human creativity and innovation, enriching our communities and the world at large.

Review

As we navigate the uncertainty of our creative journey, periodically pausing to review our creative life performance becomes essential. This reflection and self-assessment process allows us to gain valuable insights, acknowledge lessons learned, and refine our approach moving forward.

Reviewing our creative life performance involves shifting perspective from the day-to-day bustle of creative pursuits and carving out dedicated time for introspection. We might reflect on our progress at regular intervals—weekly, monthly, or quarterly—depending on the nature and scope of our creative projects.

During this review process, we ask ourselves honest, probing questions about what's working well, what challenges we're facing, and what growth and improvement opportunities exist. We examine our successes and failures with curious, compassionate eyes, seeking to extract wisdom and insights that can guide us forward. This might involve assessing the alignment between our actions and CLP Vision, evaluating the effectiveness of our time management strategies, or considering the impact of our creative work on ourselves and others.

By acknowledging lessons learned from our experiences, both positive and negative, we develop a deeper understanding of our creative process and what it takes to survive, thrive, and flourish as creative individuals. We learn to identify patterns and tendencies in our work and make strategic adjustments that help optimize performance and achieve goals more effectively.

The act of reviewing our creative life performance also helps cultivate our empowering Creative Self Mindset and sense of resourcefulness and resilience when facing challenges. By regularly assessing progress and celebrating achievements, we reinforce the value and significance of our creative pursuits, even when the path ahead feels uncertain or daunting.

This review process allows us to recalibrate goals and strategies as needed. As we gain new insights and experiences, we may find our creative aspirations evolving or certain approaches no longer serving us. The review process gives us the opportunity to make intentional adjustments to our CLP, ensuring it remains aligned with our authentic selves and current circumstances.

By embracing the power of review, we recognize that creative growth is an ongoing, iterative process requiring patience, persistence, and willingness to learn from both successes and failures. By regularly pausing to assess progress and extract lessons from our experiences, we set ourselves up for long-term creative fulfillment and success, becoming ever more capable of bringing our unique gifts and talents to the world.

Reflect

The act of reflection is a powerful process for gaining a deeper understanding of ourselves and our creative expressions. This introspection allows us to connect with our innermost thoughts, feelings, and aspirations and make intentional choices that align with our authentic selves.

Reflection involves stepping back from creative pursuits and carving out dedicated time for self-inquiry. We might reflect through journaling, meditation, or quiet contemplation, allowing ourselves to explore the deeper meanings and motivations behind our creative work. This practice goes beyond merely reviewing our actions; it goes into the underlying emotions, beliefs, and values driving our creative journey.

Through reflection, we gain insight into the unique qualities and strengths defining our creative voice, as well as areas where we may need to grow and develop. We become more attuned to our creative process, recognizing patterns and habits that either support or hinder our progress. This heightened self-awareness can lead to breakthroughs in our creative work, helping us overcome obstacles and tap into new sources of inspiration.

The act of reflection helps cultivate stronger emotional intelligence. By honestly examining our thoughts, beliefs, and behaviors, we develop a clearer understanding of how our inner world shapes our creative expressions and interactions with others. This can lead to improved relationships, more effective collaboration, and a greater ability to communicate our creative vision.

Reflection also allows us to explore the broader impact of our creative work. We can consider how our creations align with our values, how they contribute to personal growth, and how they might affect others or the world. This deeper contemplation can infuse our creative practice with greater purpose and meaning.

The practice of reflection isn't always comfortable. It may bring to light insecurities, fears, or limiting beliefs we've been avoiding. However, by facing these challenges head-on, we can work through them and emerge stronger and more resilient in our creative practice.

Overall, the practice of reflection develops a deep, abiding relationship with our Creative Self. By regularly turning inward and exploring the landscape of our hearts and minds, we cultivate self-knowledge, self-acceptance, and self-trust that enable us to show up more fully and authentically in creative work and life as a whole.

As we embrace the power of reflection, we recognize that our creative journey encompasses both external manifestations of our work and the internal process of growth, discovery, and transformation. By making introspection a regular part of our creative practice, we become more grounded, purposeful, and true to ourselves, and more capable of creating work that resonates with the deepest parts of our being and connects meaningfully with others.

Rejuvenate

As we express our creative potential through our Creative Self Expression Practice, we quickly understand the vital importance of rejuvenation. The act of creating, while deeply fulfilling, can also be mentally, emotionally, and physically taxing, as it often requires us to continually pour energy and focus into our work.

To sustain creative vitality over the long term, we must prioritize self-care and nurture our creative spirit. This means regularly setting aside time and space for activities that replenish energy, spark curiosity and imagination, and bring joy and relaxation. Rejuvenation isn't a luxury, but a necessary component of sustainable creative practice.

Rejuvenation takes many forms, depending on individual needs and preferences. For some, it involves spending time in nature, allowing the natural world to inspire and refresh the creative spirit. For others, it might mean engaging in physical exercise, which can boost energy levels, clear the mind, and stimulate creative thinking. Some find rejuvenation in mindfulness or meditation, which can quiet the noise of daily life and reconnect us with our inner creative voice.

The key is developing a keen awareness of our rhythms and cycles and honoring the natural ebbs and flows of creative energy. By tuning into our body, mind, and spirit, we can identify signs of creative burnout or fatigue and take proactive steps to replenish our reserves before they run dry. This might involve taking short breaks throughout the day, scheduling regular "creative vacations," or simply giving ourselves permission to step away from a project when feeling stuck.

Rejuvenation also involves nurturing curiosity, imagination, and playfulness. Engaging in activities purely for enjoyment, without pressure to produce or achieve, can reignite our creative spark and lead to unexpected insights. This might involve exploring a new hobby, visiting a museum, or simply allowing ourselves to daydream and let our minds wander.

Our rejuvenation process often involves connecting with others. Engaging in meaningful conversations, collaborating with fellow creatives, or simply spending time with loved ones can provide emotional support and fresh perspectives that reinvigorate our creative practice.

The practice of rejuvenation helps cultivate greater balance and perspective in our creative lives. By regularly stepping back from the intensity of our work and engaging in activities that nourish and inspire us, we maintain a fresh, vibrant outlook and can avoid getting bogged down in the inevitable challenges and frustrations of being creative.

The act of rejuvenation is about valuing ourselves and our creative well-being as much as we value the work itself. By prioritizing self-care and nurturing our creative spirit, we ensure we have the energy, inspiration, and resilience needed to show up fully and consistently in our creative pursuits and to create work that is authentic, meaningful, and impactful.

Reassert

After completing a project and moving through the essential phases of reviewing, reflecting, and rejuvenating, we arrive at the crucial final component of the Reset cycle: reassertion. This step completes the creative cycle and prepares us to begin again with renewed purpose and energy. Whether we've achieved our intended outcomes or fallen short of our expectations, reassertion positions us to continue our Creative Self Expression Practice with clarity and conviction.

Reassertion serves as the bridge between completion and new beginnings. It represents our conscious decision to re-engage with our creative journey after the necessary pause for assessment and renewal. This step is particularly vital when we've encountered significant obstacles or haven't achieved our desired results, as it prevents temporary setbacks from becoming permanent barriers to our creative expression.

As we navigate the twists and turns of our creative journey, we inevitably encounter challenges that test our resolve and commitment. In these moments, the act of reassertion becomes a powerful tool for maintaining focus, motivation, and forward momentum. It transforms the Reset phase from a potential endpoint into a launching pad for continued growth and expression.

Reassertion involves recommitting ourselves to our CLP Vision with fresh energy and perspective. It means consciously choosing to stay the course, to keep showing up and putting in the work, even when the path ahead feels uncertain or daunting. This practice is crucial for maintaining the long-term sustainability of our creative endeavors and ensuring that our practice remains vibrant and evolving.

The process of reassertion requires cultivating deep resilience and determination. After reviewing our experiences, reflecting on their meaning, and rejuvenating our creative energy, we're called upon to reframe obstacles as opportunities for growth. This perspective shift allows us to bounce back more quickly from disappointments and maintain momentum even when facing challenges.

Reassertion also involves reconnecting with the deeper purpose and meaning that drives our Creative Self Expression Practice. By realigning with our core values, passions, and aspirations, we maintain strong motivation and direction, even amid distractions or temporary setbacks. This might involve revisiting our original vision, reminding ourselves why we embarked on this creative journey, and reconnecting with the impact we hope to make through our creative expression.

The act of reassertion requires developing effective strategies for managing our thoughts, emotions, and behaviors when facing adversity. This may involve practicing self-compassion and empowering Storytelling Self-Talk, seeking support from our creative community, or breaking down ambitious goals into smaller, more manageable steps. By developing these coping mechanisms, we build the capacity to persist through challenges and maintain creative momentum over the long term.

Importantly, reassertion counters a tendency to stubbornly cling to a particular path or outcome. Rather, its focus is on staying true to our core vision and values while remaining flexible in our approach. It involves incorporating the insights gained through review and reflection, making adjustments as needed while still maintaining overall direction and commitment to our creative practice.

By consistently engaging in the practice of reassertion, we develop the mental and emotional strength needed to persevere in our creative journey. We become more confident, adaptable, and resilient in our creative endeavors, capable of navigating setbacks with grace and determination.

As we complete the Reset cycle through reassertion, we come full circle in our Creative Self Expression Practice. We're now prepared to return to the Restart phase with new insights, renewed energy, and deeper commitment. This cyclical nature of the practice ensures that every end becomes a new beginning, every challenge becomes an opportunity for growth, and every creative expression becomes a stepping stone toward living our most authentic and fulfilled creative life.

This practice of reassertion ensures that our creative journey remains vibrant, meaningful, and transformative, allowing us to navigate life's challenges and opportunities with creativity, resilience, and authenticity. Despite any circumstances we may encounter, we remain prepared to reassert ourselves and begin again—continuing the lifelong practice of Creative Self Expression.

Practice into Action: Creative Blocks and Flow

As we complete our exploration of the practice components, we turn now to a powerful application of this practice: navigating creative blocks through understanding flow.

In Chapter 15, we explored flow from a biological perspective—the remarkable synchronization of multiple bodily systems that creates what Mihaly Csikszentmihalyi identified as an optimal state of consciousness. We examined how, during flow, the brain shifts into patterns where self-consciousness decreases while neural networks involved in attention, perception, and action become highly coordinated, creating that extraordinary experience of complete immersion and peak performance.

Now, we'll see how this understanding of flow interfaces with our Creative Self Expression Practice, providing a strategic relationship for addressing one of the most common challenges on the creative journey: creative blocks.

We all encounter periods when our creative energy seems to stagnate or halt entirely. We've traditionally labeled these experiences as "creative blocks"—treating them as obstacles to overcome, problems to solve, or enemies to defeat.

Understanding What Blocks the Flow

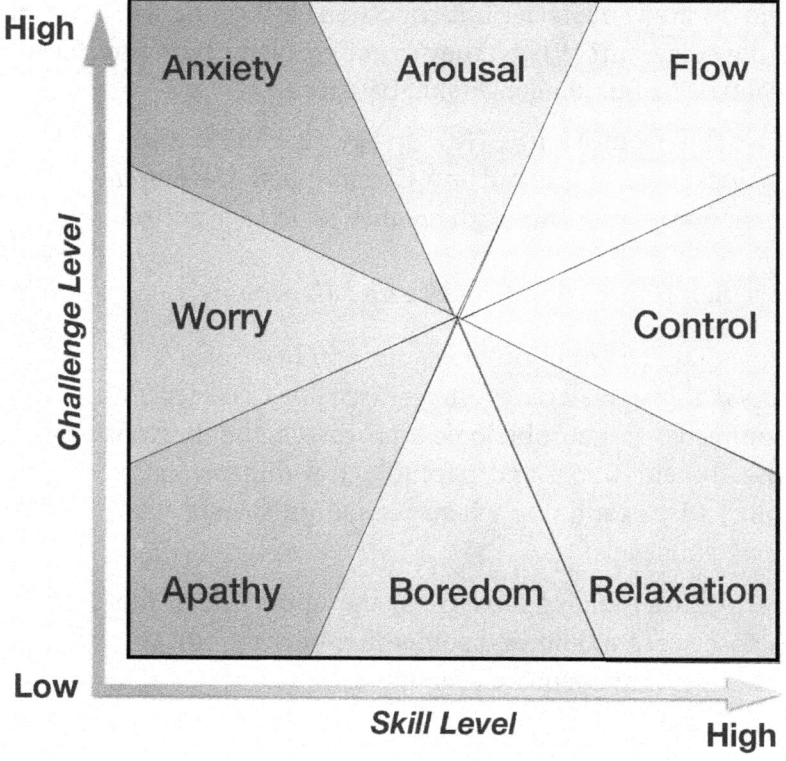

The Flow State Diagram visually represents the psychological states we experience based on the relationship between challenge and skill levels. When our skills match high challenges, we enter flow—that optimal biological state described in Chapter 15. In contrast, when these elements are mismatched, we experience states like anxiety (high challenge, low skill), boredom (low challenge, high skill), or apathy (low challenge, low skill).

Creative blocks often represent our displacement from the flow state. A quick internet search for "overcoming creative blocks" yields countless articles offering similar tactical advice: take walks, change your environment, try a new medium, or step away completely. While these approaches can sometimes provide temporary relief, they rarely address what these blocks might be communicating about our relationship with flow.

The CLP offers a fundamentally different perspective: What if creative blocks aren't obstacles but conditions indicating where we are on the flow diagram? What if they're not problems but opportunities for recalibrating our challenge-skill balance?

When we shift from asking, "How do I get past this block?" to "What is this block revealing about my Creative Self Development?" we transform our relationship with creative resistance entirely.

Creative Self Expression Practice and Flow State

The Flow State Diagram provides our first layer of strategic insight. Developed through decades of research by Csikszentmihalyi and later connected to neurobiological processes, the diagram helps us diagnose the emotional and psychological dimensions of our creative blocks by examining where we fall on the spectrum of challenge and skill levels:

- Are we experiencing *anxiety* (in the upper left of the diagram) because we're attempting something beyond our current capabilities without adequate preparation?
- Have we fallen into *boredom* (in the lower right) because we're no longer challenging ourselves in meaningful ways?
- Has *apathy* set in (at the bottom left) because we've both disconnected from meaningful challenges and aren't utilizing our skills?

- Are we stuck in *worry* because we lack confidence in our developing abilities, even though the challenge is only moderately high?
- Is our creative energy dissipating in states of *arousal* (challenged but not quite skilled enough) or *control* (skilled but not quite challenged enough)?

Rather than simply trying to "push through" these states with generic tactics, the Creative Self Expression Practice components offer a structured framework for deeper inquiry.

Revisiting Creative Blocks Strategically

Let's explore a few examples of how Creative Self Expression Practice and the concept of flow might be used together to help us learn about the root cause of our creative blocks and support our Creative Self Development.

A Writer Experiencing a Block

Traditional advice might suggest freewriting exercises or changing location. But through our strategic lens, the writer might discover that the Flow State Diagram indicates they're in a state of anxiety (high challenge, lower skill). Using the Creative Self Expression Practice components, they examine several key factors:

- **Environment**: Their physical and internal writing space has become associated with pressure rather than possibility.
- **Circumstances**: Current events in their life have shaken their confidence.
- **Context**: They've lost sight of the broader purpose of their writing.
- **Reimagine**: They need to revisit what success looks like in their writing.

The strategic response isn't simply to "write through it" but to recalibrate their relationship with their work, reassess their environment to remove pressure cues, address their current circumstances with compassion, reconnect with the context of their work, and reimagine their creative approach.

A Business Leader Struggling with Innovation

Rather than simply brainstorming more ideas (the typical tactical approach), they might use the Flow State Diagram to recognize they're in a state of boredom or relaxation (high skill, low challenge). Through the Creative Self Expression Practice components, they examine the following:

- **Environment**: Their workspace and team structure lack stimulating elements.
- **Reimagine**: They need to reconceive what innovation means in their context.
- **Refresh**: Their skills and approaches have become stale and need renewal.
- **Rejuvenate**: Their creative energy requires intentional replenishment.

The strategic response involves reimagining what innovation could look like in their industry, refreshing their approach by learning new methodologies (increasing challenge), creating an environment that stimulates diverse thinking, and taking time to rejuvenate their creative energy. This approach deliberately moves them upward on the flow diagram toward the optimal flow state.

A Musician in Creative Stagnation

Instead of simply trying new genres or instruments, they might recognize from the Flow State Diagram that they're in a state of control (high skill, moderate challenge) or relaxation. Through the Creative Self Expression Practice components, they analyze the following:

- **Recalibrate**: Their mindset has shifted from exploration to maintenance.
- **Rejuvenate**: Their creative inspiration needs revitalization.
- **Circumstances**: Their current situation has created a comfort zone.

- **Reassert**: They need to recommit to creative growth.

The strategic response involves recalibrating their mindset toward creative growth, deliberately seeking experiences that rejuvenate their creative energy, changing their circumstances to introduce productive challenges, and reasserting their commitment to artistic evolution. This strategic adjustment moves them rightward on the flow diagram into the optimal flow state, where high challenge meets their high skill level.

The Individual Puzzle of Creative Blocks

It's crucial to recognize that there are no universal, magic solutions for creative blocks. Each block presents a unique puzzle that you alone are challenged to solve. What works for someone else may not work for you because your creative journey is singularly yours—shaped by your unique blueprint, current developmental stage on the Creative Continuum, and individual circumstances.

You are called upon to approach your creative blocks from your current environment (both internal and external), circumstances, and context. The components of the Creative Self Expression Practice provide a framework for investigation, but the answers will emerge from your personal exploration and insight.

Embracing Blocks as Evolutionary Catalysts for Creative Growth

This strategic approach represents a fundamental shift in how we relate to creative resistance. Rather than treating blocks as unfortunate obstacles to be overcome through generic tactics, we recognize them as valuable signals about where we are on our creative journey and current flow state conditions.

When fully integrated into your Creative Self Expression Practice, this approach transforms the dreaded "block" into a valuable tool for Creative Self Navigation, revealing what adjustments in challenge level or skill-building your Creative Self requires to move in the direction of flow.

As psychologist Mihaly Csikszentmihalyi discovered in his research, flow is not a static achievement but a dynamic relationship we must continuously recalibrate as we grow. The biological mechanisms that create the flow state—from neurochemical changes to altered brain wave patterns—require this balance of challenge and skill. What once appeared as obstacles were actually doorways to your next level of authentic creative expression.

Closing Thoughts on Practice

As we conclude our exploration of the Creative Self Expression Practice, we're reminded of the profound impact that cultivating creativity as a life skill can have on our personal growth, problem-solving abilities, and overall fulfillment. This practice is more than a set of techniques or strategies; it's a way of life that connects us deeply to the Life Force of Creation.

By establishing this practice, we open ourselves to a world of possibilities. We become more adaptable, resilient, and innovative when facing life's challenges. Our capacity to navigate complex situations, find novel solutions, and express our unique perspectives grows exponentially.

The Life Skill of Being Creative, nurtured through this practice, fuels our Creative Self Navigation system in an ever-changing world. It guides us to approach each day with curiosity, openness, and a willingness to experiment. It empowers us to break free from limiting beliefs and societal expectations, allowing us to craft truly authentic and meaningful lives.

As we integrate this practice into our daily lives, we enrich ourselves and also contribute to a creative culture. Our individual creative expressions ripple outward, inspiring others and contributing to the evolution of ideas, culture, and society.

Let this practice be your anchor and sail as you navigate life's vast ocean. Embrace your creative potential, trust the process, and remain open to endless possibilities. By nurturing your Creative Self, you nurture the very essence of what makes you human—your ability to imagine, to create, and to shape your world.

CHAPTER 21:
CREATIVITY IN CULTURES AND RELATIONSHIPS

Creating as the essence of human life is expressed both through the actions of individuals and through the cultures, traditions, and relationships that shape societies. Every civilization has developed its own aesthetic, artistic, and problem-solving traditions, reflecting how its people engage with the Life Force of Creation to navigate, build, and live their best lives. In the CLP, this perspective extends beyond personal creativity to the collective, emphasizing that cultures themselves are the result of Creative Self Expression at scale.

Just as individuals develop and express their creativity through personal choices and actions, cultures channel creativity into their arts, traditions, values, and ways of living. Whether through music, architecture, fashion, language, or philosophy, cultures serve as macro-level Creative Self Expressions, reflecting the shared stories, challenges, and aspirations of the people who create and sustain them. The arts and aesthetics of each culture are not merely decorative or performative; they are the manifestations of creative identity, a mirror of human ingenuity and adaptability across generations.

Building Creative Cultures

In the CLP Framework, the ultimate goal is both Creative Self Development and the formation of creative cultures where innovation, expression, and collaboration thrive. A creative culture is one where individuals take responsibility for their own Creative Self Development and then engage in mutually enriching relationships, partnerships, and collaborations.

Fundamentally, every relationship—whether personal or professional—has the potential to be a creative relationship. A creative relationship is one where all parties engage in their own Creative Self work and then come together ready to contribute rather than expecting others to provide all the creativity. In contrast, relationships that lack creativity often become transactional, stagnant, or controlling, stifling the potential of those involved.

This principle applies across different domains:

- **Personal and family relationships:** Families that cultivate creativity encourage storytelling, emotional expression, and problem-solving, fostering an environment where individuals develop resilience and resourcefulness.
- **Friendships and social bonds:** Friendships based on creativity inspire exploration, shared experiences, and intellectual curiosity, deepening personal connections.
- **Business and organizational creativity:** Companies that foster a creative culture empower employees to innovate, challenge outdated models, and collaborate in meaningful ways.
- **Governments and leadership:** Societies that value creative problem-solving develop inclusive policies, resilient communities, and adaptable structures.
- **Sports and team dynamics:** Teams that embrace strategy, adaptability, and collaboration achieve greater success than those that rely solely on rigid tactics.

Regardless of the domain, the idea remains the same: a creative culture is built when individuals take responsibility for their own Creative Self Development and then bring their creative energy into interactions with others. Collaboration becomes an act of shared creativity rather than a struggle for dominance or validation.

This approach aligns with the core focus of the CLP: the ability to navigate, build, and live one's best life. When individuals and cultures engage in continuous creative growth, they build relationships and institutions that remain adaptable, relevant, empowering, and impactful.

A Global Perspective of Cultural Creativity

Beyond interpersonal relationships, creativity shapes the identity and resilience of cultures worldwide. Each society has developed unique ways of engaging with creativity—through artistic traditions, spiritual philosophies, problem-solving mindsets, or social practices—that influence how people relate to their inner potential and external world. Some cultures emphasize ingenuity in survival and adaptation, while others prioritize beauty, emotional expression, spiritual balance, or communal innovation.

The examples below offer a glimpse into how different cultures express and embody creativity, both as a *source of innovation* and as a *way of describing a creative person*. This list has been curated through cross-cultural research to highlight the diversity of meaning and expression. While not exhaustive and without claiming expertise in each cultural tradition, it aims to respectfully acknowledge the many ways creativity is understood around the world.

India: Shakti (Source) & Kalakar/Jugaadu (Person)

Shakti refers to the generative, creative energy underlying all existence. A Kalakar is an artist or performer who brings beauty and imagination to life. A Jugaadu is an ingenious problem-solver—someone who creates practical, often unconventional solutions with limited resources.

China: Qi (Source) & Wenren/Zhenren (Person)

Qi is the vital life force believed to flow through all living things and drive creativity and expression. A Wenren is a cultivated, artistic person of letters, while a Zhenren is an authentic person who lives and creates in harmony with nature and truth.

Southern Africa: Ubuntu (Philosophy/Source) & Imbongi (Person)

Ubuntu means "I am because we are" and reflects creativity as a communal, relational force. An Imbongi is a praise poet and storyteller—someone who creatively expresses truth, history, and collective spirit through language.

Japan: Gen (Source) & Shokunin (Person)

Gen means origin or source, symbolizing creativity as a natural emergence from within. A Shokunin is a craftsperson devoted to mastery, beauty, and social responsibility—someone who expresses creativity through discipline and excellence.

Greece: Metis (Source) & Technites (Person)

Metis is a form of intuitive, adaptive intelligence—cunning, skillful wisdom used in navigating complexity. A Technite is a maker or artisan who blends technical skill and aesthetic creativity in shaping the world.

France: Creativite (Source) & Createur/Faiseur d'Idees (Person)

Creativite is associated with originality, artistry, and elegance in self-expression. A Createur is a creator or artist; a Faiseur d'idees is an idea-maker—someone known for producing imaginative and conceptual innovations.

Indigenous Andes: Tikanis (Source) & Weaver (Person)

Tikanis relates to harmony, integration, and creative balance—often applied to healing, nature, and weaving. A Weaver is both literal and metaphorical—a person who brings together elements of story, tradition, and design into meaningful creations.

Polynesia: Mana (Source) & Navigator / Artist (Person)

Mana is a spiritual force or energy that fuels leadership, storytelling, and personal power. A Navigator or Artist is someone who uses intuition and inherited knowledge to create new paths, tell stories, and guide others.

Nigeria (Yoruba): Odo (Source) & Akomolede (Person)

Odo represents the energy of youth and creative innovation—bringing fresh ideas and bold problem-solving. An Akomolede is a wise speaker or wordsmith who merges tradition with new insights through language and cultural expression.

Spain/Latin America: Duende (Source) & Artista con Duende (Person)

Duende is a deep, emotional, creative force that inspires passionate, authentic artistic expression. An Artista con Duende is someone whose work moves others through intensity, soul, and raw creative presence.

Creative Self Development and Cultural Flourishing

These cultural insights reveal that creativity is not a singular concept but a rich, evolving expression of human experience. It can be a life force, a communal value, a spiritual path, or a technical pursuit—and often all at once.

The existence of these words relating to roles and forms of cultural expression for creativity across the globe further verifies that creativity is a universal human trait—not a rare talent or isolated gift. Every culture, in its own language and way of life, has developed ways to describe, value, and cultivate creativity. Whether through myth, philosophy, craftsmanship, storytelling, or innovation, these expressions reflect a shared human impulse to imagine, shape, and respond to the world.

This aligns with the CLP's functional definition of creativity. When we see creativity not only as a global phenomenon but as a natural part of being human, we begin to understand its vital role in shaping meaningful lives, resilient communities, and adaptive cultures. Creativity is how we transform what we have into what could be—and how we leave our fingerprint on the world we help build.

By understanding creativity as both a personal and collective force, we unlock its full potential to shape relationships, environments, and entire civilizations. A world shaped by creative cultures—whether in families, businesses, or nations—becomes a world where curiosity, resourcefulness, and collaboration define how we live, work, and connect. Through deliberate Creative Self Development and the shared commitment to fostering creativity in others, we lay the foundation for a future where creativity is not just expressed—it is embedded in the way we live our best lives and build a better world.

CHAPTER 22:
REVISITED—BEFORE WE BEGIN… AND WHAT'S NEXT

When you began this guide, you took a moment to reflect on your understanding of creativity and your relationship with your own creative potential. That initial self-assessment established a personal starting point—a benchmark of your beliefs, experiences, and attitudes toward creativity before embarking on this journey through the CLP Framework.

Now, as our exploration comes to a close, I invite you to return to those same questions with fresh eyes and an open heart. This is not a test of how well you've absorbed the material but rather an opportunity to observe how your perspectives may have evolved through your engagement with these ideas and practices.

Take your time with each question, answering as honestly as you did at the beginning. Notice any shifts in your thinking, any new insights that have emerged, or any areas where your convictions have deepened. Pay attention not only to changes in your intellectual understanding of creativity but also to any transformations in how you feel about your own creative potential.

After completing this post-assessment, compare your responses with those from the beginning of the guide. What has changed? What has remained consistent? Where do you see the most significant evolution in your thinking? These observations will provide valuable insights into your unique creative journey and help you recognize the growth you've already experienced.

Remember that this assessment is not about achieving a "perfect score" or reaching some predetermined level of creative enlightenment. Rather, it's a tool for self-awareness—a mirror reflecting your current relationship with creativity as you continue to discover, develop, and express your Creative Self.

The differences between your initial responses and your current perspectives offer a glimpse into the transformation that has already begun. They provide clues about which aspects of your Creative Self Development might benefit from further exploration and which areas have blossomed through your engagement with this guide.

As you reflect on your journey thus far, consider what these changes mean for your path forward. How might your evolved understanding of creativity and your creative potential shape your choices, actions, and aspirations in the days and years to come? What new possibilities have opened up that weren't visible to you before?

Now, please revisit each question from the initial assessment.

Creativity in General

How well do you understand the concept of creativity?

- Not at all
- Slightly
- Moderately
- Very
- Extremely

How important do you believe creativity is in today's rapidly changing world?

- Not important at all
- Slightly important
- Moderately important
- Very important
- Extremely important

To what extent do you believe creativity can be applied in everyday life beyond traditional artistic domains?

- Not at all
- To a small extent
- To a moderate extent
- To a great extent
- To a very great extent

How often do you consciously engage your creativity to solve problems or generate new ideas in your daily life?

- Never
- Rarely
- Sometimes
- Often
- Always

How strongly do you believe that developing and expressing creativity should be a priority for personal growth and well-being?

- Not at all
- Slightly
- Moderately
- Very
- Extremely

To what extent do you believe that creativity can be learned and developed by anyone?

- Not at all
- To a small extent
- To a moderate extent
- To a great extent
- To a very great extent

How often do you actively encourage and support others in their creative endeavors?

- Never
- Rarely
- Sometimes
- Often
- Always

How often have you received encouragement or praise for your creative ideas?

- Never
- Rarely
- Sometimes
- Often
- Always

How often have you experienced criticism or discouragement from others regarding your creative expressions or abilities?

- Never
- Rarely
- Sometimes
- Often
- Always

How much do you believe societal norms and expectations influence your willingness to think and act creatively?

- Not at all
- Slightly
- Moderately
- Very much
- Extremely

How strongly do you believe that learning about creativity and engaging in creative practices can enhance one's overall creativity?

- Not at all
- Slightly
- Moderately
- Very
- Extremely

Your Creative Potential

How strongly do you believe in your own creative potential?

- Not at all
- To a small extent
- To a moderate extent
- To a great extent
- To a very great extent

To what extent do you identify yourself as a creative individual?

- Not at all
- To a small extent
- To a moderate extent
- To a great extent
- To a very great extent

How would you assess your current level of creativity compared to what you believe is possible for you?

- Very low
- Low
- Moderate
- High
- Very high

How much time, energy, and resources do you currently invest in developing and expressing your creative potential?

- None
- A little
- A moderate amount
- A lot
- A great deal

How integral is creativity to your sense of self and your daily life?

- Not at all
- Slightly
- Moderately
- Very
- Extremely

After completing this reassessment, take some time to reflect on your journey with the following questions:

- What changed the most in your responses?
- What new insights did you gain about your creative potential?
- How do you now see creativity playing a role in your daily life?
- What are your next steps in developing your creativity further?

These reflections will help you integrate what you've learned and chart a course for your continued creative development. They serve as both a conclusion to our time together through this guide and a beginning to the next phase of your creative journey.

The Guide as a Reference for the Crafting of Your Life Story

Now that you've completed your journey through the CLP guide, you may be wondering how to best utilize this resource moving forward. This guide is designed to serve as both a sequential journey and an ongoing reference to support your creative development throughout life's changing circumstances and priorities. As you continue your Creative Self Development journey, you'll likely find yourself returning to specific sections as different aspects of your creative life take priority. The guide is structured for this "random-access" approach, allowing you to do the following:

- Revisit the Creative Self Mindset Principles when confronting limiting beliefs or mass-mindedness.
- Return to Creative Self Management roles when specific perspectives are needed for complex situations.
- Review the Life Skill of Being Creative when developing new capabilities or facing novel challenges.
- Refresh your understanding of the Creative Self Expression Practice when establishing or refining daily habits.

Use the framework diagrams and category headings as navigation tools to quickly locate the concepts most relevant to your current needs and circumstances.

Deepening Integration Through Practice

The true value of this guide emerges through consistent application and integration in your daily life:

- Focus on one concept or practice at a time for deeper understanding.
- Use the reflective questions throughout the guide to personalize the ideas to your unique situation.
- Apply the framework categories to both significant projects and everyday challenges.
- Share insights and experiences with others to reinforce your learning and inspire mutual growth.
- Periodically reassess your relationship with creativity using the questions from "Before We Begin."

This guide serves as a resource for your continuing journey of transformation from your blueprint to your fingerprint.

Making It Your Own

Over time, you may find yourself adapting concepts from the guide to fit your unique creative journey. This personalization is not only acceptable but encouraged to support your individual creative transformation.

The guide is ultimately a tool for transformation—a resource to help you discover, develop, manage, and express your unique creative potential throughout your life. Return to it whenever you need guidance, inspiration, or a fresh perspective on creativity and being creative.

CHAPTER 23:
FINAL THOUGHTS

As we arrive at the end of this guide, I find myself reflecting on my own creative journey—a path that has spanned more than five decades and traversed the realms of education, technology, business, and art. Like you, I am still discovering, developing, and expressing my Creative Self. This journey has no endpoint, no final destination where we can declare, "I've arrived at complete creative mastery." Instead, it is a continuous unfolding—an ever-expanding spiral of growth and expression that enriches our lives with each turn.

I wrote this guide because I believe deeply in the transformative power of creativity, not as an exclusive gift bestowed upon a select few, but as our shared birthright—a fundamental human trait that connects us to the Life Force of Creation and to one another. Throughout my life, I've witnessed how embracing one's creative potential can illuminate even the darkest passages, turn seemingly insurmountable obstacles into opportunities for innovation, and transform ordinary moments into extraordinary experiences.

My sincere hope is that the Creative Self Development Framework has provided you with practical tools and insights to navigate your own creative journey with greater intention, confidence, and joy. But more than that, I hope it has sparked a profound recognition of your inherent creative capacity—a recognition that will continue to flourish long after you've turned the final page of this guide.

The world we live in faces complex challenges that cannot be solved through conventional thinking alone. Climate change, social inequality, political division, technological disruption—these issues call for creative solutions that transcend old paradigms and imagine new possibilities. By developing your Creative Self, you are not only enriching your personal life; you are contributing to our collective capacity to address these challenges with wisdom, compassion, and innovation.

I encourage you to continue exploring the different facets of your creative potential. Remain curious about what you might discover. Be patient with yourself as you develop new skills and perspectives. Practice regularly, knowing that each creative act—whether deemed "successful" or not—is a step toward greater fluency and authenticity. Trust that your unique creative fingerprint has value in a world that desperately needs diverse voices and fresh approaches.

Remember that creativity flourishes in the community. Share your creative journey with others. Seek out mentors who can guide you, peers who can challenge you, and newcomers whom you can inspire. Create spaces where people feel safe to experiment, fail, learn, and grow together. Your willingness to be vulnerable in your creative expression may give someone else the courage to begin their own journey.

Throughout my years of teaching, consulting, and creating, I've observed that those who embrace their creative potential tend to live with greater purpose, resilience, and fulfillment. They approach life not as a series of problems to be solved but as a canvas awaiting their unique contribution. They see setbacks not as failures but as feedback that informs their next creative iteration. They recognize that they are both the artist and the masterpiece—continually reimagining, recalibrating, and revitalizing themselves through the creative process.

You now stand at a threshold—not an ending, but a beginning. The framework, fundamentals, principles, and practices outlined in this guide are yours to use, adapt, and expand upon as you continue to navigate, build, and live what you consider to be your best life. Your creative journey is a gift, not only to yourself but to everyone whose life you touch. As you develop and express your creative potential, you create ripples that extend far beyond what you can see—inspiring others, contributing to a more innovative culture, and helping to shape a world where creativity is valued, nurtured, and celebrated.

So go forth with creative courage and conviction. Trust in your capacity to create meaningful change. Embrace both the challenges and joys that come with living a life you have created. And remember that with each act of authentic creative expression, you are transforming your own life and contributing to making the world a better place for everyone.

One More Thing...

I'd like to leave you with a personal artifact from my own creative journey—a photograph that embodies the essence of what I've shared throughout this guide.

Years ago, I captured this image on film using a motion blur technique. When I removed the negative from the developing tank, I surprised myself by gasping aloud. There, suspended in the light and shadow of a black-and-white negative, was a visual portrait of my Creative Self—that elusive, dynamic force that exists between imagination and expression.

This moment represented a profound convergence of intention and discovery. I set out to create an image, but what emerged transcended my conscious planning. The blurred figure in flight symbolizes what I've come to understand about creativity: it is both deliberate and spontaneous, structured and free, grounded yet soaring... It's a paradox!

I share this deeply personal image not as a conclusion but as an invitation. Your Creative Self will manifest in ways entirely different from mine—through words, music, relationships, business innovations, or countless other expressions. What matters is that you seek it, recognize it, and allow it to take flight in your life.

Perhaps someday you'll experience your own moment of recognition—that instant when you see your Creative Self reflected back at you through something you've brought into the world. When that happens, I hope you, too, will feel the wonder and joy of your own Creative Self Expressions.

Creative Self Expression © 2025 Richard Altman All Rights Reserved

With the cover graphic, I imagined the Life Force of Creation; with this photograph, I captured a moment when that life force sparked my Creative Self to come out to play.

Remember, you were born creative and made to create. Your challenge is transforming your creative blueprint into the individual fingerprint you leave on your world.

I can't wait to see, hear, or feel what you create, and what, in turn, you inspire others to create as a way to nurture creative communities and make the world a better place to live for everyone.

With deep respect for your creative journey,

Richard Altman

www.ingramcontent.com/pod-product-compliance
Lightning Source LLC
Chambersburg PA
CBHW050512170426
43201CB00013B/1932